Christmas xxxx

D1447454

To Mom and
Jack -
Thank you for all of
the love, encouragement
and support.

Cheryl

Building Cultures of Peace

Building Cultures of Peace:
Transdisciplinary Voices of Hope and Action

Edited by

Elavie Ndura-Ouédraogo and Randall Amster

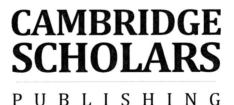

Building Cultures of Peace: Transdisciplinary Voices of Hope and Action,
Edited by Elavie Ndura-Ouédraogo and Randall Amster

This book first published 2009

Cambridge Scholars Publishing

12 Back Chapman Street, Newcastle upon Tyne, NE6 2XX, UK

British Library Cataloguing in Publication Data
A catalogue record for this book is available from the British Library

ISBN (10): 1-4438-1329-X, ISBN (13): 978-1-4438-1329-7

To my children, Star and Queen Shahuri,
In honor of the ragged road that we have travelled in search for peace
So you will always remember that faith and hope never fail us.
—Elavie Ndura-Ouédraogo, June 2009

To all the peacemakers ... past, present, and future.
—Randall Amster, June 2009

TABLE OF CONTENTS

ACKNOWLEDGMENTS

Compiling a list of those deserving thanks for inspiring and supporting this work will necessarily fall short of recalling everyone who needs to be acknowledged. The Board of Directors of the Peace & Justice Studies Association (PJSA) provided the impetus for this project specifically by framing its 2008 annual conference held at Portland State University around the issue of "Building Cultures of Peace," and Tom Hastings in particular as the conference host worked tirelessly to assemble a lineup of panels and speakers reflecting this theme. Indeed, the foundation for this volume was initially adapted from the working papers of the conference, and in this regard all of the PJSA members and conference attendees merit thanks for helping to create an enlightening forum for the incubation of the ideas that resulted in the book before you today. Prescott College generously provides me with resources for the development of peace and justice community-building, as well as support for my academic explorations of peace that make working on projects such as this even possible at all. I would especially like to express my gratitude to Elavie Ndura-Ouédraogo for her professionalism, collegiality, and good humor throughout the duration of this work. Finally, though certainly not least, my family deserves special thanks not only for their unflagging support and encouragement, but for helping to provide the *raison d'être* for writing and peacebuilding in the first place.

—Randall Amster, June 2009

The richness and diversity of voices reflected in this volume would not have been achieved without the contributions of the authors featured herein. I wish to thank the contributors for their hard work and dedication. Collaborating with Randall Amster on this book project has been a truly pleasant experience. I am grateful for his talented and caring professionalism and insightful intellect. Queen Shahuri provided invaluable assistance with the copy-editing of this book. She deserves special recognition and thank you for her generosity with her time and her sharp skills. My personal and professional journey has taught me to recognize and appreciate blessings that inspire, shape, and give meaning to each step I take. Thus, I wish to express my deep gratitude to Amanda Millar from Cambridge Scholars Publishing for taking note of the "Building Cultures of Peace" theme around which the 2008 PJSA annual conference was framed, and for reaching out and inviting us to submit a book proposal. Special thanks also go to Carol Koulikourdi and her colleagues at Cambridge Scholars Publishing for their guidance and support as we developed and finalized this volume. George Mason University sustains my journey. My colleagues in the Initiatives for Educational Transformation program and the College of Education and Human Development deserve my sincere thanks for their interest in and support for my efforts to help shape the path to peace. I am deeply grateful to my family for their love, patience, and unfailing support. Special thanks go to my husband Boureima and my step-daughters Azur, Cristal, Yasmine, and Perspective, for adding much joy to the journey.

—Elavie Ndura-Ouédraogo, June, 2009

FOREWORD

RICHARD LAPCHICK

CHAIR OF DEVOS SPORT BUSINESS MANAGEMENT PROGRAM DIRECTOR,
INSTITUTE FOR DIVERSITY AND ETHICS IN SPORT DIRECTOR,
NATIONAL CONSORTIUM FOR ACADEMICS AND SPORTS
UNIVERSITY OF CENTRAL FLORIDA

I agreed to accept a role as a Distinguished Professor at George Mason University because of the University's emphasis on social justice. One of the first people I met at George Mason was Elavie Ndura-Ouédraogo. I was immediately impressed by her sense of urgency that the world was in danger and that everyone had a responsibility to do something about it.

During the course of the year, she asked me to write the foreword to the book, *Building Cultures of Peace: Transdisciplinary Voices of Hope and Action*. I agreed to do it when I learned of its approach to the issues and because of events in my own life.

I have been a political activist for civil and human rights since the 1960s. This has included a focus on my own country, the United States, in various anti-war movements and in the Civil Rights Movement. It also included over two decades as the American leader of the sports boycott of South Africa, one of the pivotal parts of the effort to isolate that country's racist former regime.

I left for graduate school in 1967, concerned about civil rights and a war in a distant land. As I write this foreword, I am still concerned about civil rights and two wars that my country is involved with in other distant lands, as well as other wars and conflagrations across the globe.

It is also a hopeful time in my country. We have an African-American president, a dream many thought they would not live to see. Now young children of color across the nation have raised expectations that they can be anything they choose. Yet I also know that President Barack Obama faces tremendous challenges, and many are concerned that he has inherited a powder keg in which unrealistic expectations might meet stubborn realities.

In 1964 President Lyndon Johnson signed the Civil Rights Act, and a year later the Voting Rights Act. Expectations were so high. I remember thinking, "could this be the moment we achieve equality?" Then Medgar Evers, Malcolm X, Martin Luther King, Jr, and Robert F.Kennedy were assassinated and we saw riots in our cities from Watts to Detroit to Newark. In 1966, 38 American cities had broken out in violence. In 1967, 128 American cities suffered 164 riots. In the wake of his city's violence, Mayor Jerome Cavanaugh of Detroit said, "It looks like Berlin in 1945."

Almost fifty years later, the current president not only inherited two wars and the worst economy in eight decades, but he took office when more than 400 people were killed in Chicago, mostly by gangs in a major national resurgence of gang warfare. Four hundred thousand young people were taken to hospitals after violence at their schools. The same number of young people who died on that tragic day at Columbine perish each day in America from a gunshot wound.

Forty percent of high school students in Los Angeles do not graduate. One in seven college women and 26 percent of high school girls are sexually assaulted while they are enrolled at these respective schools. Thirty-four percent of girls under 20 have at least one child. Americans are the biggest consumers of drugs in the world. And the list goes on.

As the number of dead rose in the wars in Iraq and Afghanistan, enormous resources were poured into those distant lands; protest arose against the wars. As the number of dead rose in American cities, the Bush Administration poured fewer resources into those cities to stop the violence. But where is the protest against violence in our cities? Where are the resources?

While there have been slightly more than 5,000 deaths in the two wars, more than 27,000 black men have died in American streets. Now, we face that powder keg I described earlier.

As they used to say in the Navy, we need all hands on deck to fight for justice and peace. In too many places across the globe, men sexually assault women, parents and adults abuse children, and wars are waged based on conflicts that most of the world does not understand.

What gives us hope and heart is that in the face of all these challenges, there are initiatives for peace taking hold across the globe. This book, co-edited by peace educator and activist Randall Amster, raises the critical questions and calls for new partnerships to be bridged across ideological divides. As it says in the introduction, the chapters in this edited volume are informed by "a shared understanding of peace as depicting human beings working together to resolve conflicts, respect standards of justice, satisfy basic needs, and honor human rights.... [P]eace involves a respect for life and for the dignity of each human being without discrimination or prejudice." A series of authors in their chapters urge that education "must empower teachers and students to challenge hegemony, affirm diversity, and seek equity and social justice."

Ndura-Ouédraogo and Amster further make the important assertion that every person on this planet can contribute to building cultures of peace. The book strives to learn from activists as well as scholars on how best to move forward. The transdisciplinary approach encompasses not only activists, theorists, researchers, and practitioners, but also delves into art and music, literacy, global development, economics, sports, criminal justice, peace commentary, ecology, social and cultural theory, the United Nations, and current events analysis. These transdisciplinary voices may give us the fabric to wage peace instead of war.

In particular, I loved that there was a chapter on sport. I come from the world of sport, where I believe we have something special in the huddle. Those who earn a place in the team huddle have experienced the miracle of team. We learn, ever so slowly, that our differences do not matter in the huddle. It does not matter if you are African-American, White, Latino, Asian-American, Native American, or Arab-American. It does not matter if you are Hindu, Sikh, Muslim, Protestant, Catholic, Jewish, Buddhist; young or old; gay or straight. In the huddle we are all interdependent. We cannot win without becoming one unit.

Too often we talk about a white America, a black America, a Latino America, or an Asian America instead of a United States of America. Sport breaks down those barriers. There is something special about sport. But I also understand that all the other disciplines portrayed here coming together can help us form a far better understanding of the paths to peace. In this sense, the chapters collected here serve as a huddle for taking on the challenges we face.

Throughout the book, we get a sense that we have taught our children how to hate and that we have helped them learn how to wage war. The goal of this book is to teach our children how to love again and to give them the tools of peace. As the editors end their introduction, this feeling is echoed. They ask us, as we go to sleep at night, to wonder: "*What have I done today to help build a culture of peace?*"

I was lucky enough to be asked to attend the inauguration of Nelson Mandela. As I drove from Johannesburg to Pretoria, alongside the road I saw the military hardware that had been used to oppress Mandela's people for generations and I realized that the hardware would now be used by this man of peace to create freedom and equality. I knew then that anything and everything is possible.

I believe that on January 20, 2009, the inauguration of President Barack Obama was another such day for the world. We need to create days

like that across the globe because it is hard to believe in what we cannot
see in front of us. Obama was elected three years after Hurricane Katrina,
an event that I feel produced the most racist moment in American history,
as America failed the African-American population of New Orleans.

This book arrives not that long after the events of September 11th,
when anti-Muslim feelings ran rampant in America. The most beloved
Muslim in the non-Muslim world stood up to remind America that he was
a Muslim too. This man, Muhammad Ali, had been perhaps the most hated
African-American in the United States 40 years before because of his
strong stance on race and the Vietnam War.

And the book comes at a time when eight women lead governments
across the world. Indeed, the world we live in reflects a dual sense of crisis
and opportunity, of anguish and hope.

Our children need to believe in what they cannot see. *Building
Cultures of Peace: Transdisciplinary Voices of Hope and Action* will help
us build a floor on despair and a roof over the dreams of the next
generations so they can indeed believe in what they cannot see and create
it as reality. This book helps begin that arduous process of restoring hope
and fostering action.

Introduction

Calling for Individual and Collective Engagement in Building Cultures of Peace

Elavie Ndura-Ouédraogo and Randall Amster

From scarring gender-based violence and haunting instances of child abuse in families across the globe, to communities torn apart by inter-group conflict and the blood-tinged wars of opposing nations, the human condition is rife with perpetual tumult. The consequences of such conflict and violence weigh heavily on humanity: widows caring for children with uncertain futures, revolting poverty and other forms of human suffering, dilapidated schools, dysfunctional governments, shocking acts of terrorism, and an overwhelming sense of powerlessness and hopelessness that only serves to breed more conflict and violence.

Still, in the face of these grave and monumental challenges, initiatives for peace strive to take root. Seeking more effective ways to mediate peace among communities and nations, the United Nations adopted three groundbreaking declarations on the eve of the 21st century. In its resolution 52/15 of 20 November 1997, it proclaimed the year 2000 the International Year for the Culture of Peace. A year later, on 10 November 1998, in its resolution 53/25 it proclaimed the period 2001-2010 as the International Decade for a Culture of Peace and Nonviolence for the Children of the World. And the following year, on 13 September 1999, the UN adopted its Declaration on a Culture of Peace which defines what that vision looks like and the actions that must be taken to build a culture of peace.

We are nearing the end of the International Decade for a Culture of Peace, yet violence is still raging in our schools and communities around the world while warfare dominates the geopolitical landscape, and thus peace still often appears more and more like a faint dream.

That is why this edited book is important and timely. With a titular focus on "Building Cultures of Peace: Transdisciplinary Voices of Hope and Action," the book addresses the UN's charge to develop "values, attitudes, modes of behaviour and ways of life conducive to the promotion of peace among individuals, groups and nations" (*UNESCO*, p.2). This work is grounded in our firm belief that building cultures of peace calls for new critical questions to be raised and new partnerships engineered across ideological stances and disciplines. As such, it supports Johann Galtung's (1996, 1) vision of peace for the 21st century, which states: "The peace researcher must look for causes, conditions, and contexts in various spaces—Nature, Human, Social, World, Time, Culture." Although he recognizes that "this transdisciplinary spectrum makes peace studies both challenging, difficult intellectually, and problematic in praxis," Galtung warns that "a narrow focus is doomed in advance." Thus, here we bring together scholars reflecting a broad perspective on the critical issues of peace and conflict resolution that pervade our world.

The chapters in this edited volume are informed by a shared understanding of peace as depicting "human beings working together to resolve conflicts, respect standards of justice, satisfy basic needs, and honor human rights," and further that "peace involves a respect for life and for the dignity of each human being without discrimination or prejudice" (Harris & Morrison 2003, 12). The authors here stress that education must empower teachers and students to challenge hegemony, affirm diversity, and seek equity and social justice (Ndura 2007) in order to constructively and peacefully resolve issues of structural injustice and help to create long-term harmonious relationships among individuals and nations alike (Johnson & Johnson 2006).

The book is further grounded in the basic premise that every human being can contribute to the quest for building cultures of peace. It raises fundamental questions that helped to frame the proceedings at the 2008 annual conference of the Peace & Justice Studies Association (PJSA) in Portland, Oregon, where the idea to develop this book was born, and seeks to engage in a transdisciplinary discourse as an imperative for building and sustaining cultures of peace around the globe. How can we encourage systemic and critical explorations of the idea of a culture of peace, and prepare peace studies students to work effectively in their chosen fields and in life in pursuit of this outcome? How can we develop curricula and programs, and provide experiences in K-12 education and teacher preparation programs, to promote peace? What can scholarly research across disciplines contribute to the quest for cultures of peace? What can we learn from activists' struggles for peace, and how do human relations with the environment inform the dialogue? What can peace professionals contribute to our exploration and understanding of the "best practices" in peacebuilding, and how can we build upon the positive steps already being taken? These are the essential questions pursued in this interdisciplinary volume.

The book is therefore unique in its approach, contents, and broad readership appeal. Unlike any other book on this topic, *Building Cultures of Peace* draws from and appeals to theorists, researchers, practitioners, and activists with interests in nonviolent resistance, pedagogy and teacher education, art and music, critical literacy, moral development theory, economic development, sports, criminal justice, peace commentary, ecology, socio-cultural theory, the United Nations, and current events analysis. Each of these areas of exploration offers a lens through which to develop theories and practices aimed at creating a more peaceful world.

The book is organized into three parts and fifteen chapters to reflect the convergence of transdisciplinary voices in the cultures of peace discourse. Part one gathers perspectives on the role of pedagogy and education in building cultures of peace. In chapter 1, Edward Brantmeier, Antonette Aragon, and Brian Yoder discuss findings from a research study that examined their students' responses to their efforts to integrate peace education and multicultural education. They argue that such a paradigm shift allows instructors and students to critically examine cultural borderlands and include voices on the historical margins in movements toward deeper social justice. In chapter 2, Cindy Maguire introduces peace and social justice through art education grounded in a "capabilities" approach and dialogical aesthetics to promote a deeper understanding of oneself as well as the self in relation to the social and cultural environment. In chapter 3, Julie Morton draws on peace theorists, educators, and literacy specialists to construct a theoretical framework for a skills-based model of peace education that can be integrated into a secondary school language arts curriculum. Beverly Shaklee highlights the importance of preparing teachers to teach for peace in chapter 4. She provides a snapshot of our continued efforts to define peace education, to translate it into teacher preparation and classroom practice and to find ways in which to evaluate its impact. Stacia Stribling further connects literacy development and peacebuilding in Chapter 5. She uses vignettes from kindergarten, first grade and second grade classrooms to illustrate how teachers use critical literacy practices to help children understand different experiences and cultures, learn to respect these differences, and act in ways that promote equity and peace. Finally, in chapter 6, Cris Toffolo examines the psychological research on moral development and highlights relevant insights that can enhance undergraduate justice and peace studies programs.

Part two anchors the quest for cultures of peace in society and culture. Robert Baker and Craig Esherick examine sport-based peace initiatives in chapter 7. They highlight the importance of interpersonal and intergroup contact in facilitating peace and resolving conflict, and conclude that sport can be a valuable mechanism in fostering peace and social justice. In chapter 8, Michael DeValve and Cary Adkinson argue that a department-supported and diligent compassion-generative mindful practice among law enforcement officers can help cultivate a richer culture of peace in the United States by helping police agencies be more effective in their efforts to render a more compassionate, fair, and sustainable justice service to their many constituencies, and by mitigating the physical and emotional problems associated with the police job for both the officers themselves as well as their families. In chapter 9, Tom Hastings calls our attention to the missing voices of peace professors and other peace professionals in the national war-colored discourse. He contends that identifying and overcoming the barriers to such public engagement is an imperative to building cultures of peace. Pearl Hunt further broadens our conception of peace by connecting music to peacebuilding in chapter 10. In articulating music's legacy within movements of social change, she examines what making music might mean within the discourse of cultural studies and how a social justice oriented, music inclusive version of peace studies might benefit from such a practice. In Chapter 11, Elavie Ndura-Ouédraogo argues that the failure to affirm cultural diversity perpetuates oppressive systems and may contribute to violent dispositions and behaviors. Grounding the discussion of diversity, social justice, and peace within the broad human rights discourse, she discusses ways in which oppression challenges our quest for cultures of peace and contends that the main role of education should be to prepare active agents of peace.

Part three explores the role of politics, the environment, and the economy in the discourse about building cultures of peace. In chapter 12, Cheryl Duckworth examines how Iraq's war economy impacts the various peace processes currently unfolding there, offering recommendations for a way forward and discussing potential implications for peacebuilding in general. John Lango explores the ways that a reformed Security Council of the United Nations ought to counter threats to the peace in chapter 13. Using the case of genocide in Darfur as an example, he outlines a proposal for Security Council reform, and concludes that to build a global culture of peace, grassroots peace activists should advocate and promote reasonable peace actions to the Security Council. In chapter 14, Supriya Baily examines the case of Gujarat, India to highlight social, economic, and political differences that led to violence in the region and how the lack of resources affects relationships between fighting groups and hinders the effectiveness of peace education. She argues that the case of Gujarat represents not only what is happening in India, but provides broader insights about other countries where development programs and localized intolerance hamper the successful implementation of peace education programs. Randall Amster closes this section in chapter 15 by drawing upon analyses of conflict and the potential peacemaking possibilities of environmental cooperation to develop the basic tenets comprising the emerging rubric of "peace ecology." He contends that any attempt to build a culture of peace requires theories and actions aimed at promoting both social justice and environmental sustainability.

The subtitle of this book, "Transdisciplinary voices of hope and action," reflects both the necessarily inclusive nature of the cultures of peace discourse and the urgent need for individual and collective active engagement in the quest. It calls for professional collaboration beyond and across fields of study and for the broadening of academic discourses. It calls for action, and for individual and collective accountability in creating futures of peace. It calls for constant reflection and questioning of our individual and collective dispositions and motivations, as well as the relationships that we seek after or avoid. It calls for honest answers because deceit and hypocrisy only fuel mistrust and fear, and thus divert us from the path to peace. The focus of this volume also strives to stoke the fires of hope, urging that we all can do something to contribute to cultures of peace, and that we can grow better and stronger in our journey each day. Therefore, we encourage our readers to ponder with each rising new day, "What am I going to do to contribute to a culture of peace today?" And contemplate as dusk gently falls ushering in the promise of a restful night, "What have I done today to help build a culture of peace?" Maybe then we will get closer to translating our dream of peace into a reality—one educator, one student, one activist, one scholar, one person, one community, one culture, and one peaceful action at a time.

References

Galtung, J. 1996. *Peace by peaceful means: Peace and conflict, development and civilization*. London: Sage Publications.

Harris, I. M. and M.L. Morrison. 2003. *Peace education*. 2nd ed. Jefferson, NC: McFarland & Company, Inc., Publishers.

Johnson, D. W. and R.T. Johnson. 2006. Peace education for consensual
    peace: The essential role of conflict resolution. *Journal of Peace
    Education* 3 (2): 147-174.
Ndura, E. 2007. Calling institutions of higher education to join the quest
    for social justice and peace. *Harvard Educational Review* 77 (3): 345-
    350.
UNESCO. Declaration and Programme of Action on a Culture of Peace.
    http://www.unesco.org/cpp/uk/declarations/2000.htm   (accessed
    October 13, 2008).

PART I:

PEDAGOGY AND EDUCATION

When we think about building a culture of peace on any level—from a local community to the entire globe—education is central to the vision. Indeed, it may be said without exaggeration that education is the only path to peace that is both practical and sustainable. The practices of pedagogy explored here, ranging from multiculturalism and art to literacy and morality, suggest the range of dynamic possibilities for utilizing education to promote peace. Beyond this, taken together they also remind us that pedagogy is not simply a set of practices for the transmission of information and knowledge, but a shared tool for exploring and experiencing what it means to actually live in a culture of peace. And this, in the end, may be the most important lesson of all.

CHAPTER ONE

MULTICULTURAL PEACE EDUCATION: EMPOWERING PRE-SERVICE TEACHERS TOWARD A PARADIGM OF SOCIAL JUSTICE BEYOND COLORBLINDNESS

EDWARD J. BRANTMEIER, ANTONETTE ARAGON, AND BRIAN YODER

"Structural violence is silent, it does not show—it is essentially static, it *is* the tranquil waters"
—Johan Galtung 1969, 173

Promoting social justice is integral to peace education efforts in schools and is necessary for building an authentic culture of peace. Multicultural education braided with the orientations of peace education, can be understood as educative efforts toward harmonizing the tensions of diversity and unity inherent in pluralistic contexts where both direct and indirect forms of violence are present. A paradigm shift toward integrating peace and multicultural education includes generating an approach that critically examines cultural borderlands; voices on the historical margins are included in movements toward deeper social justice—conditions where both personal relationships and social structures promote racial healing and reconciliation of the past. Raising consciousness about the multicultural history of the United States seems imperative to expand a collective understanding of past injustice in a movement toward authentic social reconstruction for a more hopeful future. Raising consciousness is also imperative to prepare teachers for increasingly diverse public schools—a necessity for building cultures of peace where ethnic/racial equality and equity become the norm rather than the exception.

Based on the multiplier effect in teacher education, if teacher candidates teach in majority white schools, then these teachers who are committed to a multicultural peace education approach may prepare their students for deeper understanding of social justice, peace education, and deeper introspection concerning white privilege. However, explicit peace education courses and topics that aim to instill social justice in mainstream schools of education in the United States are a rare phenomenon (Quezada and Romo 2004). Rather, marginal and implicit approaches seem to be the norm *if* and *when* peace education is presented as an additive topic of study (Brantmeier 2008). Braiding multicultural education and peace education would be a paradigm shift toward promoting solid understandings of peace in the context of social justice (Brantmeier and Lin 2008), and in our view this is necessary for building a culture of peace.

In studies related to multiculturalism and unmasking white privilege, Carole Barlas et al. (2000) have described a process of co-operative learning in which individuals and groups reported a change in consciousness about their supremacist consciousness. Cynthia Levine-Rasky (2000) asserts that consequent to such experiences, dialogues on racism are shifting from the inadequacies of 'others' or from the race/d relations between 'us' (Whites) and 'them,' (non-Whites) to a critical examination of whiteness itself. The newly integrated textbook by Joel Spring (2006), *Deculturalization and the Struggle for Equality: A Brief History of the Education of Dominated Cultures in the United States*, helps move in the direction of a critical examination of whiteness by examining the history of schooling from the perspective of non-white groups. The critical examination of whiteness that reading this book affords is an implicit peace education approach because it allows students to deconstruct the historical narratives they have been told about how white people in the United States were the central contributors to the blossoming of American pluralistic democracy; it provides raw historical evidence suggesting both deliberate and unintended attempts of white ruling elites to deculturize and assimilate racial/ethnic "others" into a white dominance paradigm (Howard 2006). Raising consciousness about the intent and methods of deculturalization provides future teachers an understanding of the past in order to move toward transformative action for building a culture of peace in the future.

This chapter catalogues and analyzes a small component of a multicultural curriculum change process in an introduction foundations course of the teacher education sequence at a land grant institution in the West. Particularly, the curricula change process included the addition of Joel Spring's (2006) book. The process of multicultural curriculum change is explained and student responses to this new text are analyzed using qualitative data analysis methods.

The backgrounds of the researchers are important to note. Ed Brantmeier is a white male who was a first generation college student. Currently, he is a faculty member dedicated to promoting transformative peace education, social justice, and multicultural competence in schooling contexts. Antonette Aragon is a Latina woman who was also a first generation college student. She currently is a faculty member focusing her research and teaching energies on multiculturalism, cultural competence, and social justice particularly working with White teacher educators. Brian Yoder is a white male, two generations removed from the Amish community; he currently works as a graduate research assistant while pursuing his Master's in school counseling.

Collectively, the authors maintain that it is incumbent upon foundations courses in teacher education to provide students with the ability to critically examine themselves in relation to the historical and societal underpinnings of racism within society—racism that has promoted current policies and institutional practices that have ignored and forgotten the voices of oppressed people in the United States. When white students in particular examine racism critically, they move past a colorblind approach by acknowledging layers of racism that constitute the legacy of privilege, oppression, and power upon which their present world resides. A paradigm of multicultural peace education can be established as a foundation toward social justice and equity—a necessity for building a culture of peace and social justice in their own future classrooms.

Best Practices in Multicultural Education

Research on best practices in multicultural teacher education indicates that multi-dimensional, holistic approaches to multicultural reform work best. James Banks et al. (2005, 233) maintain that "all teachers must be prepared to take into account the different experiences and academic needs of a wide range of students as they plan to teach." Sonia Nieto (1999) argues that teachers' attitude, beliefs and actions are fundamental to student learning. Research indicates that when teachers use knowledge about the social, cultural and language backgrounds of their students when planning and implementing instruction, the academic achievement of students can increase (Banks et al. 2005). James Banks (1995) maintains that there are five dimensions of solid multicultural education programs: content integration, knowledge construction, prejudice reduction, equity pedagogy, and empowering the school culture and social structure.

The multicultural curriculum reform effort in this pilot study in one section of a foundations course focused on content integration and knowledge construction by introducing silenced voices of marginalized peoples and by critically deconstructing the history of schooling in the United States. The intention for including Joel Spring's (2006) book, *Deculturalization and the Struggle for Educational Equality,* was to provide pre-service teachers an opportunity to reflect on how the schooling system deculturalized non-white groups via culturally oppressive policy and assimilationist practice. Teaching and learning focused on how social memory is constructed and distorted via the perpetuation of a predominately white, mainstream version of U.S. history. The authors maintain that without deeper understanding of the legacies of power, privilege, and white dominance in the U.S., present day inequities and inequalities will be reproduced in teacher education programs, in k-12 schools, and the formal and informal curricula. Teachers who are unaware of a multicultural history may not be prepared to critically examine the historical-contextual nature of present day racial/ethnic injustice. They may not be prepared to critically examine mainstream policy discourses surrounding the achievement gap, policies regarding students of color, or examining how tracking of students of color continues to halt their achievement. Deep honesty and consciousness-raising on the part of whites and on the part of people of color are steps in the right direction. Informed by the work of Paulo Freire (1972), movement toward building a more authentic culture of peace via teacher education needs to include a critical peace education approach that includes consciousness-raising, vision, and transformative action (Brantmeier 2008).

Sonia Nieto (1999) stressed that both the *what* (curriculum) and the *how* (pedagogy) must be acknowledged as influencing student learning in a multicultural approach. In the context of this study, the instructor used a student-centered, constructivist, dialogical approach to teaching and learning. Highlighting the *how* of dialogical pedagogy, Juan-Miguel Fernandez-Balboa and James Marshall (1994, 180) maintain, "The implementation of dialogical pedagogy in teacher education establishes a normative basis for democratic participation." The article on dialogical pedagogy from which the previous quote was taken is the first reading of this foundations course. Modeling dialogical pedagogy, the instructor integrated content knowledge in a democratic classroom format. Students prepared and then co-lead discussions on Joel Spring's (2006) book; the instructor facilitated dialogue and student inquiry. Kenneth Zeichner (1998) maintains that tomorrow's educators will teach as they were taught, so it is important that multicultural educators model democratic and dialogical classrooms. Teaching strategies that have been found to raise students' awareness about race, culture, and discrimination include autobiographies, mail cultural exchanges, simulations of unequal opportunity, and teaching about white privilege. Christine Sleeter (2001, 102) maintains, "The research suggests that community based immersion experiences are more powerful than stand-alone multicultural education courses, yet it is likely that the latter are more prevalent because they are easier to institutionalize." Though students observed in a classroom for four hours in the foundations course in this study—the first required course in the teacher education sequence—classroom dialogue about the readings, on-line discussion, and simulative experiential learning were the most prevalent modes of instruction for this particular course.

Kenneth Zeichner et al. (1998) maintain that effective multicultural education programs that permeate throughout the entire curriculum in a teacher education program will have a number of impacts on the nation's future teachers. They should show teacher candidates how to learn about students, families, and communities and how to use their students' diverse experiences in planning, delivering, and evaluating instruction. Diversity classes for teacher candidates should help students reexamine their own identity and others' multiple and inter-related identities. Multicultural education programs should help prospective teachers develop the commitment to be change agents who work to promote greater equity and social justice in both schooling and society at large. We maintain that desires for creating a more peaceful world need to be integrated and cultivated along the way.

Braiding Multicultural and Peace Education

In short, peace education attempts to eliminate direct and indirect forms of violence (Harris and Morrison 2003). In peace theory Johan Galtung's (1969) distinction between negative peace, or the absence of war or direct violence, and positive peace, the absence of structural and/or indirect violence, is very helpful when positioning peace education in the context of multicultural education for social justice. Direct violence can be understood as physical violence between or among individuals, groups, and/or nations. Indirect violence can take the form of psychological violence—intimidation, bullying, fear of violence, inter-group tensions, and structural violence— political, economic, environmental, and social arrangements that privilege some at the exclusion of others (though it could be argued that psychological violence is part and parcel of structural violence). Galtung (1969, 171) maintains, "The violence is built into the structure and shows up as unequal power and consequently as unequal life chances... Above all, the power to decide over the distribution of resources is unevenly distributed." Who has control over the historical narrative or narratives taught in the curriculum in schools can influence the collective historical memory and thus the racial consciousness of a nation. Whether the history of the racial group one affiliates with is told as part of the grand narrative of history *matters* to a great extent. Further, knowing that race is a social construct developed by European colonizers to categorize, divide, dominate, and control people via colonial practices is yet another layer of understanding forms of violence (American Anthropological Association Statement on Race). Exclusionary practices in the telling of history are a form of cultural violence.

Cultural violence is a linkage concept that braids the education aims of the subfields of multicultural education and peace education. Galtung (1990, 291) introduced the idea of cultural violence to the field of peace education, "Cultural violence makes direct and structural violence look, even feel, right - or at least not wrong." Cultural violence, put simply, is exhibited when cultural formations are used to legitimate any form of violence, either direct or indirect. For example, in-group norms that legitimize, reinforce, or perpetuate violence against individuals, groups, and people within a broader society could be considered cultural violence. Cultural assimilationist practices, Eurocentric curriculum, and the denial of non-mainstream cultures (dispositions, values, behavior, and language) in school could be considered forms of cultural violence in a U.S. context. In this sense, infusing multicultural curriculum content in teacher education programs and K-12 schools can be considered a form of peace education that addresses the cultural violence embedded in exclusionary mainstream practices. However, the concept of cultural violence need be interrogated given that it presumes that there are universal human rights and values that cultural groups may violate—for example, the right for all groups to live as linguistically and cultural diverse people in a complex democracy. Other overt examples of cultural violence might include: pre-emptive war, infanticide, and female genital mutilation—though all of these examples surely are debatable.

A more complex view of peace that includes a critical examination of cultural violence need be employed for understanding the connections of multicultural peace education focused on *social justice.* A critique of the methods and motives of cultural hegemony that perpetuates overt, silent, and/or systemic racism need be employed. The semblance of peace in the form of absence of direct physical violence does not convey deeper conditions of peace that result from the elimination of intimidation, bullying, cultural violence, institutionalized racism, and political, economic, and social inequalities.

Multicultural peace education braids the theoretical and practical orientations of two interdependent subfields in education. Multicultural peace education can be understood as nonviolent educative efforts toward harmonizing the tensions of diversity and unity inherent in multicultural contexts; "intercultural borderlands are generated and distinctive primary cultures are honored and respected" (Brantmeier 2008, 70). A critique of power need be employed in this critical epistemological and diversity affirming pursuit: How is truth constructed in history? Who controls storytelling? Who benefits and who suffers? (Aragon & Brantmeier 2009) The ideal result of multicultural peace education efforts includes the building of cultures of peace, premised on positive pluralism and unity in democratic civic engagement and social life.

The authors here maintain that there are essential approaches to multicultural peace education focused on authentic racial/ethnic peacebuilding in a U.S. context: 1) A critical examination of knowledge construction (critical epistemology), deconstruction of history, white privilege, and what it means to be White; 2) An investigation into the evolution of race as a socially constructed entity and investigation of how "others" are constructed; 3) The inclusion of critical readings, particularly Joel Spring's *Deculturalization and the Struggle for Education Equality* (2006) with guided oral and written responses; 4) peaceful means for peaceful ends; opportunities for honest discussion and caring reflection about cultural violence in the past and present, as well as considerations of teachers as social change agents in the formation of a more peaceful and just future.

Meritocracy and Colorblindness

When examining what it means to be white in the United States, it is important to provide a context for deconstructing race. In today's society it is easy to dismiss color and believe that color is not important because it is often believed that we now live in a "raceless" society. Such beliefs are prevalent among people in society as well as college students because there is a sense that being white or black or brown has no bearing on an individual's or group's relative place in socio-economic hierarchy. Such beliefs are part of a colorblind perspective. Embracing color-blindness allows one to be blind to the fact that racial and ethnic minorities lag behind whites on almost every quality of life measure (Gallagher 2003). Colorblindness allows one to ignore historical implications of slavery, Jim Crow, institutional racism, white privilege and other injustices and to think of these as "a thing of the past, not relevant anymore." The colorblind

perspective removes from personal thought and public discussion any taint
or suggestion of white supremacy or white guilt while legitimating the
existing social, political and economic arrangements which privilege
Whites (Bonilla-Silva 2001). Furthermore, there is a deep-seated belief
that America is a meritocracy—Whites are able to imagine that material
success they enjoy relative to racial minorities is a function only of
individual hard work, determination, thrift and investments in education.
This perspective insinuates that class and culture and not institutional
racism, are responsible for social inequality (Gallagher 2003).

In the foundations course in this study, students are asked to critically
examine a colorblind perspective, meritocracy, and the deconstruction of
history, white privilege and what it means to be White especially as they
relate to schooling. Pre-service teachers make connections between
existing social, political and economic arrangements which privilege
Whites as a result of institutional racism, social inequality, and policy and
practice aimed at deculturalization. Students are asked to consider how
color is part of the equation of who gets access and who does not get
access in society; individual attainment and success are contextualized in
systems of dominance and privilege. In ideal form, these peace education
efforts can promote an understanding of how direct forms of violence
(land theft from Native Americans in "Manifest Destiny" policies, slavery,
Jim Crow, forced internment of Japanese-Americans) reinforce a legacy of
cultural violence apparent in white privilege, institutional racism, and the
politics of citizenship. Students can become more conscious about how
history impacts the plight of people of color today. These discussions,
analyses, writings, and careful reflections that examine historical racism,
colorblindness, and meritocracy allow students to become more conscious
of layers of racism that constitute the legacy of privilege, oppression, and
power in today's U.S. society.

Research Methods

The research question for the overarching multicultural curriculum
transformation project was, "How does newly integrated multicultural
curriculum content influence students thinking, emotions, and behaviors?"
In one pilot section of five total sections for the foundations course in the
fall of 2007, students read Joel Spring's textbook *Deculturalization and
the Struggle for Education Equality*. The participant group in this study
was somewhat consistent with broader national demographics: statistics
from the National Center of Education Statistics in 2004 convey that white
teachers comprised 83.1% of the teaching force, non-whites comprised

16.9%; female teachers comprised aproximately 75% and males comprised 25% . Of the thirty eight pariticpants in this study, thirty were female (78.9%) and eight were male (21%). Participants self-identified ethnically/racially as follows: thirty participants as White (78.9%); three students as Hispanic and White (7.8%); two participants identified as Hispanic (5%); one student as Asian (2.5%); one student as Native American, Hispanic, and White (2.5%); and one student chose to not identify her race (2.5%).

Following two classroom sessions where students discussed their understanding of the book, they were required to engage in an on-line, threaded discussion. The threaded on-line discussion format created the opportunity for students to read the responses of others, to learn from those responses, and to build on them. Participants responded on-line to the following question:

> What have you learned/unlearned from reading this book? (provide specific references and quotes from the text to validate the claims made in your response).

Data analysis of the thirty-eight responses to this question were conducted using Nvivo 8.0 qualitative analysis software. In sequence, three researchers employed an open coding technique during data analysis (Robson 2002). In the qualitative data analysis software employed, an open-code is conceptualized as a "free node" and hierarchical codes are labeled "tree nodes." The first researcher conducted open coding that aligns with Phil Carspecken's (1996) description of low-level or low-inference coding, "coding that falls close to the primary record and requires little abstraction" (p. 146). A second researcher began to make moderate inferences, speculating at the implicit meaning and overarching coding categories that emerged from the data. In sequence, a third researcher examined the primary data for high level implicit meanings and high level inferences to create umbrella coding categories that captured the major themes of the data. Axial coding and selective coding (Robson 2002) were employed intermittently during the process of open coding in order to examine emerging categories. In attempts to ensure validity and reliability, the three researchers met to discuss open coding agreements and conflicts and hierarchical coding categories in attempts to substantiate data interpretation and analysis.

A major limitation to this method included the inability to do member-checking with participants who responded to the on-line question. In some cases, sentence structure, grammar, and spelling errors somewhat obstructed researcher's interpretation of student meaning. In such instances, the researchers used low-inference interpretations whenever possible. Data triangulation through interview and systematic observation was not conducted. Also, with such a small sample size of thirty eight participants, the lessons are hardly generalizable to other contexts, though the intent of this research study was to understand student meaning making concerning the use of this text in this particular class. Finally, because individual participants were able to see the responses of others, "group think" might have impacted student responses, thus generating commonalities in some responses.

Lessons from the Case Study

Through the first researcher's process of low-inference coding, a number of codes emerged repeatedly. The most common reoccurring open codes that emerged in student responses fell under the following tree nodes: learned, unlearned, surprised or shocked, African Americans, Asian Americans, Native Americans, and sugar coating history. The graph below summarizes the open codes with the highest frequency:

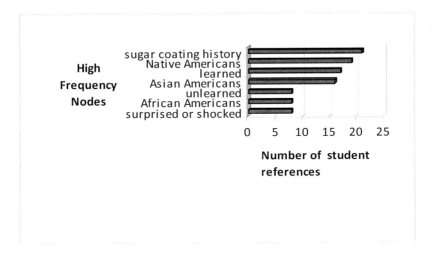

Figure 1: Themes emerged in the above nodes with the highest frequency.

Within and between nodes, the first researcher found notable patterns. In regards to exposure to history in secondary school, many students acknowledged they were familiar with the history of oppression of African Americans. Those same students wrote that they were "surprised" or "shocked" when they came to learn of the hidden history of the oppression of other minorities, notably Native Americans and especially Asian Americans. One white female student wrote "I never knew the history behind Asian Americans. I did not realize that they were considered "colored" and segregated just as much as the African Americans. That was a real eye opener for me."

Students wrote about having to "unlearn" what some described as the "innocence of the United States" and let go of the belief that America could do no wrong. Many teacher candidates wrote that they saw this belief coming from "sugar coating of history," the most common theme that emerged from the analysis. Students expressed anger or disappointment at the omissions or "glossing over" of wrong doing by the dominant white group in U.S. history. One female student wrote: "I feel a lot of history classes water down the truth of what happened so that young Americans don't have a negative outlook on the government or the countries (sic) past." Students seemed to feel that if more young Americans were exposed to all the ugly truths of past injustices, the world might be a better place for those who don't belong to the dominant culture. The use of metaphors of "eye-opening" "watering down" and "sugar-coating" imply a masking, dilution, and sweetening of some hard historical truths: some students expressed surprise, shock, or in some cases anger about the misrepresentations and voids in their own learning of U.S. history.

In the data analysis process of the second researcher, the code "selective history" was utilized to capture students' sentiments and thoughts in regard to selective versions of U.S. history that were taught to them. Student comments included:

- I feel that they publish history books for children that hide or omit the truth about what really happened. ...I go back to our class conversations about how the government wanted to take away the culture of the Native Americans and how they took the young children away from their families just to help this process be more successful. I[t] (sic) makes me want to cry almost (written by a white female student).

- I was amazed to learn about the history of Native Americans and Asian Americans in the early years of education in this country. I never learned about this side of history in any of my classes until this semester. I think it's kind of disappointing that I wasn't taught all views of history and not knowing "exactly" how other cultures and races were treated (written by an Asian male student).

• A lot of the history that I learned when I was younger always seemed to try to justify the wrongs in our past and shed whites in a more positive light (written by a white female student).

• The idea of using education as a way of destroying cultures and the idea of withholding education because of fear is ridiculous. I think that today we can attribute current racism problems to the fact that we are not educated about our country's past mistakes. Those things are hidden from us. Our society would be a lot different, I think, if everyone was aware of these things and the consequences they brought (written by a white female student).

• …I really liked how we talked about why a book such as Spring's is surprising to students because of the negligence of the government to include their mistakes and improprieties in the history taught in those very schools today (written by a white female student).

• …When flipping through the pages of this unspoken history of America, I enhanced my understanding of the oppression and brutality that so many Americans have faced (written by a white female student).

• Like the rest of my classmates, my high school history classes didn't consist of a lot of the information provided in the text (written by a white female student).

In addition to awareness of gaps in the teaching of history, several students reported awareness of white racism in U.S. history:

• A white female student wrote: One of the things that I thought was interesting was the "drop of blood" rule. I knew that people were very prejudice[d] in the past, but one drop of blood is a really extreme rule. Even if it has been generations since someone married outside their race, anyone in that family from that point on would also be counted non-white. "if a child's father was African American and the mother was European American, than (sic) the child was classified as African American and was required to attend a segregated black school" (Spring 2006, 6).

• …Wasn't America based on a "melting pot" and not on a white soup? … (written by a white female student).

- As I'm sure it is with many of the students in our class, my history classes growing up also seemed to always portray white Americans as the "superiors." If they did wrong... there *must* be a reason for it. I'm reminded of the movie, Pocahontas; it sure made John Smith and the English explorers coming to America look like bff's with the Indians. But I guess Disney (c) would NEVER show the real glimpse of history... as in these English explorers actually invaded the Indian's land and employed them for their agricultural knowledge (written by a white female student).

From reading the Spring (2006) text and discussing it, other students reported an increased awareness of cultural, linguistic, and religious assimilation:

- While reading this book, I could not believe how awful Anglo-Saxon whites treated everyone who was different than themselves. I came to the powerful and disturbing conclusion that the purpose of schooling in the United States used to be to deculturize (sic) everyone who was different than Anglo-Saxon whites (written by a white female student).

- In all my years of education, I have never been told that Missionaries were forcing Native Americans to learn English and abandon their native language and culture. This was not the first instance where the United States government tried to change an entire lifestyle to make it more like "white culture" (written by a white female).

- One thing I learned, was more about Bilingual Education, I have not heard about it until this book, and some in class, again, it makes since (sic) to have bilingual schools because the world if full of many other languages, but at the same time, I feel that we are in America and maybe because I am not fluent in a second language, but I hate walking into a store and seeing Spanish or even hearing it. I learned and now I somewhat understand the need for students to learn other languages, because it will most likely be important in the future for communication with other cultures and countries (written by a white/Hispanic female).

The plethora of student comments presented here suggests a wide range of emotions and thoughts. Awareness of past injustices is glaringly apparent. Teacher candidates received a color-blind perspective on U.S. history in their own schooling.

The colorblind perspective that students reveal was analyzed in the third researcher's examination of the primary data for high level implicit meanings. These major hierarchical coding categories (tree nodes) included a colorblind perspective, meritocracy myth, and how history shows the foundations of systems of injustice that we currently live under. When analyzing student comments related to the colorblind perspective, a white female student stated:

> I learned (and was also shocked) after reading Spring's "Methods of Deculturalization" on page 106 that these methods were used specifically to transform marginalized societies early in America's history and yet it seems these practices are still in place today. A couple that are still very apparent in today's classroom:
> - Forced to change language
> -Curriculum content that reflects culture of dominant group
> -Textbooks that reflect culture of dominant group
> -Use of teachers from dominant group
> It is enlightening, and also saddening considering the context, to realize that these methods are so familiar.

The students show awareness about what was not revealed to them in their elementary or secondary education; this reveals to them that their curricula instilled a colorblind perspective. In other words, there is a lack of color (diverse voices) presented in one's education, because only one color is represented, which is a monochromatic representation— the dominant white perspective. Students did not use the words, "colorblind perspective" in their analysis but it is implied because they show that they have a deeper understanding about how their curricula showed preference for the dominant group over the minority groups within history—and that legacy of preference continues today in linguistic assimilation practices, Eurocentric curriculum choices, and the racial/ethnic divide between high percentages of white teachers in increasingly multiracial schools. Creating awareness of the exclusionary practices inherent in U.S. history and present day reality may slowly transform the quiet waters of cultural violence into conscious awareness and action toward a more peaceful future. Another white female student wrote:

> I think that today we can attribute current racism problems to the fact that we are not educated about our country's past mistakes. Those things are hidden from us. Our society would be a lot different, I think, if everyone was aware of these things and the consequences they brought.

This student was taught to see a colorblind perspective in school because racism is "hidden" in education. If racism is hidden from students, than it is easy to believe that we live in an era free of racism. A white female student wrote:

- I came to the powerful and disturbing conclusion that the purpose of schooling in the United States used to be to deculturize (sic) everyone who was different than Anglo-Saxon whites. I cannot believe how "hush hush" our government is about our history in deculturizing people who were different than white Anglo Saxons. I believe every American student needs to be educated on the past discrimination within the school system, so that everyone can see how corrupt that system really was.

The colorblind perspective is revealed in this student's comment through a realization about how ""hush hush" the U.S. government is about history," which again signifies a form of hiding or presenting a colorblind perspective about the historical truths that show dominance of white Anglo Saxons over people who are different. There is also an understanding of discrimination, which is part of racism in society. The above quote implies that racism in the U.S. is part of a system legitimating the existing social, political and economic arrangements which privilege whites, thus maintaining conditions of indirect violence. Harris (2002, 7) defines peace education as, "Teaching encounters that draw out from people their desires for peace and provide them with …the skills for critical analysis of the structural arrangements that legitimate and produce *injustice* and *inequality.*" A critical analysis of the methods and implications of racism can be used to promote a more authentic culture of peace.

A meritocratic theme was revealed in student data as well; students are perceptive about opportunities being rendered to select groups and not to all. The quote below displays a revelation about opportunity afforded to those who are educated. Those who are not educated are taught to be compliant, inexpensive workers. Such opportunity is based upon past policies that have restricted some groups of people in our society. A white female student writes:

- A quote that really opened my eyes was in chapter three regarding the selective, restrictive policies on education: "the denial of an education or the provision of an inadequate education ensures compliant and inexpensive workers." I was taught America is a land of opportunity; this book made me question for whom these opportunities were really.

A different white female student perceives a lack of opportunity by stating:

- The shock of this book for me was the ways that people didn't just leave others out, it was how they pushed, forced, and actually took the time to ensure that others didn't obtain a fair education.

If marginalized groups were/are forced out of a fair and equitable education, then this shows that the education system limits and restricts groups from investing in their own education. Therefore, individuals and groups of people are no longer solely responsible for their education alone. Instead, limitation and restriction are revealed as a systemic process; this system is open for some but closed for those at the margins, which is how institutional racism operates. Disturbances in the silent waters of structural violence might construct new understandings of the way things are—what is natural and true might be transformed.

Another important code included how history shows the systems of power and privilege we live under. Students supported the viewpoint of how individuals are part of a bigger system that conveys privilege for some and related oppression for others. This is important because when students see how individuals no longer carry the sole responsibility for their personal successes, a systems understanding emerges. Consciousness emerges about how systems of power and privilege are in place to ensure that some people succeed, while barriers halt the success of people at the margins. A white female student wrote:

- I cannot forget the quote "It is important to understand that for some Americans, racism and democracy are not conflicting beliefs, but they are part of a general system of American values." The other main point that I got from the book is that some people in this country still deal with racism against them. I read this, I was blown away, and as I read further I began to understand how certain cultures in the United States could feel this way.

This student nudges toward understanding that social inequality is based upon institutional racism; historical racism has systematically restricted fair and equal participation for marginalized groups in U.S. society. She began to empathize with those marginalized groups and was perhaps taking some initial steps toward deconstructing a monochromatic historical narrative.

Challenges and Opportunities

The title of Gary Howard's book, *We Can't Teach What We Don't Know: White Teachers, Multiracial Schools* conveys a powerful message. If white educators do not understand how dominance paradigms operate to perpetuate privilege and oppression, if they are immersed only in a selective, monochromatic version of U.S. history, and if they affirm colorblind perspectives and the myth of meritocracy in approaches to teaching and learning, they/white educators will be hindered from engagement in transformative change of systems that de-humanize all. Unraveling the white dominance paradigm, according to Howard (2006), requires a healing response that includes: honesty, empathy, advocacy, and action. The first step, however, is honesty, "Honesty begins for Whites when we learn to question our assumptions and acknowledge the limitations of our culturally conditioned perceptions of truth" (73).

The data presented here is paradoxically both sobering and promising. Several students were sobered and surprised by their lack of knowledge about the history of Asian Americans, Native Americans, and Mexican-Americans. Several students commented that they were taught a selective history that did not include non-mainstream, white groups. Feelings of surprise, shock, amazement, and anger that the telling of history was "sugar coated" and "watered down" emerged. Awareness of white racism, of both the methods and events that reinforced white dominance in U.S. history, were reported. The beginnings of an emergence of a systems understanding of history and present day injustice that goes beyond colorblindness and the myth of individualized meritocracy are apparent.

In his foundational work in peace theory, Johan Galtung (1969) wrote that "structural violence is silent, it does not show—it is essentially static, it *is* the tranquil waters" (173). In order for the waters to be truly tranquil and authentically peaceful, they sometimes need to be stirred. If the cultural hegemony of a monochromatic version of U.S. history is not disrupted by the inclusion of multicultural historiography, then a false harmony and tentative peace prevails.

The authors suggest here that critical examination of hegemonic versions of history and inclusion of diverse voices help to alleviate legacies of structural and cultural violence.

However, a multicultural peace education approach requires peaceful means for peaceful ends. Caring, democratic, sustained dialogue about history needs to inform present conversations that hold the seed potential to actualize a better tomorrow. Such modeling of care, of dialogue, and of democracy might demonstrate how schools truly can *do* peace, diversity, and democracy in transformative ways. Awareness of past injustice alone in a multicultural peace education approach is not enough, however. Pre-service teachers need to be guided in continued inquiry and experiential immersion in culturally diverse contexts and multicultural literature where they can gain greater understanding of both "self" and "other." This study and the larger ongoing multicultural curriculum reform project in this foundations course open a dialogue about past injustice and self-reflective process that surely is emergent.

In addition, the fields of multicultural and peace education have more to learn from one another in terms of both theory and practice. With different names and sometimes different means, both attempt to eliminate direct and indirect forms of violence that emerge from culturally conditioned legacies of personal and systemic racism, sexism, classism, ableism, heterosexism, and more. Direct, indirect, and cultural violence dehumanize both the perpetrators and the victims; reconciliation requires a collective effort from all fields and sub-fields in education.

Lastly, Betty Reardon (1999, 14) affirms values for peace education that include: environmental responsibility; cultural diversity; human solidarity; social responsibility; and gender equality. Reardon (1999, 15) maintains that enacting these values requires the cultivation of the following capacities for peacemaking: ecological awareness; cultural competency; conflict proficiency; and gender sensitivity. Raising awareness about the selective telling of history potentially enacts the values of cultural diversity, human solidarity, and social responsibility. It cultivates the capacities for cultural competency and conflict proficiency in an ongoing effort of healing the wounds of the past. There are other peacebuilding values and capacities that need be cultivated in future teachers. Building authentic cultures of peace via teacher education in diverse global contexts will require consciousness raising, mobilization, and transformative action—on personal, relational, and systems levels. This timely work could greatly benefit children of the world—our greatest hope for the future of humanity.

References

American Anthropological Association Statement on Race. 1998. http://www.aaanet.org/stmts/racepp.htm (accessed May 1, 2009).
Aragon, A. and Brantmeier, E. J. 2009. *Diversity affirming ethics & critical epistemology: Institutional decision-making in community colleges*. New Directions for Community Colleges. Forthcoming.

Banks, J. A., M. Cochran-Smith, L. Moll, A. Richert, K. Zeichner, L. P.Fechner, L. D. Hammond, H. Duffy and M. McDonald. 2005. Teaching Diverse Learners. In *Preparing Teachers for a Changing World: What Teachers Should Learn and Be Able To Do*, ed. L. E. Darling-Hammond and J. E. Bransford, 232-274. Indianapolis: Jossey-Bass.

Banks, J. A.. 1995. Multicultural education: Historical development, dimensions and practice. In *Handbook of Research on Multicultural Education*, eds J. A. Banks and C. A. McGee Banks, 3-24. New York: Macmillan.

Barlas, C., E. Kasl, R. Kyle, A. MacLeod, D. Paxton, P. Rosenwasser and L. Sartor. 2000. *Learning to unlearn white supremacist consciousness*. Paper presented at the 41st Annual Adult Education Research Conference, 26-30. Vancouver, Canada.

Bonilla-Silva, E..2001. *White Supremacy and Racism in the Post-Civil Rights Era*. Boulder: Lynne Rienner Publishers.

Brantmeier, E. 2008. *Toward mainstreaming critical peace education in U.S. teacher education*. Paper presented at the Comparative and International Education Society Conference, August in New York, USA.

Brantmeier, E. 2008. Building empathy for intercultural peace: Teacher involvement in peace curricula development at a U.S. Midwestern High School. In *Transforming Education for Peace*, ed. J. Lin, E. J. Brantmeier and C. Bruhn, 67-89. Greenwich: Information Age Publishing.

Carspecken, P. 1996. *Critical ethnography in educational research: a Theoretical and practical guide*. London, Routledge.

Fernandez-Balboa J.-M. and J. Marshall. 1994. Dialogical pedagogy in teacher education: Toward and education for democracy. *Journal of Teacher Education* 45 (3): 172-182.

Freire, P. 1970. *Pedagogy of the Oppressed*. London: Penguin Books.

Gallagher, C. 2003. Color-blind privilege: The social and political functions of erasing the color line in post race America. *Race, Gender & Class* 10 (4): 1-17.

Galtung, J. 1969. Violence, peace, and peace research. *Journal of Peace Research* 6 (3): 167-191.

Galtung, J. 1990. Cultural violence. *Journal of Peace Research* 27 (3): 291-305.

Harris, I. 2002. Peace Education for a New Century. *Social Alternatives*. The University of Queensland. 21 (1).

Harris, I. and M.L. Morrison. 2003. *Peace Education*. 2nd ed. Jefferson: McFarland & Company Inc.

Howard, G. 2006. *We can't teach what we don't know: white teachers, multiracial schools*. 2nd ed. New York: Teachers College Press.

Levine-Rasky, C. 2000. Framing whiteness: Working through the tensions in introducing whiteness to educators. *Race Ethnicity and Education* 3 (3): 271-292.

National Center of Education Statistics. 2004. http://nces.ed.gov/surveys/sass.tables.state_2004_18.asp (accessed January 20, 2009).

Nieto, S. 1999. *The light in their eyes: Creating multicultural learning communities*. New York: Teachers College   Press.

Quezada, R. and J. Romo. 2004. Multiculturalism, peace education, and social justice in teacher education. *Multicultural Education* 11 (3): 2-11.

Reardon, B. 1999. Peace education; a review and projection. *Peace Education Reports* 17. Sweden: Malmo University School of Education.

Robson, C. 2002. *Real World Research*, 2nd ed. Oxford: Blackwell Publishers.

Sleeter, C. E. 2001. Preparing teachers for culturally diverse schools: Research and the overwhelming presence of whiteness. *Journal of Teacher Education* 52 (2): 94-106.

Spring, J. 2006. *Deculturalization and the struggle for equality: A brief history of the education of dominated cultures in the United States*, 5th ed. New York: McGraw-Hill

Zeichner, K. M., C. Grant, G. Gay, M. Gillete, L. Valli,and A. M. Villegas. 1998. Research informed vision of good practice in multicultural teacher education: Design principles. *Theory into practice* 37 (2) 163-171.

CHAPTER TWO

FOSTERING CAPABILITIES:
THE PRACTICE OF PEACE AND SOCIAL JUSTICE
IN CONTEMPORARY ART EDUCATION

CINDY MAGUIRE

In the spring of 2005, art education and art therapy students at Loyola
Marymount University (LMU) in Los Angeles facilitated participation by
students from kindergarten through eighth grade (K–8) in the *10,000 Kites*
project. Israeli artist Adi Yekutieli and Palestinian artist, George Nustas,
initiated *10,000 Kites*. In this project Israeli and Palestinian children and
families, invited to set aside differences, gathered together to fly kites in a
public display of their desire to end the regional conflict. Children from
around the world were invited to participate in their own communities as a
show of solidarity. LMU created an interactive presentation about the
conflict in the Middle East and its impact on children and youth for two
local schools. A poem by Israeli poet Yehuda Amichai, *Jerusalem*, was
read aloud as an entry point into the discussion and subsequent art making
experiences, utilizing the arts as a tool for cultivating "insight into the
experience of another" (Nussbaum 2002, 391). On the day of the kite-
flying event, students from the schools went to the LMU campus to
participate in opening ceremonies and to fly their kites. The day began
with a greeting from the Dean of the art program followed by an official
procession to the field to kick off the event. For four hours, students,
faculty, and staff flew kites. The initial anxiety of the college
participants—would the kites fly, would the children and youth from the
two schools get along—were allayed once the event started. There was no
obvious animosity as students and adults, many who had never met each
other outside of the workshop, collaborated to get the kites up and flying
despite numerous logistical and engineering problems. In fact, as the day
progressed, increasingly more people found their way to the field as word
spread about the event. The joy that can be generated by participating in

the arts in connection with acts of subversion and cultural criticism can often "produce an endurable and even attractive dialogue with the prejudices of the past" (Nussbaum 2006, 392). Such embodied activities allowed these students and adults, representative of a variety of religious, cultural, and socioeconomic backgrounds, to move beyond fear and defensiveness in ways that are often not possible in more traditional classroom settings. By working together in what Kester (2004) refers to as a *dialogical aesthetics model* wherein the interactive nature of art projects is emphasized, everyone involved in the kite-flying event accepted a position of dependence on and vulnerability relative to one another, allowing for the possibility of individual and collective transformation.

If education is understood as integral to the health of democratic societies, then teacher-training programs in higher education have a role to play in promoting peace and social justice in K-12 educational settings such as those exemplified in *10,000 Kites*. Yet, according to countless research findings, and as specifically cited in a comment posted to the LeadCast Blog on November 6, 2008, Donna Young notes, "too few courses and programs have been created and designed to equip future and current educators with the knowledge, skills, and dispositions to work with our nation's increasing diversity." Such skills are integral components to any education program concerned with peace and social justice. Furthermore, research indicates that teacher education programs that strive to incorporate issues of justice often show minimal effective change in actual curriculum and pedagogical practices (Cochran-Smith 2003; Ladson-Billings 2006). Compounding this problem are the increased demands for accountability through standardized testing in K-12 urban public schools. Finding the spaces for cultivating peace and social justice in these education settings is particularly challenging. The proactive work and achievements of family, school, and community networks are pushed to the margins of school discourse, and policies that instead emphasize, conformity and standardized testing, come to the fore. Preparation of student teachers to resist these patterns upon entering the field requires the cultivation of systemic thinking and critical explorations that foster the knowledge, skills, and dispositions needed to teach within a peace and social justice paradigm. This chapter proposes using aspects of Amartya Sen (1993; 1999) and Martha Nussbaum's (2002; 2006a; 2006b) capability approach, which refers to "what people are actually able to do and to be—in a way informed by an intuitive idea of a life that is worthy of the dignity of the human being" (Nussbaum 2000, 5), and Kester's (2004) dialogical aesthetics as a means of framing how to understand and teach peace and social justice in post-secondary art education programs.

To begin the discussion, I define my understanding of peace and social justice education before providing an overview of Sen and Nussbaum's capability approach and its relationship to post-secondary art education. Following this, I analyze how Kester's (2004) notion of dialogical aesthetics and contemporary art education practices can be used as a means of creating spaces for the fostering of capabilities and skills associated with building a culture of peace. Specific examples of curricular and pedagogical practices are provided. I do not argue that such an approach provides a full accounting of peace and social justice in post-secondary art education programs. Rather, I argue that the approach is one of many that can help clarify and further efforts towards understanding the components critical to build cultures of peace through art education.

Framing Peace and Social Justice in Teacher Education

I work with Thich Nhat Hanh's understanding of peace when I speak about personal and social transformation within art education. "Peace," he says, "is not simply the absence of violence; it is the cultivation of understanding, insight, and compassion, combined with action" (Nhat Hanh 2003, 5). The work of creating just societies requires that we recognize and bring to bear a critical understanding of social injustice, as well as practical action through the promotion of self-determination and solidarity with others (Watts and Guessous 2006). What is called for is a curriculum and pedagogy that promotes a deeper understanding of oneself as well as oneself in relation to the social and cultural landscape in which one lives. The arts are often the sole remaining place in the curriculum where embodied, experiential learning still exists—where interacting with materials forms the basis for extended critical learning. But even as we profess to train art educators in peace- and justice-oriented curriculum and pedagogy, the limited research available indicates a low rate of transference into the post-secondary art education classroom.

Resistance to Social Justice Practices in Higher Education

In a comment posted to The Huffington Post on January 2, 2009, Ayers argues that democratic societies ideally view education as a tool for fostering the intellectual, emotional, physical, spiritual and creative forces that exists within every student as well as a tool for participation and engagement with the broader society. Within a peace and social justice paradigm, addressing the inequities and biases that exist in the world, as well as sharing stories, inspires work towards making the world a better place to live (Hunt 1998). Yet resistance to peace and social justice curriculum and pedagogy crosses multiple disciplines and perspectives including teacher education (Cochran-Smith 2003; Chizhik and Chizhik 2005; Ladson-Billings 1996; hooks 1994). A meta-analysis of research on teacher education concludes minimal effective change in the ways teachers are prepared in college and university-based programs despite more than two decades of multicultural reform (Cochran-Smith 2003; Ladson-Billings 2006). Milbrandt (2002) investigated the current attitudes and practices of Georgia State public school art educators towards addressing social issues in their lessons. Teachers expressed interest in and support for teaching social issues within the art classroom; however more than 50% of the respondents indicated that the lessons they taught were instead directed at "tolerance or appreciation for cultural diversity" (146). According to Milbrandt, "more teachers presented the effects of mass media before racism, homelessness, and gender issues even though they reportedly valued those issues as more important to include in their teaching" (147). Fear of negative responses to the curriculum influenced the choices these teachers made. A need for more preparation to teach social issues through their post-secondary art education programs was expressed.

Although the academy can potentially function as an engaged learning environment that supports respectful and sensitive explorations of self and others, the process to achieve such a space necessitates the solidarity of everyone across cultural differences and power differentials (Cervenak et al. 2002). Simply connecting these ideas via theoretical coursework and/or constructed art lessons in the university classroom does not necessarily translate into meaningful action, particularly if the arts continue to be taught primarily through a skills- and materials-based curriculum. Aspects of Sen's and Nussbaum's capability approach provide a framework for identifying some of the knowledge, skills and dispositions—hereafter referred to as *capabilities*—necessary to foster in students in order to further peace and social justice in teacher preparation programs and, by extension, K-12 classrooms. Contemporary art education programs that integrate critical inquiry and embodied learning opportunities through artmaking are uniquely positioned to foster these capabilities.

Capability Approach and Higher Education

The *capability approach* is "about freedom and the development of an environment suitable for human flourishing. Capability refers to what people are actually able to be and do, rather than to [only] what resources they have access to. It focuses on developing capabilities to choose a life that they have reason to value" (Walker 2005, 103). The belief that all human beings deserve the opportunity to participate and engage in building lives of personal value and dignity is at the root of educational programs concerned with peace and social justice. The capability approach suggests the need to look at people's beings and doings—their capabilities of functioning—rather than only outcomes, such as standardized test scores, to understand whether movement is closer towards or further away from peace and social justice in education.

The difference between a *capability* and a *functioning* parallels the difference between an opportunity to achieve and the actual achievement, between potential and outcome (Walker 2005). Functionings range from the basic (being able to write a lesson plan) to the more complex (being able to write and critically analyze a lesson plan in relation to student needs). Choice also plays a critical role in the capability approach. Opportunities for choice, in the case of education means that a student, having the requisite set of capabilities, exercise her choices from a range of options and alternatives such that the choices she makes benefit her well-being, and in the case of teaching, the well-being of her students (Walker 2005). The approach also takes into account the freedoms and constraints that accompany an ability to perceive and make choices for oneself. Walker and Unterhalter (2007) note that "our choices are deeply shaped by the structure of opportunities available to us so that a disadvantaged group comes to accept its status within the hierarchy as correct even when it involves a denial of opportunities" (6). Aspirations and hopes for the future can become circumscribed by these adapted preferences. Moreover, the choices of advantaged individuals are also shaped by structures of opportunities, making it difficult for them to see and understand situations and circumstances that impact the opportunities of others outside of their own socioeconomic status. Sen (1999) locates the individual within the context of one's social arrangements and recognizes how one's social context can enrich or diminish capabilities. Integral to the capability approach is this connection between interpersonal development and broader social, cultural, and economic constraints: critical understandings for any program concerned with peace and social justice.

The recognition of the heterogeneity of human experience is especially useful for teachers engaged in peace and social justice education. While students should be held accountable for assuming responsibility in their own learning, it is imperative for teachers to recognize that when a system is implemented, those who fall outside of the normative structure will have to acclimate to that system while others will not have to acclimate (Walker and Unterhalter 2007). For example, in the context of a diverse, urban public school system such as New York City, where 42% of public school students report speaking a language at home other than English (Insideschools.org 2008), a monolingual school with no programs in place for bridging the language and cultural differences poses a major obstacle for those students trying to maximize the utility of their learning experience. It is not that these students lack the mental capacities to learn as much as students whose primary language is English, but rather that the educational institution lacks the overall infrastructure to foster those capabilities. Teachers concerned with peace and social justice need to strategize a curriculum that bridges the gap between normative structures and divergent student needs for an enriching learning experience. "A more complete perspective," says Hoffman (2006, 2), "would be the concept of equitable access to an education that specifically enhances capability." In this view, education must account for the "inter-relatedness of teaching, learning and human development" as well as quality to foster the capabilities that enable all students to, for example, "think critically and creatively, solve problems, make informed decisions, cope with and manage new situations, and communicate effectively" (2). To maximize capabilities to achieve valued functionings, it is necessary to question how "individual conceptions of justice and propriety, which influence the specific uses [we] make of [our] freedoms" have become circumscribed (Sen 1999, 31). Through a critical reflection of the world and self, a process of dialogue and action begins that provides multiple opportunities for the development of capabilities necessary for democratic citizenship and mapping global connections to one another.

Today art education communities concerned with peace and social justice in the United States understand the range of interpersonal, sociopolitical, and economic issues generated by the impact of contemporary imagery and the values inherent in such representations (Freedman 2003). It is also understood that such imagery can profoundly influence "student identity, notions of citizenship, [and] beliefs about democracy" (94). Students learn early on, for example, whether or not to ask questions, to imagine themselves as members of a homogenous group or as members of a nation state. The definition of what it means to be a "good" citizen is directly colored by these early educational experiences. If students find themselves victimized and powerless, overwhelmed by external circumstances, the freedoms and opportunities for developing valued beings and doings, including those associated with democratic citizenship, are restricted. Peace- and social justice-based art education has the potential for uncoupling the predictable ties between race, class, gender, and first language. Individual and collective art projects ask students to engage in self-expression as well as to participate in collaborative productions that necessitate moving beyond established comfort zones. When students negotiate design decisions in a collaborative wall mural or participate in classroom dialogue regarding a social issue in relation to creating a political poster, there is a "responsiveness and interactivity" (Nussbaum 2006) that is characteristic of political processes in healthy democracies. The aim is to provide multiple, intersecting opportunities for the fostering of individual and collective capabilities associated with understanding, insight, and compassion, combined with thoughtful action. The creation of this *capability space* in higher education art classrooms provides fertile ground for all students, regardless of socioeconomic status, to develop, expand, and act on the capabilities associated with a culture of peace.

An array of post-secondary art education approaches, including multicultural, social reconstruction, visual culture, and community-based art education fall under the rubric of peace and social justice art education (Garber 2004). Such an education seeks to decenter "student identities in order to allow students the opportunity to reexamine and (hopefully) reconstruct their notions of selfhood and assumptions of practice" (Butin 2005, 10). Without this "decentering" it is difficult for students to enter into an understanding of other people's experiences and stories, including those of their future K-12 students. As Butin notes, such a process is neither direct nor easy. Deliberate preparation, intensive discussion, and reflections are integral to the process as is a willingness to let go of "total control of over what our students learn" (10). Regarding curriculum, linear progress is questioned, the separation of fine arts from craft and popular culture is breached and normative ideas regarding identity, race, class and gender are challenged (Efland, Freedman and Stuhr 1996). Furthermore, links between local communities, national concerns, and international issues are explored and established (Delacruz 2004; Zimmerman 1990), providing the foundation for students to recognize their ties to "fellow citizens who live at a distance, or who look different from [them]selves" (Nussbaum 2002, 296). The fostering of capabilities associated with peace and social justice are integral to contemporary art education theory and practice. Melanie Walker (2003) proposes a tentative list of specific, interdependent capabilities associated with social justice in higher education from which we can begin to delineate the specific opportunities, skills, and capacities necessary for building cultures of peace in post-secondary art education classrooms.

A Capabilities List for Peace and Social Justice Art Education

The capabilities in the following list are grounded in the notions of agency and freedom, integral components to peace and social justice education program. Walker's (2003) aim is to create a list that enables understanding and delineates a potential criterion of justice in higher education while at the same time inviting review and refinement of such a list within specific higher education contexts. In doing so she reminds us that the capability approach,

- Incorporates both rationality and freedom,
- Is for equality and quality,
- Is for complexity and for multidimensionality, not for single capabilities,
- Is for educational development, and
- Above all, is for agency (constructing oneself as an actor) and well-being (Walker 2006, 129).

Proposed capabilities for post-secondary art education programs:

1. Practical reasoning: Being able to make well-reasoned informed, critical, independent, intellectually acute, socially responsible, and reflective choices. Being able to construct a personal life project in an uncertain world. Have good judgment. Being able to put ideas into action. Being able to reflect on self, attitudes, feelings, beliefs, habits, and behaviors.
2. Educational resilience: Able to navigate study, work and life. Able to negotiate risk, to persevere academically, to be responsive to educational opportunities and adaptive to constraints. Self-reliant. Having aspirations and hopes for a good future.
3. Knowledge and imagination: Being able to gain knowledge of peace and social justice through the arts—its form of academic inquiry and standards. Being able to use critical thinking and imagination to comprehend the perspectives of multiple others and to form impartial judgments. Being able to debate complex issues. Being able to acquire knowledge for pleasure and personal development, for career and economic opportunities, for political, cultural and social action and participation in the world. Awareness of ethical debates and moral issues. Open-mindedness.
4. Learning disposition: Being able to have curiosity and a desire for learning. Having confidence in one's ability to learn. Being an active inquirer.
5. Social relations and social networks: Being able to participate in a group for learning, working with others to solve problems and tasks. Being able to work with others to form effective or good groups for collaborative and

participatory learning. Being able to form networks of friendship and belonging for learning support and leisure. Mutual trust.

6. Respect, dignity, and recognition: Being able to have respect for oneself and for and from others, being treated with dignity, not being diminished or devalued because of one's gender, social class, religion or race, valuing other languages, other religious and spiritual practices, and human diversity. Being able to show empathy, compassion, fairness and generosity, listening to and considering other person's points of view in dialogue and debate. Being able to act inclusively and being able to respond to human need. Having competence in intercultural communication. Having a voice to participate effectively in learning; a voice to speak out, to debate and persuade; to be able to listen.

7. Emotional integrity, emotions: Not being subject to anxiety or fear, which diminishes learning. Being able to develop emotions for imagination, understanding, empathy, awareness and discernment.

8. Bodily integrity: Safety and freedom from all forms of physical and verbal harassment in the higher education environment (Walker 2006, 128-29).

Post-secondary art education programs concerned with peace and social justice can use Walker's list of capabilities as an entry point into crafting a list that is responsive to the needs of specific programs concerned with peace and social justice education. Kester's (2004) dialogical aesthetics approach to art-making provides a pedagogical platform on which to create the spaces that in turn foster the kinds of capabilities Walker proposes.

Dialogical Aesthetics and Art Education

Dialogical aesthetics is derived from Russian literary theorist, Mikhail Bakhtin. According to Kester (2004), Bakhtin argues, "that [a] work of art can be viewed as a kind of conversation—a locus of differing meanings, interpretations, and points of view" (10). In such an approach, the *interactive* character of projects is emphasized, replacing "the conventional, 'banking' style of art…in which the artist deposits an expressive content into a physical object, to be withdrawn later by the viewer" (10). Through the creative facilitation of dialogue and exchange in the art making process, as well as willingness on the artist's part for "active listening and empathetic understanding" meaning occurs and is developed "in the exchange between the artist and viewers, ultimately affecting the identities of both" (Garber 2004, 4). Such an approach can be used in post-secondary art education classrooms that also resist the banking style of education.

Kester (2004) argues that two important shifts need to occur in the understanding of aesthetic experience for a dialogical aesthetic experience to occur. First, a more nuanced account of communicative experience is needed that is sensitive to specific identities and "dialogical exchange based on reciprocal openness" (90). Secondly, an understanding is needed of a work of art "as a process of communicative exchange rather than a physical object" (90). Kester identifies three concepts that are of particular relevance to this approach: Habermas' (1998) discourse ethics and discussion of the ideal speech situation; connected knowing arising from the book, *Women's Ways of Knowing* (Belenky et al., 1997); and empathetic insight.

Habermas (1998) provides a theory of communicative democracy as a means towards social justice within the public sphere—the ideal speech situation. Discursive forms of communication are differentiated from more instrumental or hierarchical forms of communication in that "material and social differentials (of power, resources, and authority) are bracketed and speakers rely solely on the compelling forces of superior argument" (Kester 2004, 109). These interactions are intended to create a "provisional understanding… among the members of a given [classroom] when normal social or political consensus breaks down" (109). Such a breakdown is inevitable and, in fact, is sought after in art classrooms concerned with peace and social justice to enable addressing issues of difference that move beyond a tolerance model. Dissent allows a deeper examination of the root of the differences and therefore gives voice to a liberating dialogue. Furthermore, by participating in such encounters, participants not only have the chance to see themselves from other people's points of view, they also carry within them the potential for more critical self-awareness and creative transformation (Kester 2004). Such an approach, however, assumes an egalitarianism in the classroom that may or may not exist due to prevailing social and/or power structures. Connected knowing helps mediate the gaps that exist across these differences.

Connected knowing is based on a conversational mode where classroom students and faculty strive to identify with the perspectives of each other (Belenky et al. 1997). The social context from which others speak, judge, and act is recognized as "it attempts to situate a given discursive statement in the specific material conditions of the speaker" (Kester 2004, 113). Both students and teachers are encouraged to question and explore the stereotypes and assumptions that emerge in the classroom. The aim is to transform "personal anecdotes into critical reflections by *connecting* them to the larger sociopolitical, historical, and economic contexts" (Cervenak et al. 2002, 344), and in the case of this practice, artmaking. For example, students can be asked to create a poster aimed at a social justice issue of their choosing. The dialogue preceding and during the artmaking, as well as the subsequent critical examination of the artwork in light of sociopolitical, historical and economic contexts provide opportunities for students to identify with and critique the perspectives of others in the course. Kester's notion of empathetic insight helps lay the ground for the safe spaces necessary to engage in this type of critical discourse.

In classrooms that utilize aspects of connected knowing, there is the danger of difference being negated through sameness, that is, a dismissal of the ideas and individuals different from oneself or those that or who threaten to undermine notions of collective solidarity as they related to issues of peace and social justice. Engaging in empathetic insight enables creation of safe spaces where individuals learn to listen closely and to recognize divisions that exist among people as well as to analyze how these differences are produced (Cervenak et al. 2002). Such classrooms strive for "respect and appreciation for the integrity of difference", which in turn, allow "us to love in complicated ways, acknowledging that our love for ourselves and each other is circuitous, growing deeper with the introduction of new knowledge" (352). Post-secondary art education classrooms concerned with peace and social justice embrace difference, conflict, and contradictions, recognizing that the process of learning to listen is more important than unity.

Within these classroom spaces, the art education professor acts as a facilitator and co-creator with students as they individually and collectively perform the role of the educator *and* artist. Notions of individual identity and how these identities intersect with race, class, gender, sexuality, citizenship, ideological values, and the group dynamic play an integral role from concept to finished product. In dialogical practices and aesthetics, a student artist's own expectations can be challenged through a process of direct collaboration and feedback with viewers: consciousness of the world is transformed through a dialogical encounter that is mediated by the art process and product (Kester 2004). In the U.S., there are numerous individual and collaborative contemporary artists who facilitate civic dialogue and transformation through arts and cultural activities. Using a dialogical aesthetics approach to teaching art promotes a deeper understanding of one's self as well as one's self in relation to the social and cultural landscape in which we live, necessary components of any education program concerned with peace and social justice.

The Capability Space in the Post-Secondary Art Education Classroom: Theory into Practice

The art education program presented in this chapter uses art making through a dialogical aesthetics model as a means of fostering a range of capabilities associated with cultures of peace. The curricular and pedagogical practices described in following text are drawn from the art education programs at LMU in Los Angeles, CA, and Adelphi University in Long Island, NY. As stated earlier in this chapter, the components are not intended to be stand-alone activities or to represent an overarching static model. Rather it is a fluid and integrated framework for cultivating the understanding, insight, and compassion necessary for students to foster peace in their future K-12 classrooms.

Components of the Capability Space in Post-secondary Classrooms

- *A working definition and framing of peace and social justice to coordinate readings and activities that support, reinforce, and—when appropriate—challenge these definitions.* The definition and framing of peace and social justice makes transparent the professor's sociopolitical positions, directs their teaching and learning practices, therefore impacting students' depth of knowledge in relation to course content, particularly as it relates to any service-learning activities (Westheimer and Kahn 2004).

- *Studio art-making directed at exploring personal identity before moving outwards into exploring local and global community issues.* A variety of verbal and written assessments and critiques on individual and peer artwork are included. By using art to explore individual experiences and perspectives, teachers create the ground on which students can move beyond broad cultural generalizations. In essence, their experiences and perspectives, expressed through artmaking, become the starting points to mapping areas where connections either are or not made with others.

- *Directed critical readings and discussions covering peace and social justice issues from a range of perspectives and geographic locations followed by reflective journal writing on assigned readings as well as classroom and service-learning experiences.* Guided critical reflection provides students with the opportunity to reexamine and reconstruct notions of selfhood and assumptions of practice (Butin 2005).

- *Service-learning opportunities to reinforce and embody classroom learning with the goal of assisting students in linking their own artistic pedagogical processes in the higher education classroom to the lessons they devise for students in the K-12 service-learning component*. Not only do students have the opportunity to put their knowledge into action, they are called on to negotiate risk, be responsive to educational opportunities and adaptive to the constraints of the K-12 classroom.

- *Finally, the professor acts as a co-facilitator in the classroom—providing the space, materials and supports for students to engage in the content of the lessons.* In her role as facilitator, the professor is open to inviting individuals into the classroom as well as facilitating panel discussions, across disciplines, with individuals and groups on campus and the broader community who are directly involved in peace, social justice, diversity and intercultural affairs. Such practices embody for the art education students in the classroom the transdisciplinary nature of education programs committed to peace and social justice.

Conclusion

Peace and social justice education in this research is concerned with curriculum and pedagogy that promotes a deeper understanding of oneself as well as oneself in relation to the social and cultural landscape in which we live. As noted by Desai and Chalmers (2007), such an approach reflects Dewey's (1957) understanding of the purpose of democratic social institutions, that is "to set free and develop the [capabilities] of human individuals without respect to race, sex, class, or economic status… the test of [social institutions'] value [being] the extent to which they educate every individual into the full stature of [their] possibility" (Dewey 1957,186, as quoted in Desai and Chalmers 2007, 11). As social disparities persist, regardless of race, class, and/or gender, the movement to rectify those disparities is the collective responsibility of all citizens and the work of any educational program concerned with peace and social justice. In art education, students must examine and map their roles in the social structure and identify the problems from which action can then be predicated. Art education programs work to reconcile the disparate range of class, race, and educational experiences inside and outside of school. At the same time these classrooms are also "constructed out of the specific identities of its members in a process that will, inevitably, promote or legitimate some aspects of these identities at the expense of others" (Kester 2004, 130). These tensions must be acknowledged and incorporated into the process to facilitate a culture of peace. Grounding the capability approach within a dialogical aesthetics art classroom provides a framework towards understanding and evaluating individual student experience. It also helps us understand how to support and foster the capability development of prospective teachers and by extension, their future K-12 students.

The arts are a physical as well as psychic location, "a place in the mind where one allows for a recombination of experiences, a suspension of the rules that govern daily life" (Becker 1994, 117). If it is possible to experience alternative realities, perceptions, or beliefs in the process of making and viewing art, then it becomes feasible to conceive of such moments in the unfolding of daily life. The fostering of capabilities through the arts can provide students with the freedoms and tools that make building cultures of peace and civic transformation possible, not only in higher education classrooms but also in a democratic society.

References

Becker, C. 1994. Herbert Marcuse and the subversive potential of art. In *The Subversive Imagination: Artists, Society, and Social Responsibility,* ed. C. Becker, 113-29. New York: Routledge.

Belenky, M., B. Clinchy, N. Goldberger, and J. Tarule. 1997. *Women's ways of knowing: The development of self, voice, and mind.* New York: Basic Books.

Butin, D. 2003. Of what use is it? Multiple conceptualizations of service learning within education. *Teachers College Record* 105 (9): 1674-92.

Cervenak, S. J., K. L. Cespedes, C. Souza, and A. Straub. 2002. Imagining differently: The politics of listening in a feminist classroom. In *This bridge we call home,* ed. G. E. Anzaldúa and A. Keating, 341-56. New York: Routledge.

Chizhik, E. W. and A. W. Chizhik. 2005. Are you privileged or oppressed? Students' conceptions of themselves and others. *Urban Education* 40 (2): 116-43.

Cochran-Smith, M. 2003. The multiple meanings of multicultural teacher education: A conceptual framework. *Teacher Education Quarterly* 30 (2): 7-118.

Delacruz, E. 2004. Art education in civil society. *Visual Arts Research* 30 (2): 3-9.

Desai, D. and Chalmers, G. 2007. Notes for a dialogue on art education. *Art Education* 60 (5): 6-12.

Dewey, J. 1957. *Reconstruction in philosophy.* Boston: Beacon.

Efland, A. and K. Freedman, and P. Stuhr. 1996. *Postmodern art education: An approach to curriculum.* Reston, VA: National Art Education Association.

Freedman, K. 2003. *Teaching visual culture.* New York: Teachers

College.

Garber, E. 2004. Social justice and art education. *Visual Arts Research* 30 (2): 4-22.

Habermas, J. 1998. *The structural transformation of the public sphere.* Cambridge: MIT Press.

Hoffman, A. M. 2006. The Capability Approach and educational policies and strategies: Effective life skills education for sustainable development. In *Amartya Sen: Un économiste du dévelopment?*, ed. V. Reboud, 81-94. Paris: Agence Française de Développement. http://www.afd.fr/jahia/Jahia/home/publications/NotesDocuments/pid/ 2756.

Hooks, B. 1994. *Teaching to transgress: Education as the practice of freedom.* New York: Routledge.

Hunt, J. A. 1998. Preface to *Teaching for social justice: A democracy and education reader*, ed. W. Ayers, J. A. Hunt, and T. Quinn, xiii-xv. New York: Teachers College Press.

Kester, G. 2004. *Conversation Pieces: Community and Communication in Modern Art*, Los Angeles, CA: University of California Press.

Ladson-Billings, G. 1996. Silences as weapons: Challenges of a Black professor teaching White students. *Theory into Practice* 35: 79-85.

—. 2006. *Educational Research in the Public Interest.* Presentation at the University Wisconsin, March 30, in Madison, Wisconsin.

Milbrandt, M. 2002. Addressing contemporary social issues in art education: A survey of public school art educators in Georgia. *Studies in Art Education* 43(2): 141-57.

New York City Department of Education. DOE and Learning Leaders Sponsor Sixth Annual English Language Learners Conference. http://schools.nyc.gov/Offices/mediarelations/ NewsandSpeeches/2008-2009/10222008.htm.

Nhat Hanh, T. 2003. *Creating true peace: Ending violence in yourself, your family, your community, and the world.* New York: Free Press.

Nussbaum, M. 2000. *Women and human development: The capabilities approach.* Cambridge: Cambridge University Press.

—. 2002. Education for Citizenship in an Era of Global Connection. *Studies in Philosophy and Education* 21: 289-303.

—. 2006a. Teaching humanity: In our globalized world, an arts education is more crucial than ever as a way to cultivate sympathy for others. *Newsweek,* August 21.

—. 2006b. Education and democratic citizenship: Capabilities and quality education. *Journal of Human Development* 7 (3): 385-95.

Sen, A. 1993. Capability and well-being. In *The Quality of Life,* ed.

Martha Nussbaum and Amartya Sen, 30-53. Oxford: Clarendon Press.
—. 1999. *Development as freedom*. New York: Random House.
Walker, M. 2003. Framing social justice in education: What does the 'capabilities' approach offer? *British Journal of Educational Studies* 51 (2): 168-87.
—. 2005. Amartya Sen's capability approach and education. *Educational Action Research* 13 (1): 105-22.
—. 2006. *Higher education pedagogies*. Maidenhead: Open University Press.
Walker, M. and Unterhalter, E. 2007. The capability approach: Its potential for work in education. In *Amartya Sen's capability approach and social justice in education,* ed. Melanie Walker and Elaine Unterhalter, 1-18. New York: Palgrave MacMillan.
Watts, Roderick. J. and Omar Guessous. 2006. Sociopolitical development: The missing link in research and policy on adolescents. In *Beyond Resistance: Youth Activism and Community Change*, ed. Shawn Ginwright, Pedro Noguera and Julio. Cammarota, 59-80. New York: Routledge.
Westheimer, J. and J. Kahne. 2004. What kind of citizen? The politics of educating for democracy. *American Educational Research Journal* 41 (2): 237-69.
Zimmerman, E. 2002. Intercultural education offers a means to promote tolerance and understanding. *Journal of Cultural Research in Art Education* 19 (20): 68-80.

CHAPTER THREE

READING AND WRITING PEACE: THE CORE SKILLS OF CONFLICT TRANSFORMATION AND LITERACY

JULIE MORTON

We live in a tremendously violent world. Even at home, the statistics are shocking. Widespread violence tears at the seams of families in the United States. In 1999, an estimated 791,210 individuals were victims of violence at the hands of former or current intimate partners (Rennison 2001). Violence is a problem in our communities as well. For young people between the ages of 10 and 24, homicide was the second leading cause of death in 2005 (Center for Disease Control and Prevention 2007). A staggering 2.2 million people populate U.S. prisons, and another 5 million are on probation or parole (Lazare 2007). While the United States claims five percent of the world's population, it incarcerates twenty-five percent of the world's prisoners (Liptak 2008). All this to add to the obvious: a growing death toll in Afghanistan and Iraq, massive casualties in the Congo and the Sudan, and more explosive conflicts looming on the horizon.

Is this epidemic of violence inevitable? Peace theorists believe it is not. Johan Galtung proposes that there are three levels of peace, corresponding to three levels of violence, including: direct, structural, and cultural. Direct peace is the protection of humans against "deliberate intention to hurt and harm" (Galtung 1997, ¶ 4), structural peace demands that basic needs of human beings are met, and cultural peace supports all individuals as they strive to realize their potential. All three levels are vital to establishing real, lasting peace.

To achieve peace, many leading conflict workers turn to conflict transformation. John Paul Lederach (2003, 14), who coined the term "conflict transformation" in the 1980s, describes it as the following:

To envision and respond to the ebb and flow of social conflict as life-giving opportunities for creating constructive change processes that reduce violence, increase justice in direct interaction and social structures, and respond to real-life problems in human relationships.

Solving a problem often implies that there is a final, potentially static end-goal in sight. However, the word transformation acknowledges the dynamic, evolving process of learning to bridge difference with our own selves intact.

As a teacher, my calling is to prepare the next generation to grow, even flourish in an interconnected but violent world. I believe passionately that violence needs to be addressed directly in our classrooms, yet the current education reform trends make this difficult. Today, the high-stakes testing of No Child Left Behind (NCLB) defines U.S. public education, and while President Obama may alter the course, the emphasis on accountability is here to stay. Many standards-based tests, intended to raise the caliber of all schools, tragically focus on low-level thinking skills (Resnick 2001). In the frantic race to keep up with the pace which testing companies have set, there is no time and no resources for a comprehensive peace and conflict transformation curriculum as a core course in public schools alongside English, math, science, and social studies. With public schools cornered by NCLB, how can we address pervasive violence through proactive education?

I propose that we can teach conflict transformation in public schools today by integrating peace skills into literacy classes. Literacy implies an active and investigatory approach to text, and conflict transformation entails the same active and investigatory approach to conflict. After careful analysis, I isolated four core skills essential in both literacy and conflict transformation: research, dialogue, critical thinking, and creativity. A language arts teacher can teach both literacy and conflict transformation simultaneously by examining literature, both fiction and nonfiction, with an ongoing focus on conflict. For example, when reading *To Kill A Mockingbird*, students might focus on literary research by using evidence from the text to explain the significance of the relationship of Atticus and Mrs. Dubose. Students can use these same research skills to study conflict transformation by preparing for and holding a simulation of a hearing to ban the school's use of the novel. Each skill can be modeled, scaffolded, and applied in paired activities, one project focused on literary analysis and the other on conflict transformation. By creating parallel activities that use the same skills in conflict transformation and literacy, students will learn how to transfer and apply these skills in a variety of contexts.

When literacy is linked with conflict transformation, I believe students will have the skills to effectively navigate challenging text as well as complex conflict. This integrated, skill-based approach can be applied today in schools without special funding and without disrupting testing schedules. In this paper I will outline the four central skills of conflict transformation and literacy so as to create a theoretical framework for an integrated peace and language arts curriculum in public schools.

Research

Understanding is one of the beginning levels on Bloom's taxonomy of intellectual behavior (Bloom et al. 1956). When faced with a problem, this is where we start. When learning to write an article, the first question is always: What happened? Gather the facts. Research the problem. As the initial step, it ought to be the easiest. Yet the word research spells out the process itself: Search again. Stand under the problem. Question the official narrative and look for overlapping stories and conflicting truths. Research is itself a conglomerate of four subskills: self-reflection, questioning, finding and evaluating resources, and finally, tracing the complexity of the problem or event. All four of these essential subskills fundamentally inform peace work and literacy.

Self-reflection serves as the bedrock of research in both conflict transformation and literacy because it helps us to acknowledge our own lenses before we gather and interpret information. This is a metacognitive tool, meaning something that helps us think about our thinking. "The goal of education…" writes Arthur Costa (2001, xviii), "should be to support others and ourselves in liberating, developing, and habituating greater self-thought and reflection. Thinking about our own thoughtfulness becomes the force directing us toward becoming increasingly authentic, congruent, and ethical." For Paulo Freire (2006, 109) this kind of reflection is the "very condition of existence." All too often we fumble in murky situations without defining them. Thus, a first step in the research process in both literacy and conflict transformation is to determine how we are predisposed to frame a particular conflict or question, why we are drawn to that frame, and how we use it to understand the issue.

The second skill of research is questioning. Questions can break apart binary thinking and uncover submerged assumptions. Lederach proposes what he calls paradoxical curiosity as an essential habit in conflict transformation. With it one "approaches social realities with an abiding respect for complexity, a refusal to fall prey to the pressures of forced dualistic categories of truth, and an inquisitiveness about what may hold together seeming contradictory social energies in a greater whole" (Lederach 2005, 36). When students learn to ask questions—good probing questions—they learn to enter into conflict from a place of inquiry rather than assumed knowledge.

Questions are also essential in the research process in literacy. Mortimer Adler and Charles Van Doren (1972, 123) explain that an important "part of reading ... is to *be perplexed and know it*. Wonder is the beginning of wisdom in learning from books as well as from nature." Good focusing questions, which are open-ended yet cogent, inspire deeper reading. Adler and Van Doren (1972, 46) argue that there is one rule to active reading: "Reading a book on any level beyond the elementary is essentially an effort on your part to ask it questions." Questioning transforms a passive reader into an active one. It encourages readers to use metacognition skills to check their own understanding, and it helps writers determine a starting point for further research.

The third skill in research is finding and evaluating resources. To whom do we ask these questions? From where do we gather our data? "Perceptions differ because our experiences differ, and because we select from among our experiences," observes Roger Fisher, Elizabeth Kopelman, and Andrea Schneider Kopelman (1994, 21). "Depending on our specific perspective, our perceptions vary." Understanding varying perceptions will prepare a conflict researcher to identify bias, predispositions, and fact-framing tendencies. Determining the perspectives of different sources in a conflict is also another way to focus the parties involved on underlying interests rather than positions. Collecting facts, perceptions, and theories from both sides helps the researcher identify points of agreement.

Selecting and evaluating resources is important in literacy as well. Adler and Van Doren (1972, 32) suggest that skimming and pre-reading "is a threshing process that helps you to separate the chaff from the real kernels of nourishment." It allows us to select appropriate sources of information from the vast options available. When writing research papers, many of my enthusiastic seventh graders rush at any type of information to confirm their opinions, lugging back assertions made by their grandfather at suppertime or an unclaimed Internet resource. They soon discover that finding relevant and revealing sources can be challenging and eye-opening.

The final subskill of research is the ability to navigate complexity. Many of us shy away from complexity. Paradoxically, Galtung (2004, 34) argues that the simpler the problem, the harder it is to transform. His remedy? "Introduce more goals, possibly by differentiating the goals that are there; introduce more parties to whom the outcome of the conflict is important enough to become a goal, and then we may get closer to transcendence and transformation." Complexity helps, not hurts, according to Galtung. Lederach (2005, 120) agrees. "Patterns of relationship, like complexity, offer up a sense of the larger picture and myriads of small openings and opportunities." As a result, the first step of peacemaking is rejecting sound bites, and searching for the potential of peace in complexity.

Literacy, like conflict transformation, is enriched by complexity. Literacy bequeaths us membership in discussions that stretch back to the beginning of recorded history and around the globe. It is the tool of revolutionaries and oppressive regimes alike (Frye 1964). To use it, rather than be used by it, we need to know how to embrace complexity. Yet, according to 2005 ACT college-prep test results, only half of those tested (most of whom intend to go on to college) were prepared for college-level reading (ACT, Inc. 2006). Half the students tested failed "to comprehend *complex* texts" (ACT, Inc. 2006, 2). The study bemoans a blanket silence in state standards on the topic of text complexity. Most complex texts "will contain multiple layers of meaning, not all of which will be immediately apparent to students upon a single superficial reading. Rather, such texts require students to work at unlocking meaning by calling upon sophisticated reading comprehension skills and strategies" (ACT, Inc. 2006, 7). Reading complex texts and then comparing and contrasting information gleaned from other sources is a fundamental literacy skill, yet students still struggle to demonstrate competency.

Self-reflection, questioning, finding and evaluating resources, and embracing complexity are all skills that work together to help a researcher construct overlapping understandings in both literacy and conflict transformation. Coordinating these subskills into the research process helps students be more aware of their own consumption of information. By introducing research as a technique applied in different contexts, students will be better prepared to use it on their own, both inside and outside of the classroom.

Dialogue

Dialogue is a collective journey into the participants' truths, with a shared commitment to root out assumptions and prejudice. It requires two main elements—an individual construction of meaning and the reception and clarification of this meaning, resulting in a collective act of creation that the exchange engenders. Reflective speech, engaged listening, and the generation of new ideas through shared exploration are all necessary elements of the dialogue process.

Dialogue begins with an individual naming something that he or she considers true. Yet often this truth is rooted in our unconscious and must be uncovered through the process of articulation. Thinking "is often merely the reporting or acting out of patterns already in our memory. Like a prerecorded tape, these thoughts (and feelings) are instantly ready for playback," writes William Isaacs (1999, 59). The more we try to name the unnamable, the better we can understand our perspectives and articulate them. When we speak in dialogue, we uncover truths and inconsistencies, revelations and assumptions.

In conflict transformation this engaged speaking—this self-conscious sharing of personal truth—reveals the submerged interests and perspectives of the opposed parties. A party's interests are defined by their "needs, desires, concerns, and fears" (Fisher and Ury 1983, 42). Our interests often remain concealed, while our positions drive negotiations. When we focus on positions rather than interests, negotiations can stagnate. Dialogue dislodges positions, because it asks parties to reflect on their own assumptions as well as their needs, hopes, and fears. Speaking from this kind of truth can transform the communication dynamic from competitive to cooperative.

The same process defines literacy. Like the dialogue that generates conflict transformation, the writing process requires the transference of ideas or feelings into words. The symbolic structure of language, further structured by the conventions of writing, forces a writer to rethink ideas so that others might follow his or her arguments. The dialogue of thought and language, unified on the page, often requires multiple revisions. Even E.B. White was known to revise his pieces an average of nine times (Zinsser 1989). The result is a progressively deeper trough cut through an issue to its heart as the writer strips away unnecessary digressions on his or her way to the goal.

The second element of dialogue is listening. Listening—real, active, present listening—is the cement that holds dialogue together. Without it, we speak only to confirm ourselves. Thich Nhat Hanh (1992, 87-88) writes that "deep listening is the basis for reconciliation . . . To promote the work of reconciliation, we have to refrain from aligning ourselves with one party or another so that we understand both . . . . After listening to both sides, we can tell each side of the suffering of the other." Deep listening allows us to consider conflicts in different ways; the focus can shift from the people with whom we differ, to the problem we want to transform.

In the dialogue of literacy, listening is equally important. The reader essentially listens to the writer, the same way those in dialogue strive to understand a speaker. Catherine Snow (2002) suggests that reading comprehension takes great effort because rather than extracting meaning from text, readers have to construct meaning themselves. Sometimes we simply read for information (just as we listen with agendas), selecting facts that support our preconceived ideas. Reading for understanding, however, is a different skill entirely, which not only offers readers new facts, but also sheds a "revealing light on *all* the facts [the reader] knows" (Adler and Van Doren 1972, 9). Like dialectic listening, reading for understanding involves self-awareness. "To construct meaning," writes Snow (2002, 32), "students must monitor their understanding... They notice when something they are reading is incongruous with their background knowledge or is unclear, then they take action to clarify their understanding, such as rereading or reading ahead." We need to read holistically, which is why good readers periodically paraphrase and summarize difficult material (ibid). To gain new insights and to grow from reading, we need to get to the heart of text rather than fragment it.

The exchange of speaking and listening in conflict transformation invites new ideas to spring forth as a collaborative "act of creation" (Freire 2006, 89). This act of invention, fueled by the truths of individuals, holistically shared and examined, becomes a generative act of love. "The naming of the world, which is an act of creation and re-creation, is not possible if it is not infused with love," writes Freire (2006, 89). "Love is at the same time the foundation of dialogue and the dialogue itself." The joint revelation of truths offers the individual meaning and empowerment and gives the group a tool for communication, exploration, and exchange. It is, if Freire is right, the very face of equitable power.

Like conflict transformation, dialogue in literacy can become a generative experience of love. Myles Horton recalls that although he read voraciously all his life, he grew particularly passionate about it when "I was beginning to deal with real problems in life. When I'd read, I was informed by that reading. I'd get ideas from the reading. I'd get emboldened by it, especially poetry, and it took a new meaning" (Freire and Horton 1990, 30). Horton could draw knowledge from his reading to approach his life in new, more intentional ways. Freire recalls that his love affair with books inspired him as well. "I discovered that reading has to be loving event," (ibid, 26) he explained. Theories, conjectures, or stories intimately shared, whether in person or on paper, often elicit empathy and produce a cross-pollination of ideas.

Dialogue, both in conflict transformation and literacy, is love because it shares, it seeks, and it grows. Whether through spoken word or written word, humanity has a dynamic medium for connection. When we focus on understanding and making meaning rather than winning, the possibility of transformation emerges.

Critical Thinking

Research and dialogue both encourage a holistic exploration of perspectives and facts. Yet we live in the information age, a button-click away from exponentially growing stores of knowledge. Today, information doubles every five years; by 2020 it is projected that it will double every 73 days (Costa 2001, xv). Although we can strive to be open and accepting, we also need to be able to identify faulty logic, recognize prejudice, and unpack generalizations using the structured reasoning of critical thinking. The word critical is formed from the Greek *kitikós*, meaning to be "able to judge" (Barnhart 2005, 236) and the verb to think is derived from old English *thencan*, meaning to "conceive of in the mind" (Barnhart 2005, 1134). Critical thinking, both in the realm of conflict transformation and literacy, is thinking based on criteria that use both analysis and evaluation to make judgments. Critical thinking offers a system of judging fairly, or at least more fairly than we might if we judged without structure or stratagem.

In critical thinking, we begin with analysis. "Analyzing skills are used to clarify existing information by examining parts and relationships," write Robert Marzano et al. (1988, 91). If you go to a mechanic, explains Linda Elder and Richard Paul (2006, 2), you would be shocked to hear, "I'll do my best to fix your car, but frankly I've never understood the parts of the engine." Just as knowledge of specific parts in an engine helps a mechanic understand the functioning of the car, knowledge of the components of ideas help thinkers analyze arguments or events. Marzano et al. (1988) distill analytical skills into three main categories: identifying components and attributes, identifying relationships and patterns, and identifying purpose or main ideas. This technique is championed by Galtung, who frequently analyzes conflicts in terms of win/win, win/lose, lose/win, and lose/lose outcomes. This lens helps him break down options into clearly identifiable parts.

Analysis is an important element in literacy as well. Adler and Van Doren (1972) suggest first classifying a text, then identifying its unifying idea, next determining its organizational parts, asking what problem the author is trying to answer, searching for the author's key words, finding the author's leading propositions, and finally enumerating the author's arguments. All of this, according to Adler and Van Doren, breaks down the pieces of a text to make sense of the main argument and its primary supporting ideas. Once we understand the structure of the text, we can move on to analyzing the content of its parts. While we might agree with a statement superficially, upon closer scrutiny we might discover the supporting evidence is vague or erroneous.

The second component of critical thinking is evaluation. After breaking down the parts of an argument or issue in analysis, we evaluate the pieces in order to determine their worth. "Judging is the act of selecting and weighting the bearing of facts and suggestions as they present themselves, as well as of deciding whether the alleged facts are really facts and whether the idea used is a sound idea or merely a fancy," writes John Dewey (1933, 119-120). Judgments, in his eyes, are "units in reflective activity."

To judge effectively, Dewey suggests, we must first select which data is significant. Dewey explains that "till we have reached a final conclusion, rejection and selection must be tentative or conditional. We select the things that we hope or trust are cues to meaning. But if they do not suggest a situation that accepts and includes them . . . we reconstitute . . . the facts of the case" (1933, 122-123). To do this effectively, we can use certain criteria as a lens through which we view problems along with a certain sensitivity to context (Lipman 1991). Judgment is essential both in peace work and in literacy to determine our focus, strip away prejudice, and clarify our aims.

Critical thinking is a higher-order thinking technique built on a flexible variety of skills and strategies used to analyze, evaluate, and judge ideas. It is equally applicable in conflict transformation and in literacy, although by nature it resists formulas and scripts. With it we can deconstruct and examine complex issues, just as we can piece together essays in organizational units that guide the reader deep into the writer's logic. Critical thinking also helps us evaluate ideas. For critical thinking to be productive, it serves the vision of an integrated whole—a transformed conflict or a unified text. Critical thinking is like pruning a tree to inspire stronger, greener growth.

Creativity

Creative thinking identifies the mental patterns that structure the way we see reality so that we can peer beyond them. It is deliberate, active thinking that considers problems through multiple frames and focuses on resulting action (De Bono 1994). "Characteristically, the creative person has the ability to look at a problem from one frame of reference or schema and then consciously shift to another frame of reference, giving a completely new perspective," explain Marzano et al. (1988, 26).

Edward De Bono (1994, 45-46) describes the human brain as a "self-organizing information system," which creates patterns of thinking based on previous experiences. "In practical life most thinking takes place in the perception area: how we get to look at things. It is only in rather specialized situations that we then have to proceed to elaborate processing" (ibid, 38). De Bono argues that our brain constantly compares patterns in order to avoid this elaborate processing. It is only when we practice interrupting ingrained thinking patterns that our creativity emerges.

We teach children to learn their ABC's and times-tables, while creative thought is often left to the naturally gifted or inspired. Inner city schools that have repeatedly failed NCLB assessments require test-taking classes instead of art and music so that they can meet Adequate Yearly Progress and avoid losing accreditation. Some districts have turned to scripted curricula, where booklets contain both the teachers' instructions, explanations, and questions, as well as the students' potential responses (Kozol 2005). This rigidity only fossilizes thinking, instead of inspiring innovative problem solving. I've witnessed the results myself as an experienced teacher, new to an inner-city school. After panic and uproar when I asked students to create collages of a character in a story we read, they assured me that they were much better at filling in worksheets. Students do need basic skills, but not at the expense of higher-order thinking.

Creative thinking fuels conflict transformation because it shifts us out of entrenched patterns of violence, oppression, and indifference. Peacemakers "embrace the possibility that there exist untold possibilities capable at any moment to move beyond the narrow parameters of what is commonly accepted and perceived as the narrow and rigidly defined range of choices," writes Lederach (2005, 38). This ability to jump between paradigms allows a creative peacemaker to identify alternatives on many levels—alternative allies, alternative next steps, and alternative ways to meet both parties' needs. Lederach (2005, 121) calls this "peripheral vision," where "multiple avenues are held simultaneously within the panorama of the possible." Peripheral vision, then, is a strategy for flexible thinking, scanning endless options for action. Galtung (2004, 5) concurs, explaining, "The broader the spectrum of solutions, the more alternatives there are to violence."

Creative thinking is an essential element in literacy, no matter how marginalized it has become in this age of NCLB. First, literature offers a variety of storylines; each narrative can serve as a different model for how to interpret the human experience. Literary critic Northrop Frye (1964, 134) argues that "literature speaks the language of the imagination, and the study of literature is supposed to train and improve the imagination." Without creativity, we recycle words, stories, and myths until they become hollow patterns, learned by rote. "The area of ordinary speech," writes Frye (1964, 148), "is a battleground between two forms of social speech, the speech of a mob and the speech of a free society." According to Frye (1964, 148) the mob speaks a language of "cliché, ready-made idea and automatic babble, and it leads us inevitably from illusion into hysteria." The free individual, by contrast, imagines better, more just, equitable societies, and so rejects the myths of the mob for inspired alternative narratives. Literature trains the imagination because it offers a myriad of possible models for self-reflection, social imagination, and independent thought. When readers are active and curious, when they question stereotypes and assumptions, both trite stories and rich literature offer insight into culture, language, power, and possibility.

Creative thinking illuminates the world we live in and inspires us to open our minds to other experiences and choices. It produces transformative fiction and provoking prose. And it can be taught. While it engages the imagination, it is not ephemeral or exclusive. By learning to see beyond old patterns, we can look at our world with new eyes again and again.

Conclusion

With nuclear weapons, terrorism, and fundamentalism intensifying conflicts today, we cannot afford to focus narrowly on reading, writing, and arithmetic in schools. Instead we might ask: How can we cultivate alternative habits of thinking? "There is nothing in the inherent nature of habit that prevents intelligent method from becoming itself habitual; and there is nothing in the nature of emotion to prevent the development of intense emotional allegiance to the method," writes Dewey (1997, 81). By targeting strategies and skills through intentional teaching, by using rich content, and by offering repeated practice, new studies indicate that these strategies and skills can evolve into "proclivities" and then habits (Resnick 2001).

If we design language arts classes with paired activities—one focusing on a skill's application in the context of conflict transformation and one focusing on the application of that same skill in literacy—students will have broader opportunities to integrate skills and develop habits of intelligent methods. For example, I recently observed in an informal review that my students in Thornton were better able to summarize the main idea of a text when teachers in other content areas identified and required proficiency in the same skill. Similarly, I propose that the practice, reinforcement, and repetition of essential conflict transformation and literacy skills will support flexible application in a variety of contexts when we deliberately intertwine them in language arts classes. Teachers can select literary material based on the instruction and mastery of each skill. In every text students can utilize one of the four skills in the context of the conflict in the text or surrounding the text and in its literary application. The result would be a curriculum that cycles through each skill repeatedly, using the same fertile literary soil for a practice ground.

By turning important literary and peace skills into habits, we can offer students strategies for reading the world rather than simply giving them an ideology to define it. Conflict transformation and literacy skills can empower students to grow into active world citizens, who will be prepared to labor with others to shape and share a deeply complex world.

References

ACT, Inc. 2006. *Reading between the lines: What the ACT reveals about college readiness in reading.* Iowa City, IA: Author. www.act.org/research/policymakers/pdf/reading_summary.pdf (accessed January 20, 2008).

Adler, M.r J., and C. Van Doren. 1972. *How to read a book: The classic guide to intelligent reading.* New York: Simon and Schuster.

Barnhart, R. K, ed. 2005. *Chambers dictionary of etymology.* New York: Chambers.

Bloom, B. S., M. D. Englehart, E. J. Furst, W. H. Hill, and David R. Krathwohl, ed. 1956. *Taxonomy of educational objectives: The classification of educational goals. Handbook I: Cognitive domain.* New York: David McKay.

Center for Disease Control and Prevention. 2007. Youth violence: Facts at a glance. http://www.cdc.gov/ncipc/dvp/YV_DataSheet.pdf (accessed February 5, 2008).

Costa, A. 2001. Introduction: The vision. *Developing minds: A resource book for teaching thinking*, ed. Arthur Costa, xv-xviii. 3rd ed. Alexandria, VA: ASCD.

De Bono, E. 1994. *De Bono's thinking course.* Rev. ed. New York: Facts on File.

Dewey, J. 1933. *How we think.* Boston: D.C. Heath and Company.

—. 1997. *Experience and education.* New York: Touchstone.

Elder, L, and R. Paul. 2006. *The thinker's guide to analytic thinking.* Dillon Beach, CA: Foundation for Critical Thinking.

Fisher, R. E. Kopelman, and A. K. Schneider. 1994. *Beyond Machiavelli: Tools for coping with conflict.* Cambridge, MA: Harvard University Press.

Fisher, R. and W. Ury. 1983. *Getting to yes: Negotiating agreement without giving in.* Ed. B. Patton. New York: Penguin Books.

Freire, P. 2006. *Pedagogy of the oppressed.* London: Continuum.

Freire, P. and M. Horton. 1990. *We make the road by walking: Conversations on education & social change.* Ed. Brenda Bell, John Gaventa, and John Peters. Philadelphia: Temple University Press.

Frye, N. 1964. *The educated imagination.* Bloomington, IN: Indiana University Press.

Galtung, J. 1997. Peace education is only meaningful if it leads to action. *UNESCO Courier* 1:4.

—. 2004. *Transcend and transform: An introduction to conflict work.* Boulder, CO: Paradigm Publishers.

Hanh, T. N. 1992. *Touching peace: Practicing the art of mindful living.* Ed. Arnold Kotler. Berkeley, CA: Parallax Press.

Isaacs, W. 1999. *Dialogue and the art of thinking together.* New York: Currency.

Kozol, J. 2005. *The shame of the nation.* New York: Three Rivers Press.

Lazare, D. 2007. Stars and bars. *The Nation* 285: 29-36.

Lederach, J. P. 2003. *The little book of conflict transformation.* Intercourse, PA: Good Books.

—. 2005. *The moral imagination.* New York: Oxford University Press.

Lipman, M. 1991. *Thinking in education.* New York: Cambridge University Press.

Marzano, R.J., Brandt, R.S., Hughes, C.S., Jones, B.F., Presseisen, B.Z., Rankin, S.C., and Suhor, C. 1988.   *Dimensions of thinking: A framework for curriculum and instruction.* Alexandra, VA: ASCD.

Rennison, C. M. 2001. *Bureau of Justice statistics special report: Intimate partner violence and age of victim, 1993-99.* (October). U.S. Department of Justice. http://news.findlaw.com/hdocs/docs/doj/usdojipva93-99.pdf (accessed May 23, 2008).

Resnick, L. B. 2001. Making America smarter: The real goal of school reform. In

Developing minds: A resource book for teaching thinking, ed. A. Costa, 3-6. 3rd ed. Alexandria, VA: ASCD.

Snow, C. 2002. *Reading for understanding: Toward a R and D program in reading comprehension.* Santa Monica, CA: Rand Education.

Zinsser, W. 1989. *Writing to learn.* New York: Harper and Row.

CHAPTER FOUR

PROMOTING PEACE EDUCATION THROUGH TEACHER EDUCATION

BEVERLY D. SHAKLEE

During the course of writing this chapter, it came to the day of Barack Obama's inauguration as President of the United States and the world took note. Change is his mantra and hopefully peace will be the means. Throughout the day many people commented that in times of great turmoil we seem to find great leaders, I hope this is true. I also am reminded that it continues to be timely to discuss peace education, teacher education and the ways in which we promote peaceful change in classrooms throughout the world. As it has been throughout the history of peace education, it is time to remind ourselves again of the power and importance teaching about and for peace.

Introduction

As noted at the United Nations Cyber-school website (2008,1), "Peace education brings together multiple traditions of pedagogy, theories of education, and international initiatives for the advancement of human development through learning. It is fundamentally dynamic, interdisciplinary, and multicultural and grows out of the work of educators such as John Dewey, Maria Montessori, Paulo Freire, Johan Galtung, Elise and Kenneth Boulding, and many others. Building on principles and practices that have evolved over time, responding to different historical circumstances, peace education aims to cultivate the knowledge, skills, and attitudes needed to achieve and sustain a global culture of peace." Recognizing the power of that statement and the history of peace education we also note the historical failure of Colleges of Education to make peace education a transparent part of teacher education.

Bjerstedt (1994, 4) in his early review of teacher education through his work with the Peace Education Commission network, noted that "if teachers do not get acquainted with peace education possibilities and procedures in their training then we cannot expect them to do a good job as peace educators." The results of his research, with responses from some thirty-three countries, indicated that while teacher education was seen as highly important in its relationship to fostering peace education the complexity of the task was constrained by national views, requirements in teacher preparation programs, lack of resources as well as issues of financing or the approaches to peace education which should be used (e.g. knowledge/awareness, value oriented and/or skills approaches). A number of recommendations also accompanied this report.

At the close of the century, Brock-Utne outlined the challenges for peace education (1999). In her article for *The Journal of Peace Studies*, she outlines a distinction between education about peace and education for peace. This included intercultural awareness (cognitive); global ethics (values); and, action (readiness to engage in social justice) (1999, 1). At this juncture the definition of peace education was still a contested concept (1999, 3), with a broad definition open to many different political interpretations making it very difficult to provide school (or teacher education) curriculum guidelines. The division of the field into different topics or elements such as human rights education, conflict resolution, peace building or development education may, as noted by Brock-Utne, be an attempt to make the broad field of peace education more understandable and acceptable across political environments.

Ten years after Bjerstedt and Brock-Utne's investigations, it is relevant to ask a similar question, 'to what extent is or should peace education be a part of teacher education programs?' It appears that there has been little systematic and consistent change in the field of teacher education in relation to peace education. Quezada and Romo (2004), argue that while Colleges of Education have addressed issues of peacemaking, conflict resolution and mediation as management tools in the classroom they have yet to systemically address the knowledge, skills and attitudes needed to sustain a culture of peace. According to the Quezada and Romo, part of the failure can be directly linked to teacher education programs which espouse peace but fail to systematically implement peace education within teacher education. The structure of teacher education programs, state or national requirements coupled with the authoritarian manner in which curriculum, experiences and activities are transmitted and the failure to allow for individual development of teachers are also incongruent with the aims of many peace education programs. "It is of no help if the subject matter taught is of a critical nature selected to further democratic values and the character formation of the individuals if the methods used to convey the subject matter are authoritarian, do not engage the students and do not appeal to their emotions" (Brock-Ute 1999, 5). Further the violent environments (both structurally and physically) in many of the schools make it seemingly impossible for teachers, even if prepared to be peace educators, to actively engage and implement a peace education curriculum.

The purpose of this chapter is to examine the following questions: in what ways do we model and engender peace in our teacher education programs; are there models of embedded peace education principles within teacher education programs; in what ways can we insure that the principles being taught are also being fully implemented; and, how can we assess the effectiveness of such programs on student growth, school climate and environments?

A Brief History

The history of peace education is rich and varied across the world. Numerous documents attest to the long term interest and commitment of educators to embed peace education within the framework of teacher education (e.g., Dewey 1897; UNESCO 1945). While the purpose of this chapter is not to repeat history some notable efforts are important to our understanding of where we have been and how peace education is currently visible in teacher education. Hathaway (2007) in her review of peace education in international contexts notes that UNESCO has provided a consistent call for over sixty years for curriculum which promotes the peace process within teacher education calling for curricular reform throughout education to include the skills and attributes associated with peaceful change. Others within national and international contexts have also been deeply associated with creating pathways to peace education (e.g. Elise Boulding, Paulo Freire). The 10th Triennial World Conference of the World Council for Curriculum and Instruction focused entirely on creating cultures of peace within pedagogy and practice (2001). In addition, authors Miller and Ramos (1999) examined teacher training across the world to determine the ways in which teacher education extends the notion of building a culture of peace. Innovative teacher education programs in Bolivia, Namibia and Egypt have been studied to determine how they began the transformative process.

Unfortunately, the field itself is not clear on the definitions of peace education, peace studies, peaceful change, global education, international education much less the attributes or curriculum associated with each definition. Further, the notion of peace itself is bound by culture, traditions, religion, and other elements that define the notion of peace. For example, Palestinians in Gaza may view peace as very different from some Israeli citizens. Governments negotiate peace based on economic and political factors which may or may not be beneficial to their citizens and how private citizens find peace within their homes and families depends on highly subjective variables. Peace education has been described as seeking to transform changing social structures and patterns of thought that have been created (e.g. Reardon) or as a process of listening, reflecting, problem solving, cooperation and conflict resolution. It has been differentiated to describe those elements that are peace keeping, peace making and peace building and ways in which to address each of those elements.

The field is complex, the definitions and parameters boundless and yet, the strong feeling among many is the peace must come through education and commitment of teacher educators throughout the world to teach children for peace in order to foster a long term sustainable peace in the world. For our purposes we rely on Johnson's broad definition of peace education curricula which would involve instruction in conflict resolution; cooperation and interdependence; global awareness; and, social and ecological responsibility (2009, 5). Johnson's definition provides the link to implementation that seems to be missing in teacher education programs and while not a theoretical perspective such as Danesh (2006) and others (e.g. Reardon) have proposed to think about peace education, Johnson's definition provides a means by which to look directly at instruction within teacher education programs.

Teacher Education

Within the field of teacher education in the United States, peace as an educative process can still be found within two main areas of the field. One is in the development of content knowledge and pedagogy such as Social Studies education in elementary school/middle schools with high school and secondary programs focusing within the content fields of Civics, History, Politics/Economics and Government to name a few. The second area has been in classroom management (e.g. conflict resolution) primarily in elementary/middle school programs. Occasionally peace education elements may also be found within programs that focus on environment, conservation and global education. Finally, teacher education programs that use models of culturally responsive curriculum or embedded standards that focus on social justice, respect for diversity and inclusion may be counted among peace education programs. In fact the elements of peace education have become transdisciplinary and perhaps, lost as a focal point in teacher education.

Within content domains such as social studies, politics or history, elements of peace education are taught to novice or practicing teachers. Merryfield in her work at The Ohio State University has systematically explored the notions of global mindedness, peace education and education for diversity within her extensive body of work. The website TEACHGLOBALED.net hosted by Merryfield and her colleagues across the university provides teachers with access to "high quality scholarship, primary sources, and web-based connections to the five world regions." (Merryfield 2009, 2). The advent of web-based sites has resulted in a proliferation of excellent resources for teachers on peace education but the question is still implementation. To what extent do teachers access and use resources on these sites and to what end?

If providing resources is not sufficient to the recognition of peace education in teacher education then in what other ways are teachers in teacher preparation programs exposed to peace education? One way is the integration of peace pedagogy and skills within specific course requirements. However this approach can be hampered in the United States by state requirements, time, resources and the skill of the instructor or even their philosophical stance toward peace education. For example, many mission statements in College's of Education espouse language that includes social justice, inclusion, respect for diversity or equality of access but to what extent do those concepts find themselves deeply embedded in day to day instruction? To what extent do instructors embrace those concepts and to what extent are they associated with peace education? Is it important that they are taught or linked to peace education?

In the elementary program at one institution the social studies methods course enumerates the following elements that could be associated with peace education: examine issues related to multiculturalism and diversity as related to elementary students; promote elementary students abilities to make informed decisions as citizens of culturally diverse democratic society and interdependent world; and national standards from Interstate New Teacher Assessment and Support Consortium (INTASC) related to the development of problem solving skills, critical thinking, positive social interaction and respect for diversity (2007). Even with a skilled instructor to what extent can we determine whether novice teachers taking this class transfer and implement those skills in the classroom? The National Association for Colleges of Teacher Education (NCATE 2008) has attempted to answer this question through their assessment system. As part of the NCATE assessment model, all teacher education candidates are to be regularly assessed through performances that indicated their ability to demonstrate the content knowledge, skills and dispositions identified by the faculty. In this example, teacher candidates in the elementary social studies class would be assessed on a regular basis through a variety of means to demonstrate their acquisition of the identified elements. Since this is a relatively new process for institutions accredited by NCATE it has yet to be proven as a viable means to determine the effectiveness of teaching elements of peace education through implementation into an elementary classroom. However, it does show some promise for the future in answering the implementation question.

Harris (2003) in his study of the evaluation of peace education programs noted the difficulty in assessing the impact of a program on the participants to determine whether they transfer their knowledge and awareness to real world and 'act in ways that contribute to the creation of peaceful cultures' (Harris 2003, 3). He suggests that as we consider peace education initiatives, formal or non-formal, we are not able to answer the question whether or not the peace education initiative brings peace to the world but rather what is the effect on the individual participant. In the case of teacher educators then it would not be how they affect even their school but rather how they themselves change, their understandings, knowledge, skills and values to promote peace both personally and professionally. Additionally, we would need to study the formative development of teacher educators as peace educators and the summative effect of their development in relation to their pupils. Finally, we may never know the full or long-term effect of what happens in each individual classroom on the students who were engaged in peace education within the classroom. How, if or when peace education becomes action in their lives may be undiscoverable.

Resources, a mission statement and a content course focused on peace education principles are all good examples of ways in which peace education has found a home in teacher education however, these are insufficient for full implementation into a teacher education program. Full implementation would include a deeply running thread beginning with the faculty and found throughout the program from mission statement to conceptual framework; from conceptual framework to coursework; from coursework to assessments; from assessments to implementation, evaluation and impact on children. If peace education became teacher education what would it look like?

Peace Education AS Teacher Education

In a review of programs that propose teacher education as peace education there are a few programs such as Teacher's College that provide an opportunity for teacher educators to study peace education as part of their formal program. There were also programs such as EURED (Europe-education as Peace Education) that were created to develop curriculum for teacher raining programs based on peace education (Wintersteiner 2002). Finally, a significant number of master's degree and doctoral programs are found that focus primarily on elements of peace education such as George Mason's Institute for Conflict Resolution (ICAR 2009), the first institution in the United States to grant a doctoral degree in this area. However, there were very few programs that aligned the elements of peace education with the requirements of teacher education.

Looking at more contemporary programs and efforts that focused on peace education as integral to teacher education and that specifically used the term peace education as a focal point; few were located. A selection of programs are used here as examples of the kinds of approaches that seem to be used. Each of these descriptions is based on published articles or artifacts retrieved from websites and each demonstrates an aspect related to the questions under study.

A Curriculum of Hope Initiative was created by The Curriculum of Hope for a Peaceful World Committee which is a Standing Committee of Alpha Kappa State. The Committee focus is threefold: promote peace, protect the environment, and celebrate diversity. As part of the original Resolution for Peace in 1985, the educators in the group specifically adopted responsibilities for teachers with regard to their students that included: providing students with the critical thinking, conflict resolution, and cooperative learning skills necessary for them to become responsible and active citizens striving for positive change and a peaceful world (www.paxeducare.org).

Of interest to this work is the consortium of four Connecticut universities that began the conversation of how to move peace education into the curriculum of teacher education. The focus groups included both teacher educators and liberal arts faculty at the four institutions and began with conversations around six questions include definitions of Peace Education, student interest in peace education elements, faculty and course offerings, requirements for peace education courses, relationship of standards to peace education (2008). The information generated discussion points to continue the conversation through a forum on peace education. Comments from the participants echoed earlier concerns expressed in this chapter: elements of peace education that related to: classroom management, equity and diversity discussions are taught; decision making, peaceful environments for learning and power relationships in classroom were discussed; and, students were particularly interested in skills related to conflict resolution. Of concern from these focus groups were issues related to national and state standards, whether peace education was embedded or additive; time commitments, and, testing requirements prevent the inclusion of peace education (www.paxeducare.org). As noted peace education appears to exist as a distributed concept in many teacher education programs but do we find peace education as a central concept in teacher education?

In the article, *Multiculturalism, Peace Education and Social Justice in Teacher Education*, Quezada and Romo (2004,1) explore the role of programs in multicultural education to support the elements of peace education and the responsibility of teacher education programs to promote multicultural education, peace education and social justice. In preparation for accreditation the faculty undertook a series of discussions which resulted in the creation of a conceptual framework that focused on six areas: inquiry and reflection; value; service; technology; social justice; and, diversity and inclusiveness. Six elements of peace education were embedded in coursework, these included "cross-cultural communication, justice, nonviolence, cultural democracy and decision-making" (2004, 5). As part of their study they document the changes in pre-service teachers from the first course to the last course working toward demonstrated commitment rather than simple use of language related to peace education or social justice.

Narrative examples from reflective responses in the beginning of coursework indicated that students began to understand power, privilege, equality, advantage, and demonstrated a better understanding at both a personal and institutional level (2004, 9). At the end of the program data was retrieved from student culminating portfolios and analyzed in comparison to state standards for evidence of the themes of diversity, inclusiveness and social justice, all elements of peace education. In the portfolios examined, students gave specific evidence from classroom practice, reflections on teaching/learning events and documented both conceptual and literal understanding of the issues of multiculturalism, peace education, social justice, equity, and diversity (2004, 12). The implementation and demonstration of tangible examples are of paramount importance moving from awareness or comprehension into authentic action of peace education elements.

The example provided by Quezada and Romo is important because, in conjunction with their faculty colleagues, they examined the curriculum of the teacher education program in light of the conceptual framework, reoriented or strengthen coursework to reflect that framework and studied the results. A gap in the field of peace education has been the direct relationship between teaching about peace education in teacher education and the influence or impact that has on teaching and learning in the K-12 classroom. Longitudinal studies of graduates from this or similar programs may reveal the differences in implementation and the effectiveness of specific elements of peace education (e.g. conflict resolution) on the day to day life of teachers and children.

In a third example, *Supporting Peace Education in Teacher Education Programs* (2008), authors Baker, Martin and Pence explore the decision of a team of faculty to focus precisely on peace education within their elementary teacher education program. Faced with similar barriers based on US state content and assessment standards, the team selected three courses in which peace education could be more visibly and methodically instituted. The three courses were social studies education, a course in creativity and the arts and a course in children's literature. Specifically selected texts, resources and activities were designed to reflect elements of peace education. In addition, they studied changes in the faculty and changes in pre-service teachers as a result of these efforts. Throughout their discussion the authors noted that they capitalized on the existing curriculum by highlighting those elements which reflected the goals of peace education. For example in their discussion of children's literature selections they integrated the state requirement to examine historical events by looking at children's literature related to internment camps. In doing so, they highlighted issues related to peace education (e.g. social justice) while meeting the state mandates. In another course, students became social activists by engaging in an authentic learning experience within their own context. The elements of social justice and active engagement are part of a peace education curriculum and while the authors note anecdotal evidence of pre-service teacher change and faculty implementation of peace education curricula the question of the pre-service teacher's active use of peace education curriculum within their own classrooms has yet to be answered. If peace education can be made visible in three courses required in the teacher education sequence could it be elevated in all courses in the teacher education sequence?

Turning from US based examples which occur in *relatively* tranquil settings more dramatic efforts are being addressed internationally in post-conflict countries that are trying to stabilize the country in part through universal education based on high quality teacher education. Historically colonized countries inherited their education systems directly from the colonizer so that a country would reflect, for example, a British or French model of education that was designed to primarily prepare a class of persons to interact between the local population and the colonial government. The education provided was often out of context, irrelevant to the needs of the population and focused on maintaining the status quo (Shaklee & Blackwell 2004). In these situations education was not used to encourage peace or peaceful change but rather conformity and compliance.

As these countries became independent they began to craft their own views of education. Unfortunately in some situations access to education perpetuated an elite population and denied others opportunity. Along with other political and economic factors some countries became engaged in bloody civil and intercultural wars. In parts of Africa, as peace began to take hold a new wave of understanding and determination also came to introduce and embed peace education into the education of all.

Gbesso (2006) provides an illuminating description of the state of peace education in West African countries. Among the recommendations from the research study is the following: *Teacher education, especially the ones relating to peace and development, should be decentralized and brought closer to the local communities for maximum functionality* (Gbesso 2006, 1). Within the description of the countries under review (Benin, Burkina Faso, Cape Verde, Côte-d'Ivoire, Gambia, Ghana, Guinea, Guinea Bissau, Liberia, Mali, Niger, Senegal, Sierra Leone, and Togo), Gbesso specifically addresses the importance for West African nations to consider peace education as the means to provide a quality education for all As pointed out by Gbesso, the majority of peace education initiatives are undertaken by non-governmental organizations (NGOs) and have little influence on teacher education. However, several university systems are noted as including peace education among the areas of study and a few embrace peace education components as a driving force in teacher education. Similar to some of the US based models, the elements are embedded in areas such as citizenship, government, student development or teacher characteristics. Gbesso further notes the need to train teachers on new methods of teaching and help them design a clear curriculum for peace education programs while providing resources such as texts, teaching materials and finally, access to the internet (2004, 25).

In Rwanda, the post-conflict reform of teacher education included an attempt to reconstruct teacher perceptions, eliminate prejudice (most particularly between Hutu and Tutsi teachers/students) and reform teaching pedagogy to include critical, creative and self-directed strategies.

The Kigali Institution of Education was established to create a force of highly qualified teachers prepared to use best-practices including those that can be framed from a peace education perspective (Njoroge 2007). As noted on their website, the Mission of the Faculty of Education at Kigali Institute of Education, *is to prepare teachers, teacher educators, education managers and other education practitioners, instilling among other academic values, the beliefs, attitudes and practices that professionally contribute to the building of a peaceful and just society for all* (http://www.kie.ac.rw/spip.php?article234).

Teacher Educators: Standards

In the search for information specific to teacher education, the *Standards for Peace Education* (Carter 2006, 8) from the Florida Center for Public and International Policy, University of North Florida were retrieved. Within the body of the standards, Carter illuminates recommended standards for students, teachers, teacher educators, and school administrators. Of interest to this chapter are the recommended standards for teacher educators. While too lengthy to add to this chapter, Carter's work gives significant attention specifically to teacher educators and their work. She highlights specific institutional examples (e.g. inclusion in course syllabi and content) as well as process examples (e.g. social and environmental action projects) which when bundled together provide a comprehensive view of peace education as part of mainstream teacher education programs in the United States.

Conclusion

There is no doubt the field of peace education faces challenges as does the field of teacher education. Each has a wide variety of researchers who contribute their expertise and knowledge to the field and the variables that influence the fields are similar (e.g. political, economic, social). To some degree both lack conceptual clarity for example in what ways are the concepts peace education, peace studies, peace building similar or different; do those differences mean that implementation for teacher education is different? In teacher education there is a significant difference between training and preparation. Training is associated with the acquisition of information not the implementation or use of the information so peace education associated with training may only be sharing information with teachers but not having the teachers successfully use the knowledge with students. If we are going to see peace education

AS teacher education then both need to be transformed into a new entity rather than as a seemingly simple process of adding elements of peace education to a program which is still dependent on the beliefs of instructors and the whims of state and/or national standards for implementation. Many of the programs under review have elements of Johnson's original definition: conflict resolution; cooperation and interdependence; global awareness; and, social and ecological responsibility (2009). Few programs acknowledge the historical dimensions of the origin of these elements in peace education.

Is it important that peace education as a construct become visible and public within teacher education programs to be effective? Yes, it is. Peace education is currently the warp and weft of a tapestry of teacher education, within but not visible, binding together elements of social justice, respect for diversity, awareness of global issues, political/social concerns all of which have significant impact on the students we teach, their communities and the ways in which they come to view the world. Without naming, peace education becomes invisible, and teachers do not necessarily see the connections nor make the connections for their students. Instead of having a focal point of peace, the learning can become diluted and distributed into small pockets of disconnected strategies or activities without meaning. In addition, no vision of a peaceful future for schools, children, families and communities can be constructed from loosely coupled activities; many children do not have the wherewithal until much later to make those connections independently. Without a clear understanding and vision of a peace education in teacher education, we will continue to fail at implementation.

References

Baker, M., D. Martin and H. Pence 2008. Supporting Peace Education in Teacher Education Programs. *Childhood Education* http://www.blintz.com/news/2008/11/04/Supporting_peace_education.

Benton, J. and P. Swami, Eds 2001. *Creating Cultures of Peace: Pedagogical Thought and Practice*: Selected Papers from the 10th Triennial World Conference, ED 503385 http:eric.edu.gov/ERICWebPortal

Bjerstedt, A. 1993. *The "Didactic Locus" of Peace Education: Extra-Curricular, Mono-Curricular, Cross-Curricular or TransCurricular.* ED 374 036 http:eric.edu.gov/ERICWebPortal

Bjerstedt, A. 1994. *Teacher Training in Relation to Peace Education in Schools.* ED 383686 http:eric.edu.gov/ERICWebPortal

Brock-Utne, B. 1999. The Challenges for Peace Educators At The End of
  A Millenium. *The International Journal of Peace Studies.*
  http://www.gmu.edu/academic/ijps/ 1:1:1-13
Carter, C.C. 2006 *Standards for Peace Education*: A Florida Center for
  Public and International Policy Paper. University of North Florida.
  http://www.unf.edu/thefloridacenter/
Curriculum of Hope 2008. *A Curriculum of Hope Initiative: Talking
  Points on Peace Education.*
  http://www.paxeducare.org/CofHopeTalkingPoints.shtml)
Danesh, H.B. March 2006. Towards an integrative theory of peace
  education. *Journal of Peace Education* 3 (1):55-78.
Gbesso, A. December 2006. The Status of Peace Education in West
  Africa. www.tc.columbia.edu/PeaceEd/docs/PEwestfrica.pdf
Harris, I. M. 2003-04. Peace Education Evaluation. Paper presented at
  AERA, Chicago, 2003. ED 480 127 http:eric.edu.gov/ERICWebPortal/
Hathaway, D. M. 2007. *Understanding Peace and Peace Education in
  International Contexts*, unpublished manuscript, George Mason
  University.
Interstate New Teacher Assessment Support Consortium (INTASC)
  www.ccsso.org/projects/Interstate_New_Teacher_Assessment_and_Su
  pport_Consortium/
Johnson, M. *Trends in Peace Education,* ERIC Digest
  http://www.ericdigests.org/1998-3/peace.html
Miller, V. and A. Mucci Ramos. *Transformative Teacher Education for a
  Culture of Peace.* ED 435606,
  http://eric.edu.gov/ERICWebPortal/custom/porlets/recordDetails/)
National College Association of Teacher Education (NCATE)
  www.ncate.org
Njorge, G. 2007. The reconstruction of the teacher's psyche in Rwanda:
  The theory and practice of peace education. *Addressing ethnic conflict
  through peace education: International perspectives,* eds. Z. Bekerman
  and C. McGlynn 215-229. New York: Palgrave McMillan:
Reardon, B. 1997. Human Rights as Education for Peace.
  http://www.pdhre.org/book/reardon.html.
Shaklee, B. D. and M. Blackwell. 2003. *Post-colonial Remnants of
  Pedagogy and Practice: Influences on the Bahamianization of the
  Public Schools.* Paper presented at the 30th Annual Research Forum,
  The College of The Bahamas: Nassau.
TeachGlobalEd.net: Online resources for Global Educators
  http://www.coe.ohio-state.edu/globaled/home)

Quezada, R. and J. J. Romo 2004. *Multiculturalism, Peace Education and Social Justice in Teacher Education* http://findarticles.com/p/articles/mi_qa3935/is_200404/ai_9386584.

United Nations Cyberschool.bus. *Teacher as Learner: about peace education.*(retrieved http://www.un.org/cyberschoolbus/peace/frame.htm.

Vroemen, L. 2004. What do we mean by peace education? sPace for Peace, www.spaceforpeace.net.

Wintersteiner, W. 2001. *EURED—Europe education as peace education.* http://siu.no/isoc.

CHAPTER FIVE

CRITICAL LITERACY: A BUILDING BLOCK TOWARD PEACE

STACIA M. STRIBLING

The second graders were working at their literacy centers, practicing skills such as spelling, word building, reading with expression, and writing. All of a sudden a conflict erupted in the corner where two girls and three boys were playing a game of contraction bingo. Sarah came running over to report that "they" were cheating. When I approached the group to get the full story, Roberto explained that a girl (Sarah) was about to win the game, and that wasn't fair; so, he told Joaquin to put a bingo marker on his space so that he would win.

This vignette represents the typical conflicts that emerge on a daily basis in elementary school classrooms throughout the United States. While on the surface it might seem like a trivial conflict, the ways in which classroom teachers choose to address these disputes lay a powerful foundation for how students might eventually solve larger conflicts that surface in their lives. Therefore, elementary school teachers are tasked with fostering not only the academic growth of young children, but their social development as well. This effort often falls under the heading of "character education" and is taken on either by the guidance counselor who drops into classrooms for specific lessons and/or by the classroom teachers. Either way, the typical approach is to read a story focused on one of the "pillars" of good character such as trustworthiness, respect, responsibility, fairness, caring, or citizenship followed by a discussion of appropriate and inappropriate behaviors exhibited in the book and an art project or written product that illustrates the lesson. While "peace" is not an explicit component of this program, educators often fall back on character education programs when asked how they address peace in their classrooms (Joseph and Efron 2005). Getting along with others is therefore hinged on ensuring that all citizens exhibit good character.

There are several flaws with relying on programs such as this to do the work of peace education. For one, they focus on individual behaviors and do not address the ways in which people can work together to resolve conflict; peace building is a collaborative effort and requires group accountability, not just individual "good" children who act in appropriate ways. So, in the example above, it is not simply Roberto's responsibility to follow the rules of the game and treat others with respect, but rather the responsibility of the group to examine why winning appears to be the most important outcome of the literacy learning activity; what other ways might they approach the purpose of this learning center? Furthermore, the lessons associated with character education are often taught in isolation without being connected to other important academic lessons such as math, science, social studies, or literacy development. An integrated model, in contrast, implies that issues should be seriously addressed as they arise; so, rather than waiting for the character lesson to cover the behaviors that should have been exhibited in the contraction bingo center, the classroom teacher takes the time to discuss the situation as it unfolds allowing all voices to be heard and highlighting the intricate connections between what we learn and how we engage in that learning. Finally, and perhaps most importantly, using character education as a form of peace education does not begin to address a fundamental cause of conflict—difference. The conflict in the contraction bingo game appeared to be about winning, but I propose this competition was complicated by the issue of gender—Roberto said he did not think it was "fair" that a girl was going to win the game, so he convinced another boy to cheat so that a boy would win. How can we use peace education to explore the differences among us and approaches for creating environments where those differences become strengths in a community rather than sources of conflict?

This chapter will present a pedagogical approach that emphasizes collaboration, integration, and difference in building peace. This approach is critical literacy, which requires that students read the word (decode/encode words and make meaning of those words) and read the world (decode/encode people, communities, and the visible and invisible messages embedded in texts and experiences). It uses literacy practices such as reading and writing as the conduit through which to examine issues of social justice such as race, class, gender, etc. It is through this examination of social justice that students learn about difference of experience and of culture. Understanding different experiences and cultures, learning to respect these differences, and acting in ways that promote equity for all are critical components of learning how to peacefully coexist in a democratic society. Teachers, who have embraced critical literacy practices, use these practices to help students build a healthy classroom community and envision a healthier global community.

Connecting Critical Literacy to Peace Education

A main goal of peace education is to teach students how to address potentially violent conflicts using non-violent means. Instructive approaches fall under one of three different levels: peacekeeping, peacemaking, and peacebuilding (Harris and Morrison 2003). In peacekeeping efforts, the onus is on the educators to create a learning climate that is orderly and safe while peacemaking efforts place more responsibility on the students as they develop conflict resolution skills. The final approach, peacebuilding, is more proactive; rather than creating a safe environment or merely reacting to conflict, educators work to build foundations for peaceful co-existence. While critical literacy practices address each of these levels to some extent, the main focus is on peacebuilding—teaching students to collaborate, to understand the ways in which peaceful existence is integrated in all that we study, and to appreciate the diversity of the world's citizens.

An examination of the history of critical literacy reveals roots in the work of Paulo Freire as he helped peasants in Brazil recognize their oppression and use literacy learning as a means to empowerment and peaceful liberation (Freire 1970). Freire emphasized the power of not only reading the *word*, but reading the *world* (Shor and Freire 1987, 135). He stressed the importance of critically examining the world in which we live and work in order to name existing inequities and begin to transform oppressive structures through the power of words (spoken, read, and written). The connection between literacy and peaceful liberation is at the core of critical literacy.

In the United States these issues of power and politics dominate conversations in social sciences and humanities, but are only recently finding their way into the discourse of literacy education. Historically, reading research was grounded in quantitative methods where reading was treated as a skill that could be observed and measured independent from issues of culture and power. There was a shift in the 1970's that placed "reading" in the larger context of "literacy," recognizing the socio-cultural context of literacy practices (Siegel and Fernandez 2000). In the past forty years, researchers and educators have acknowledged not only the ways in which literacy is embedded in culture but how literacy can be used to impact society in order to create more equitable, just, and peaceful practices.

Because critical literacy has only recently entered the discourse of literacy education, there is no single definition for what it is and how it is enacted in classroom settings. Lewison, Flint, and Van Sluys (2002, 382), however, offer one of the most complete definitions that has strong connections with the goals of peace education; they identified four dimensions of critical literacy: "1) disrupting the commonplace, 2) interrogating multiple viewpoints, 3) focusing on sociopolitical issues, and 4) taking action and promoting social justice." Disrupting the commonplace requires students to question what is considered "the norm." In the context of peace, this might mean questioning how conflicts are typically resolved; how, as a nation, do we model appropriate and/or inappropriate responses to conflicts? Supporting students to explore multiple viewpoints means teaching students how to listen and consider the perspectives of all including those voices that are often marginalized. This skill is a critical component of peaceful conflict resolution. Focusing on sociopolitical issues means that students have an opportunity to explore issues of power and ways in which subordinate groups do/do not have a chance to participate in social processes. This approach connects to peace education because violence is so often associated with power; students can examine other manifestations of power and how that power can be shared in more peaceful and equitable ways. Finally, critical literacy promotes action and socially just change, a goal that is consistent with peaceful endeavors.

This critical literacy framework, and hence many peace education goals, fit within the larger theory of critical pedagogy (e.g. Giroux 1988; McLaren 2003; Wink 2005). Critical pedagogy is the process of naming, reflecting critically, and acting on issues of social justice (Wink 2005, 3); critical literacy names, reflects, and acts through literacy practices in order to peacefully move toward a more just and equitable world. As such, critical literacy is not "a piece of knowledge" to be fed to our students but is rather "a culture of thinking" that engages students in observing their world in ways that move them toward re-envisioning equity and access (Hadjioannou and Fu 2007). Furthermore, Vasquez (2004, 1) reminds us that

A critical literacy curriculum needs to be lived. It arises from the social and political conditions that unfold in communities in which we live. As such it cannot be traditionally taught. In other words, as teachers we need to incorporate a critical perspective into our everyday lives with our students

in order to find ways to help children understand the social and political
issues around them.

This perspective is consistent with the idea of peace education as "both
a philosophy and a process involving skills including listening, reflection,
problem solving, cooperation and conflict resolution" (Harris and
Morrison 2003, 9). This philosophy/process provides students with the
knowledge (e.g. self-awareness, multiculturalism, peace strategies), skills
(e.g. analysis of communication, inclusion, cooperation), and dispositions
(e.g. acceptance, empathy, service) to contribute to a more peaceful world
(Carter 2006). In both critical literacy and peace education approaches,
students are encouraged to observe their surroundings, reflect on issues
and conflicts that emerge within those surroundings, and find ways to
address those issues and conflicts collaboratively and peacefully.

Difference is often the root of conflicts that arise; people have different
perspectives on who has power, who should have power, and what should
be done with that power. That power is often embedded in more concrete
differences such as race, class, gender, religion, sexuality, etc.
Multicultural education theorists recognize the conflicts that arise from
difference, but they also note the benefits of living in a diverse society;
therefore, they argue for educational practices where students have an
opportunity to examine the conflicts related to racism, sexism, classism,
etc. and to deepen their understanding and acceptance of difference (Banks
& Banks 2007; Banks 20008; Nieto 2000). Banks (2008) discusses the
importance of "prejudice reduction strategies so that all students will
develop the knowledge, attitudes, and skills needed to function in an
increasingly diverse, tense, and problem-ridden world" (103).

Early childhood educators who embrace critical literacy practices
recognize the awareness children have of these differences at an early age.
Children's awareness is often grounded in their experiences, and effective
teachers will use those experiences to guide instruction in ways that
facilitate development of healthy attitudes towards those who may differ
from them as well as a healthy sense of their own unique identities
(Derman-Sparks and ABC Task Force 1989; Derman-Sparks and Ramsey
2006; Schniedewind and Davidson 2006). Young children are more than
capable of engaging with ideas around diversity through the use of critical
literacy practices. As Van Ausdale and Feagin (2001, 179-82) found:

> Close scrutiny of [children's] lives reveals that they are as intricate as
> adults' lives, even though children have a more limited experience with the
> social world. The limitations to children's experience derive from their
> relatively brief time in social contact with others, not from deficits in

ability, engagement, or facility with interaction…Most children are accomplished at deciphering and manipulating the social world and its complexities… They take the language and concepts of the larger society and experiment with them in their own interactions with other children and adult caregiver.

Teachers who incorporate critical literacy practices take advantage of this experimentation with roles and identities in order to foster a deeper understanding and tolerance of difference in young children and to help them recognize the issues of equity and justice in the world around them.

At a pedagogical level, critical literacy encompasses multiple strategies for engaging students to critically read the word and the world. A review of the literature reveals three different approaches to critical literacy: 1) critically examining texts for voice and perspective, 2) using texts as a vehicle through which one can examine larger social issues, and 3) using students' lives and experiences as the text and incorporating literacy practices (Stribling 2008). These three approaches are not mutually exclusive and, in fact, intersect in very natural and powerful ways. Furthermore, each of these approaches has the potential for incorporating the collaboration, integration, and diversity awareness that contribute to a peaceful co-existence.

Possibilities for Peace

In my experiences in elementary school classrooms as both a teacher and a researcher, I observed the ways in which critical literacy uncovers the root of conflict as well as introduces possibilities for forging harmonious relationships. Critical literacy supports collaborative problem solving, can easily be integrated into the required academic standards, and addresses the differences among us that often lead to conflict. Each of these foci of critical literacy—collaboration, integration, and difference—is further explored below through the experiences of young children and their teachers. In the reality of classroom communities, collaboration, integration, and diversity awareness are not addressed in mutually exclusive ways, so even though the experiences described are used to highlight one specific focus, they often emphasize multiple ways in which critical literacy can build a foundation of peace.

Collaboration

A commotion erupted at the writing center. Naomi and Olivia were visibly upset, so the teacher called them over to the carpet to figure out what the problem was. Apparently their friendship was precariously hinged on the actions of another student, Samantha. When Samantha joined the conversation, it was discovered that she wanted to be friends with Naomi on the condition that Naomi would not be friends with Olivia. The teacher listened intently to each girl's feelings. Then together they developed a plan where Samantha understood that both she and Olivia could be friends with Naomi; Naomi would finish up at the writing table with Samantha and then read big books with Olivia.

Critical literacy is most effective when focused on the students' real life experiences related to issues of equity and fairness; for young children these issues often revolve around friendships and the ways in which they interact with their classmates. The key aspect of a critical literacy framework that is addressed in this example is the exploration of multiple perspectives and using those multiple perspectives to create practices that are more fair and equitable for all. The teacher did not step in as the authority telling the girls that they must get along, nor did she praise or punish based on standards of "good character." Instead the teacher gave the students space to voice their concerns, to hear the concerns of their peers, and to find ways to solve the conflict peacefully.

An important aspect of critical literacy practices, particularly with young children, is the modeling of this collaborative problem solving. In the following example, the teacher uses a student's struggle with fairness to illustrate for the rest of the class how to peacefully resolve issues as well as how to carefully examine our assumptions around these issues.

The kindergarten class was writing their own version of the folktale, The Mitten. The class could not agree on whether the character should be a boy or a girl. The teacher decided to solve the dilemma with a vote; all six girls and three of the boys voted for a girl character while the remaining five boys voted for a boy character. Some of the boys, particularly Sam, were not happy with this outcome. Instead of dismissing the issue, the teacher engaged the whole class in processing their thinking around this outcome. She asked if it was okay for a boy to vote for a girl character. Madison said yes, and added that you can also be a girl and vote for a boy character. Sam was still upset declaring that he did not like girl characters. The teacher then began naming books the class had read and loved that had girl characters. Some of the students joined in the naming and agreed that they loved these characters. The teacher then checked in with Sam to see how he now felt about the decision. He was still upset, so as the rest of the class went to their seats to work in their journals, Sam sat with the teacher to further discuss the character choice. When writing workshop time ended and the students returned to the carpet, the teacher, along with Sam, reported back to the class about how he resolved the issue he was having with the character being a girl. Apparently Sam thought that the other versions of the story they had read already had girl characters, therefore to him, the class choosing yet another girl character was not fair. Once he looked back at the books, however, he was able to reflect on his feelings and broaden his understanding of the issue so that he was now okay with the class' decision.

Because the teacher took the time to check in with Sam and allowed him the opportunity to voice his perspective and examine his assumptions, Sam was able to resolve his issue with the character choice. All of this happened in collaboration with the teacher, a process that was then shared with the rest of the class. Collaboration is a time consuming effort, but the teacher was committed to dedicating that time in order to resolve the conflict.

Opportunities to practice collaborative problem solving are also important for young children. The next example illustrates how a kindergarten teacher took advantage of such an opportunity.

The students were singing a morning song where they pair up with a partner to greet them with a series of hand motions and movements. Once the greeting is over, the students switch partners and repeat the greeting. Students looking for a new partner are supposed to raise their hands and pair up with the first person they see whose hand is also raised. On this particular morning, students were walking right past students with raised hands in order to pair with particular students such as their friends. After the greeting, the teacher gathered the students on the carpet and shared this observation with them. She then asked how, as a class, they might solve this problem. Students responded with ideas for pairing up with the first person they see or the person next to them as well ideas for helping their classmates notice those students who are looking for partners.

In this situation, the teacher did not reprimand the students for not following the proper protocol for the greeting song, but rather presented the students with her observation and gave them the space to solve the problem as a collaborative group. The responsibility did not only lie with those students who were looking for particular friends with whom to pair, but with the class as a whole to be accountable to each other as friends and peaceful problem solvers.

Integration

During reading centers, Vanessa was helping Sarah at the recording station when Morgan approached and yelled at Vanessa to give the microphone to Sarah. This upset Vanessa since she was only trying to help Sarah. Before having an opportunity to resolve the issue, the students were instructed to return to their seats to work on a writing activity. Because Vanessa did not have an opportunity to talk with Morgan, she decided to write her a letter. In the letter she expressed how she felt when Morgan yelled at her. Vanessa discretely passed the note to Morgan since the students were supposed to be working on a reading response piece. After reading the note, Morgan wrote a response apologizing for making Vanessa feel that way and discretely passed it back to her. The note writing/passing continued for a few more minutes as the girls expressed feelings, responded to feelings, apologized, and accepted apologies ultimately resolving their conflict in a peaceful manner.

These second graders illustrate how powerful the written word can be in contributing to peaceful problem solving. Vanessa and Morgan capitalized on the power of literacy to express needs and find resolution and space where they could once again be friends. When the teacher introduced this grade level skill at the beginning of the year, she told the students how useful letter writing was for sharing feelings with others. She even made letter writing a center so students could practice using this medium for sharing thoughts/feelings/ideas with their friends. Vanessa and Morgan definitely found value in this literacy lesson and ended up using it to solve a very real and personal conflict.

Literacy lessons are a very natural way to integrate peace education. The following example illustrates how a read aloud lesson can simultaneously address assumptions based on gender/race differences, conflict resolution around those assumptions, and important literacy skills such as comprehension.

The kindergarten teacher was reading "Amazing Grace" to the students, a story about a little girl, Grace, who wants to play the part of Peter Pan in the class play; however, some of her classmates claim that she cannot have this part because she is not a boy, and she is not white. In the story, Grace's mother and grandmother support her dream to play the part, and in the end her audition is by far the best so she is chosen to be Peter Pan. The teacher chose to share this story since the children had been learning about slavery and segregation leading up to the birthday of Dr. Martin Luther King Jr. They spent a lot of time discussing skin color and the ways in which our different shades should not be the basis for inclusion or exclusion. When discussing the story, the students noted that Grace really want to play the part of Peter Pan. The teacher asked, "Why would Grace want to be Peter? What do we know about her?" The students responded by citing what was read earlier about Grace's favorite activity— pretending to be story characters. She particularly enjoyed the most adventurous characters, and Peter Pan was a pretty adventurous character.

In this vignette, the teacher posed comprehension questions that pushed the students to think back to what was read earlier in order to find support for their claim. This teacher developed a lesson that grew out of a social studies concept (segregation and Dr. Martin Luther King Jr.) and addressed a conflict or social justice issue (fairness and conflict resolution) through reading while reinforcing important literacy skills (comprehension).

While literacy and social studies lessons are a natural fit for lessons on peace building, they are not the only place where fairness and equity issues emerge. Science and math activities also present opportunities to integrate a critical literacy perspective where foundations for peace can be laid (Gutstein and Peterson 2006; Pelo 2008; Schniedewind and Davidson 2006).

Difference

The previous example where the teacher used "Amazing Grace" to address fairness issues in conjunction with literacy skills, also highlights the ways in which critical literacy practices contribute to a greater awareness and appreciation of human diversity. More specifically, "Amazing Grace" teaches that neither race nor gender should be pieces of our identity that keep us from participating in activities. Just because Grace was a black girl did not mean that she could not imagine and fulfill her desire to play the part of Peter Pan in the class play.

Helping children to examine assumptions they might have around their own identity and the identities of their peers can help build a greater understanding and awareness of diversity and hopefully reduce the conflicts that might stem from our differences. In my experiences in elementary school classrooms, I have heard children poignantly reveal assumptions around issues of gender, ethnicity, and class. The following vignette is from a second grade class and highlights gender assumptions:

Six boys and one girl were sitting in the back of the room diligently working on their reading contracts. Almost out of nowhere, one of the boys announced, "Boys are braver than girls." Other boys joined in repeating this notion. Sarah, the only girl sitting in the vicinity, protested this idea. Reggie insisted that the claim was true and offered evidence to prove it when he stated, "When girls get scared, they get behind boys." Sarah was not convinced and countered, "Boys do that too." Unfortunately the boys were not convinced.

The next example, from a first grade classroom, focuses on issues of ethnicity:

> *The first-grade class was sitting on the carpet for morning meeting. It was Erica's turn to share what she did that weekend. She reported to the class that she went to the mall so she could use her "heelies" (sneakers that have built-in wheels that allow the sneakers to double as roller-blades). I asked if she went to the North Mall as this is the closest one to our community. Erica, a Korean-American student, wrinkled her nose in disgust and declared that she had gone to the South Mall in a neighboring community. The North Mall, in her words, had "too many Hispanics."*

The final example reveals interesting assumptions regarding class:

> *In a discussion about the story, Rumplestiltskin, Danny pointed to an illustration of the king in the book and announced that he was rich. I asked how he came to that conclusion, and Danny offered his "valuables" (the jewels on his crown and clothes) as evidence. I then asked if the girl in the story was rich, to which Danny replied that she was not because the only "valuables" she had were one necklace and one ring. I followed up by asking Danny if he thought I was rich. Danny quickly responded that I was not. When asked how he knew that, however, Danny became flustered and asked another student to answer that question for him. Angela decided that I was not rich because "rich people are mean, but you are nice." Danny agreed adding that "rich people brag about the money they have, but you don't."*

From a critical literacy perspective, these examples represent opportunities to help children examine these assumptions in order to come to a greater understanding of the possibilities and humanity of all people regardless of race, class, gender, etc. For example, a teacher might address the gender misconception with an examination of storybook characters and historical figures who exhibit bravery and the ways in which that bravery transcends gender and does not rely on physical size and/or strength. Similarly lessons and activities around the contributions of Hispanics and the ways in which people, both rich and poor, have cared for the well-being of others can help students examine assumptions and make them less likely to see and treat groups of people as "others" with whom they have little in common. Awareness and acceptance of the diversity and the similarities of all contributes to peace education efforts and the desire for harmonious co-existence.

The classroom experiences shared in this chapter are not earth shattering examples of conflict or extraordinary instances of peace building efforts, but they do represent important aspects of the realities of elementary school classrooms in the United States and suggest ways in which critical literacy can be incorporated to build a foundation toward understanding and peaceful problem solving. Just like learning how to read or how to complete math computations, peace building involves skills that must be purposefully taught and practiced in meaningful contexts. It is critical to teach these skills and lay the foundation for peaceful problem solving with young children—a foundation that rests on collaboration, the integration of conflict resolution into classroom practices, and an awareness of the differences that too often create the walls between us. While this chapter suggests ways in which critical literacy can help build this foundation, there is certainly more to explore regarding the explicit connections between peace education and a commitment to collaboration, integration, and diversity awareness. Educational researchers, peace educators, and classroom teachers must work together to find ways to transform PK-12 schools into spaces where students engage in critical literacy practices that help foster commitments to social justice and peaceful coexistence. Critical literacy can empower young children to create for themselves a more peaceful and just world.

References

Banks, J. A., and C.A. Banks. 2007. *Multicultural education: Issues and perspectives.* Hoboken, NJ: Wiley.

Banks, J. A. 2008. *An introduction to multicultural education.* Boston: Pearson.

Carter, C. 2006. Standards for peace education: Florida Center for Public & International policy paper. University of North Florida, http://www.unf.edu/thefloridacenter/PeaceEdStdsForWebsite.pdf (accessed January 15, 2009).

Derman-Sparks, L., and ABC Task Force. 1989. *Anti-bias curriculum: Tools for empowering young children.* Washington, D.C.: National Association for the Education of Young Children.

Derman-Sparks, L. and P.G. Ramsey. 2006. *What if all the kids are white? Anti-bias multicultural education with young children and families.* New York: Teachers College Press.

Freire, P. 1970. *Pedagogy of the oppressed.* New York: Continuum.

Giroux, H. 1988. *Teachers as intellectuals: Toward a critical pedagogy of learning.* South Hadley, MA: Bergin & Garvey.

Gutstein, E. and B. Peterson. 2006. *Rethinking mathematics: Teaching social justice by the numbers.* Milwaukee, WI: Rethinking Schools.

Hadjioannou, X., and D. Fu, 2007. Critical literacy as a tool for preparing prospective educators for teaching in a multicultural world. *The New England Reading Association Journal* 43: 43-8.

Harris, I. M., and M. L. Morrison. 2003. *Peace education.* London: McFarland & Company, Inc.

Joseph, P. B., and S. Efron. 2005. Seven worlds of moral education. *Phi Delta Kappan* 86: 525-33.

Lewison, M., A.S. Flint, and K. Van Sluys. 2002. Taking on critical literacy: The journey of newcomers and novices. *Language Arts 79*: 382-92.

McLaren, P. 2003. *Life in schools: An introduction to critical pedagogy in the foundations of education.* 4th ed. Boston, MA: Allyn & Bacon.

Nieto, S. 2000. *Affirming diversity: The sociopolitical context of multicultural education.* New York: Longman.

Pelo, A. 2008. *Rethinking early childhood education.* Milwaukee, WI: Rethinking Schools.

Schniedewind, N., and E. Davidson. 2006. *Open minds to equality.* Milwaukee, WI: Rethinking Schools.

Shor, I., and P. Freire. 1987. *A pedagogy for liberation: Dialogues on transforming education.* Westport, CT: Bergin & Garvey.

Siegel, M., and S.L. Fernandez. 2000. Critical approaches. In *Handbook of reading research ,Volume III*, ed. M. Kamil, P.B. Mosenthal, P.D. Pearson, and R. Barr, 141-151. Mahwah, NJ: Lawrence Erlbaum Associates.

Stribling, S. M. 2008. Using critical literacy practices in the classroom. *The New England Reading Association Journal* 44, 34-8.

Van Ausdale, D., and J.R. Feagin. 2001. *The first R: How children learn race and racism.* New York: Rowman & Littlefield.

Vasquez, V. M. 2004. *Negotiating critical literacies with young children.* Mahwah, NJ: Lawrence Erlbaum Associates.

Wink, J. 2005. *Critical pedagogy: Notes from the real world.* New York: Addison Wesley Longman.

CHAPTER SIX

EDUCATION OF HEART:
WHAT JUSTICE AND PEACE STUDIES
CAN LEARN FROM MORAL DEVELOPMENT
LITERATURE

CRIS TOFFOLO

The discipline(s) of justice and peace studies (JPS) investigate the causes and effects of violence and injustice at various levels of human interaction, as well as the ideologies of hierarchy, and the practices, policies, and structures of oppression that produce various forms of injustice. JPS programs also teach strategies to transform unjust and violent situations. In these ways they differ from the mainstream of other social sciences. This difference produces somewhat different education goals, in that JPS programs seek to develop not only the cognitive and theoretical abilities of their students, but also their desire and ability to act wisely and morally to transform systems and stop injustices. Archbishop Desmond Tutu and the Dalai Lama call this the "education of the heart" and argue that while we have advanced technical and scientific education, which has resulted in much material progress, we still know very little about how to educate people to act morally, especially under pressure. Given that we live in unjust, hierarchical, and violent social systems, such action is often controversial and counter-cultural. These are the challenges of our age.

If our educational aspirations are different, do we need to approach the educational task in a different way? Many JPS educators would say yes, and many use praxis-oriented and interactive pedagogies (i.e., peer learning, service learning, case studies, study away, etc.) because we intuitively understand their efficacy, and because they fit logically with theories of multiple intelligences and different learning styles which are consistent with JPS commitments to honor diversity and provide meaningful opportunities for all.

This paper examines the field of moral development in order to better understand, justify, and develop the kinds of pedagogy and curriculum JPS programs must have in order to fulfill their educational mission. Moral development literature within the field of psychology can help to explain why and how certain pedagogies and curriculum content can stimulate the ability to act morally under pressure. The paper also makes suggestions about incorporating these findings into JPS programs.

An important caveat: This paper does not provide a philosophical critique of the presuppositions of the field of moral development, which is needed because much of the field has been guided uncritically by Kantian ethics, liberalism's universalistic claims about rights, and a Rawlsian theory of justice. While such commitments provide important insights, they are not necessarily compatible with the philosophical commitments of some JPS programs. This of course is a complicated conversation. Suffice it to say that contemporary work in the field is increasingly self critical about these issues. Indeed, most psychological theories of cognitive moral development are grounded in moral philosophies that focus on fairness, justice and rights. For example, Piaget relied on Kant's categorical imperative to frame his research on the moral development of children. Kohlberg is even more explicit about his commitment to Kantian ethics and Rawls. The field has now incorporated insights from feminism (initially thanks to Carol Gilligan), Marxism (a la renewed interest in Vygotsky), and post-modernism (with the growing interest in both cross-cultural comparison and religious aspects of moral action). The field also is replacing Kohlberg's formalism with a new interest in how adults understand and seek to act morally in the course of their daily lives.

The First Generation: Piaget and Kohlberg

Psychological moral development research began where philosophy had always dwelt, by assuming morality was primarily a cognitive achievement. Traditional moral development theory, as developed by Jean Piaget and furthered by Lawrence Kohlberg, focuses on children's evolving concepts of fairness and justice, and examines how children apply moral principles to their peers and family. At its center this research is concerned about: the universality of conceptual moral categories; the differentiation of moral rules from social conventions; understanding inhibitive verse prohibitive morality; distribute justice; and distinguishing rights from freedoms (Killen et al. 2006, 157)

Piaget married these philosophical interests to methodologies from the social sciences, to challenge Durkheim's view that morality was transmitted by socialization, a process whereby children internalize the norms of their culture. Instead Piaget claimed moral truths and judgment are most effectively learned through "social construction," which consists of exchanging perspectives with others. In social exchanges children practice perspective taking, which leads them to become "decentered" in their view of the world. Social construction is different from internalizing a norm through imitation or following orders because it involves a dialectical process of social interaction and collaborative learning, which produces an understanding of phenomena that is epistemologically distinct and unique (Gibbs 2003, 31-33).

At stake for Piaget was to refute the relativistic implications of Durkheim's view of morality, as being merely the contingent product of a particular culture. He argued instead that moral judgment is analogous to logical truth. An example used to demonstrate Piaget's claim is the development of "conservation knowledge" (e.g., if the same amount of liquid is poured into two different containers, the amount of liquid in each remains equal, no matter what the appearance). Conservation judgments have a logical quality about them such that once they are learned, they no longer require further empirical verification. From then on they are experienced as necessary, as illogical imbalances violate the laws of logic and thus cannot exist. Learning this about the physical world produces a cognitive preference for equality and reciprocity that carries over into morality. In other words, morality is grounded in our perception of how the universe necessarily functions. This produces a natural preference for balance, congruency, consistency and non-contradiction, which then predisposes us to know reciprocity and equality are right in that they are logically consistent. "Morality is the logic of action just as logic is the morality of thought" (Piaget 1965, 398).

Social interactions that violate reciprocity and equality generate strong feelings that can motivate moral behavior. That motivational power is stronger because the norm is internalized through social construction, rather than merely by being taught. Violations of justice and reciprocity just shouldn't exist and must be challenged when they do occur. In other words, mature moral judgment can be a motive to moral behavior in its own right. Piaget called this "cognitive primacy" (Gibbs 2003, 32-35, 58).

Kohlberg followed Piaget in describing moral development in terms of cognitive development and cognitive primacy. Like Piaget he believed mature morality is a necessary logic that is inherent in social relations. Kohlberg also followed Piaget's claim that cognitive moral development progresses through a series of invariant stages that are linked to parallel gains in cognitive development. This development is linear, invariant in its sequence, and universal across cultures. As one progresses through the stages one's cognitive structure gets reorganized to become more inclusive.

Drawing upon Dewey's ideas, Kohlberg elaborated and expanded upon Piaget's stages. Kohlberg saw Piaget as proving Dewey empirically, having observed that young people on Israeli kibbutzim were more advanced in their moral development than other youth. Dewey believed there were three completing moral orientations: impulsive (hedonistic desires); group conforming (rules and customs); and reflective (principles). Kohlberg argued that Dewey's three orientations were related developmentally, and he relabeled them the pre-conventional, conventional, and post-conventions stages of moral development. He went on to argue that within each stage there were two different levels, bringing to six the total number of moral development stages. These he articulated in great detail.

Like Piaget, Kohlberg argued that at each stage people use a cognitively different structure of moral justification (reasons) to support a decision about what is right or good. As such, these stages describe *how* people approach moral issues, not *what* specific moral beliefs they hold. With each move to the next stage a person's way of thinking gets reorganized, such that his or her perspective on justice becomes more inclusive. Gains in moral reasoning include: movement from superficiality to depth in moral judgments; deeper understandings of rights and wrong; one's own welfare and self-interest increasingly seen in the context of the welfare of others; and an expanded understanding of fairness that comes to encompass everyone.

For Kohlberg moral development is stimulated by participation in groups that allow one to take on different roles and gain skills at joint decision-making. Mayhew and King (2008) in fact tested over 400 undergraduates in an effort to figure out what types of pedagogy are best at facilitating students' ability to reason about moral issues. As with similar studies, their results were somewhat inconclusive. To the degree that they were able to identify trends, they found that "explicitly including moral content [into courses] … appears to foster growth of moral reasoning." This, however, might just be because students learn a better language with which to discuss moral issues, or because such courses encourage perspective taking and opportunities to practice moral decision making. Also important was how instructors structured their classroom and communicated: "Creating supportive and safe learning environments for students to ask questions and … engage in thought-provoking discussions about moral issues and to critically reflect on substantive topics are important for spurring growth in moral reasoning" (Mayhew and King 2008, 36). In addition, the frequency and quality of faculty student interactions was found to be critical to promoting moral reasoning development, especially when the teacher modeled a stage of reasoning that is a step ahead of where the students are (Mayhew and King 2008, 21).

In the end, it appears that the more social stimulation of various kinds, the faster the rate of moral development. Especially crucial are opportunities to be exposed to different kinds of people in social institutions that promote trust and connection, for such social interactions mitigate inter-group stereotyping and help to prevent and control cycles of escalating violence and vengeance (Gibbs 2003, 44-45).

Gilligan's Kuhnian Revolution

Carol Gilligan's work in the 1970s radically challenged Kohlberg's methods and assumptions. After observing that girls rarely reach the highest stages of moral development, as determined by Kohlberg's methods and tests, she concluded not that girls are less moral than boys but that they approach moral problems using a different logic of care, which is invisible within Kohlberg's schema.

Gilligan's thesis completely upset Kohlberg's stage theory, for in place of logical moral reasons, grounded in cognitive abilities, and unchanging truths about the universe, Gilligan put the need for caring connections to other people. Recently Gilligan has expanded her critique to include Piaget's view of relationships as being incidental to the construction of the self. Instead, Gilligan argues relationships are constitutive of the self. Even "the existence of autonomous selves is itself a product of relationships." (Hekman 1995, 16)

Susan Hekman claims Gilligan's work is revolutionary in the Kuhnian sense of a scientific revolution (paradigm shift) because not only did it open a flood of criticism of Kohlberg's invariant and universal stage theory, but it also raised the possibility that morality was about more than training cognitively grounded faculties of judgment (Kuhn 1970). Vis-à-vis JPS, Gilligan's work raises a question about whether our pedagogy and curriculum should include mechanisms to help our students develop caring connections with people who are suffering injustice and violence. In our individualistic culture, that also is economically stratified, as well as socially, culturally and racially segregated, and shaped by for-profit media, it is very easy to be oblivious to the suffering of all but one's immediate friends and family, or to assuage one's guilt simply by writing a check. In this kind of a world JPS programs must endeavor to break through distance and indifference. We should help students forge bonds of solidarity with other people. This means helping students form respectful relationships with those who are adversely situated. It also means critiquing individualistic ideologies of self-help that compel some students to break with their own communities in order to achieve the American dream for themselves alone.

Why might such educational strategies work? According to Hoffman care is an innate human capacity for empathy, which is the glue that makes social life possible. Empathy is a "feeling with" another's emotion; suffering with another imaginatively. Hoffman argues empathy is the exclusive motivation for moral behavior in that it transforms caring ideals into "hot cognitions," which provide the motivation to rectify injustice (Gibbs 2003, 96). Empathy gets its energy and power by being a natural biological endowment that is enhanced and expanded through cognitive development and socialization, such that we become predisposed to care about others, especially those within our own group.

Although Hoffman agrees with Piaget and Kohlberg that perspective taking is key, he argues this is so because it teaches us that other people have inner emotional states, histories, futures, and an ongoing life conditions that can be unpleasant (Gibbs 2003, 87-89). A mature sense of empathy is developed by socializing children to see the hurt they cause to others. By pointing this out, children develop an empathy-based sense of guilt which is at the core of moral motivation. This may help to explain why introductory JPS courses that starkly reveal the suffering caused by illegal, violent and immortal government policies (at home or abroad) can disrupt many students' settled view of their country as basically good (at most in need of some policy corrections). Not only does information and graphic images (e.g., of the US invasion of Panama, atrocities in Vietnam, post-Katrina government inaction, etc.) create serious cognitive dissonance, but to the degree that Americans believe they have a stake in their democracy, empathy-based guilt might also be triggered. One or both are powerful motivators that propel students to continue to desire to educate themselves about issues of justice and peace.

Returning to Hoffman's theory, moral development is not a function of the child constructing more complex moral schemas, in the Piagetian/Kohlbergian sense. Rather, as children mature, they build up moral scripts of social sequences and gain motivation from empathic affect. However these moral scripts are Janus-faced. While they do channel our natural empathy into moral responses, they also can lead us to anti-social behavior, as when we blame victims for their own misfortune (Ryan 1972), or when these scripts limit empathy to in-group members.

In response to these phenomena teachers often attempt to broaden the scope of their students' social perspective taking to include all people, thereby extending those covered by our empathy. Maccoby called this "relabeling" or "reframing" (Maccoby 1980). Such work is critical to JPS programs because typically most of the moral scripts/narratives we are socialized to accept reflect the bias of the powerful. As Michel Foucault has adroitly explained, power is most absolute not when using brute force but when it is never questioned (Foucault 1980). This happens when a population accepts its leaders' narrative about what is right and true. Yet every system contains those at its margins who are the victims of harsh government treatment (e.g. Guantanamo Bay, police brutality in poor neighborhoods). And every system's narrative, even those of democratic nations which officially extol at least legal equality, contains ideologies which justify certain inequalities (of race, class, gender, disability, sexual orientation, etc.). Given such injustices JPS programs must expose their students to atrocities and offer critiques of these ideological justifications. Deconstructing dominant ideologies is therefore a necessary part of expanding our students' scope of empathy, which is part of helping them to include all people within their moral frame of reference.

Given this task let us take a moment to review the literature on inter-group relationships which examines stereotyping, prejudice and discrimination. Work by Turiel, has revealed several things about the nature of inter-group relations (Turiel 1998). First, from laboratory research, we know that after being artificially divided into arbitrary groups most people quickly favor their in-group and exhibit negative biases toward the out-group, even attributing stereotypes, biases and prejudices to them. This phenomenon was most famously demonstrated by Jane Elliot's "blue-eyed/brown-eyed" exercise, as documented in a 1971 documentary that was featured on the PBS program "Frontline." This is related to three other phenomena. The "out-group homogeneity effect" is the tendency to see heterogeneity in one's own group but to assume homogeneity of other groups. This contributes to stereotyping and thus to inter-group conflict. The "shifting standards" phenomenon refers to the use of different measures for members of another group (which typically are linked to stereotypic expectations about the group). Finally, people who view other peoples' personal qualities as static, and believe innate traits cause behavior, are more likely to stereotype than those who see traits as malleable and believe context influences behavior. This same research reveals that peoples' view of whether exclusion is a moral transgression depends on the target, and that the use of stereotypical expectations increases as one ages (Killen 2006, 162-172).

All of the above must be carefully responded to by JPS programs, and in repetitive ways. For another finding is that students have a much easier time remembering stereotypic than counter-stereotypic information. In addition, stories about traits are better remembered than stories about social relationships. These tendencies are especially apparent in students who openly endorse more stereotypes: they have worse memories for counter-stereotypical information.

What these findings indicate is that there are many aspects of daily life that intervene in the process of moral decision making, and therefore we cannot simply presuppose that if individuals' cognitive moral development is attended to that they will typically act in moral ways. One of the people most responsible for helping us understand this, Gus Blasi, identified the gap between moral judgment and action. He also has conducted research to help bridge this gap (Walker 2004, 1). Blasi makes several key points. First, identical behaviors can be supported by different moral criteria, and the same moral criteria can lead to different behaviors. Second, better moral reasoning is predictive of better behavior, however moral cognition alone plays only a modest role in explaining the variability in moral action—maybe 10 percent. This means we need to develop a more comprehensive view of moral functioning (Walker 2004, 2). This has been provided by James Rest, who posited four components of moral behavior:

1. Moral sensitivity (awareness of the moral dimension of a situation)
2. Moral reasoning (to determine which action is morally justified)
3. Moral motivation (putting moral values first)
4. Moral character (following through on one's convictions, which is related to ego strength, perseverance, willpower and volition) (Rest 1994).

To these Gruber has added the importance of creativity and imagination, arguing that moral situations are those that lack clear means to moral action (Gruber 1993, 3-15). People who exhibit a high level of moral responsibility also exhibit "creative altruism" which is similar to other creative work in that both require awareness of the possibility of something new, followed by patient evaluation of the problem, and the ability to translate that analysis into actions that can produce a different possible future. Essential aspects of creative altruism include empathic awareness of the needs and feelings of the others; the ability to take the initiative; willingness to live constantly with the knowledge of unmet need, while seeking to transform the status quo to address that need; and being willing and able to undertake exceptional actions (Rostan 2005, 105).

Recently Blasi has added self identity to the list of attributes that explain moral functioning. His model points out that some people have morality at the core of their self identity. Such people have a very high sense of responsibility to act morally. This conceptual system is distinct from their moral ideals. Instead it relates to the way their identity is constructed, such that in order to retain a positive self-image, their actions must be in congruence with their moral judgments. For such people "the self's very identity is constructed, at least in part, under the influence of moral reasons" (Blasi, as quoted in Walker 2004, 3-5).

Blasi's thesis is compatible with Gilligan's claim that relationships are constitutive of the self. This is demonstrated by research conducted by Anne Colby and William Damon who studied adults, whom others identified as highly moral, in order to explain differences in people's amount of pro-social behavior. In *Some Do Care* Colby and Damon record their study of 23 people who were exceptional in their levels of moral commitment (Colby and Damon 2002). According to Colby and Damon central to adult moral development is an on-going and gradual transformation of goals through experiences in relationships and social contexts that transform an individual's existing goals, beliefs, and propensities in the direction of expanded commitment to the common good. In certain circumstances, social influences trigger a person to reevaluate his/her existing moral goals and commitments. This occurs most often when the context contains respected people who can provide moral guidance (Colby and Damon 2002, 342-43).

One person they studied was a southern white woman who began her adult moral journey when she agreed to sit at a table with a black student in order to fulfill her goal of staying at Wellesley College. In the process she came to admire that student's intelligence and civility, and this gradually led her to question the segregationist ideology with which she had been raised (Colby and Damon 2002, 347). She then had the opportunity to work in the women's movement alongside women whom she greatly admired, though they held more progressive views about race than she did. This again forced her to reconsider her views and goals. At some point during this process critical events triggered an abrupt change in both her goals and views, and she became a life-long anti-racism activist.

In this story four key processes are at work. The first is "goal transformation." This activist's original goal was to remain at a college she liked, but that led her to a different set of beliefs, which in turn, imposed new moral goals. Second, this story highlights the influence of personal relationships, both the original one with her fellow student, and later on with women she admired but who held views on race different from her own. Third, she engaged in sustained social change work with a group of people she admired. People who continually immerse themselves in social networks engaged in moral issues experienced much moral development (Colby and Damon 2002, 344). Lastly, people who lead lives of moral courage are open to moral change. All people enter into situations in order to meet a particular set of goals but while engaging in the situation, the possibility arises that their original goals will be changed. Moral exemplars seemed more open to embrace such change.

A fifth key process for moral development is highlighted by the case of an anti-poverty activist whose moral development was spurred on when someone in a position of authority responded to a key event in her life. A pastor invited this woman into his church and soon put her into a leadership position that drew on her talents (Colby and Damon 2002, 356). She then had a vision, which her church and family encouraged her to pursue. In a very short amount of time she went from teaching Sunday school, to moving her family to another town to help feed, cloth and heal very poor children. Key to this woman's development was the recognition she received from someone in authority and from her community. Secondly, in the process of responding to the needs of others, she naturally set new and more ambitious moral goals for herself (Colby and Damon 2002, 360). This is related to another of Colby and Damon's findings: moral exemplars typically do not act out of any explicit logical argument or well-articulated belief system. In fact they don't score particularly high on Kohlberg's scale (though their scores are somewhat higher than those of other people) (Colby and Damon 2002, 366-67).

In contrast to Kohlberg's portrayal of moral exemplary individuals in terms of their high stage moral reasoning abilities, current scholarship reveals these people are distinguished by high levels of caring, compassion, self-sacrifice, consistency, honesty, open-mindedness, and the fact that they act habitually, without inner struggle (Walker 2004, 8). This likely is because they exhibit a very high degree of integration of their personal identities with their moral goals, which causes them not to view their moral choices in terms of self-sacrifice or exceptionality but simply as part of attaining their own goals. This unity also is likely to be what produces their ability to inspire others. Beyond that, the only other things that most moral exemplars share is an optimistic attitude about what they can achieve, and an enjoyment of their work.

Based on this study, Colby and Damon suggest several ways to promote the development of deep moral commitment and to sustain altruistic action:

1.   Support deeper moral engagement for all people, including for mature adults.
2.   Use educational and other programs to engage people's most urgent personal goals and needs, in a way that moves these goals in an altruistic direction. This can be done through providing powerful collaborative experiences. This naturally leads people to encounter others with different points of view, which in turn challenges, changes and broadens their own perspectives.
3.   Develop and support people's central moral convections while helping them to consider new information and its implications for themselves.
4.   In order to make sacrifices, take risks, and sustain commitment, people must feel a sense of moral effectiveness and empowerment. One goal of education programs thus should be to help people gain experiences of being effective in contributing to the welfare of others. They need to feel that their efforts are valuable and make a difference.
5.   Since a positive and optimistic approach to life is also important to sustaining moral work, help people find ways to creatively deal with setbacks, and to identify work that they enjoy doing.
6.   Get students to work directly with local moral exemplars who are present in all communities (Colby and Damon 2002, 368-69).

In terms of what these recommendations mean for the development of JPS curriculum and pedagogy, this study (as well as several of the others discussed above) confirms the necessity of putting our students into situations where they are forced to question the beliefs they were raised with as a result of new experiences that include sustained direct contact with people of different races, classes and ideologies.

Further, as Elise Boulding advocated, students should be encouraged to dream and imagine alternative futures. Teachers should help students to link their visions to their current goals. Teachers, as authority figures, have an important role in affirming the importance of these dreams and encouraging students to act upon them. This means knowing one's students and taking the time to help them articulate solutions to the problems that they find most pressing. It also means helping them to connect with others who are engaged in similar work.

This study also suggests that resources should be spent on co-curricular activities, in order to help create and sustain a sense of just community and identity for JPS students. This not only will help them work together to form bonds of solidarity that can sustain them as they explore unusual ideas and morally challenging situations, but it also can help generate a running discourse about moral topics, which other research confirms is very important to moral development (Mayhew and King 2008). Further, by creating a morally defined community, a JPS program can help students develop a morally centered self-identity, which now is increasingly recognized as being central to sustained moral work. Key here is that morality is a social enterprise, both in its origins and its functions: it prescribes people's activities, regulates their social interactions, and arbitrates conflicts. Also, morality is multifaceted in that it entails the interplay of behavior, thought, and emotion (Walker 1995, 372). Thus, although we typically view reasoning as an individual activity, in fact it also fundamentally is a social process of group interchange, with individual reasons a derivative phenomenon involving internalized aspects of the group process or, alternatively, that individual and collaborative reasoning are developed in tandem by a complex process of reciprocal influence (Moshman, in Gibbs 2003, 42).

Conclusion

Higher education has primarily paid attention to the first of Rest's components (moral reasoning) because it fits with how material is taught in the classroom (ala traditional philosophy and ethics), and because it is related to the priority universities have in promoting critical inquiry. Certainly JPS programs should provide training in moral reasoning and the development of an ethical vocabulary, including the different types of philosophical arguments used by different schools of ethics (utilitarian, situationalist, virtue-based, teleological, and deontological). However it is also increasingly clear that this is not a complete formula for helping people become able to act in moral ways. So what else must our curricula include? I would argue it must include lessons and practical engagements that help students expand the scope of their empathy, as well as lessons and exercises to challenge ideologies and practices that stereotype and demean certain groups. Also key are activities and community building exercises that help students develop a moral self-identity. And we need to incorporate examinations of practical successes and other material that engenders hope, including exposure to exemplary individuals.

In addition to these things which are directly suggested by the moral development literature, it can be inferred that JPS programs should also teach theories of social solidarity, including the complexities that come when one is not an organic member of the community in which one is working. We should follow this with opportunities for students to practice solidarity, both within the student community and with other groups. This is linked to social movement theory which is still a relatively new field. Although we now know a bit about how people get motivated to become involved, and something about what sustains engagement, the theory is still weak in its explanatory and predictive power, and thin in terms of what aspects of these phenomena have been analyzed to date.

This review of moral development theory can also help JPS programs sort through charges of bias, for the field of moral development theory provides an academically respectable empirical basis that backs up JPS curriculum and pedagogical choices.

Finally, this literature can help us achieve greater clarity concerning difficult choices that our programs face. One of these concerns what we should teach about violence. Certainly, we teach Galtung's theory about the relationships between structural, cultural and direct violence, and we expose and excoriate the many instances of all three in our world, as well as the processes by which one form of violence reinforces another. We also typically teach conflict resolution/conflict transformation techniques to deal with conflict (a normal and necessary part of human interaction) without resorting to any form of violence. And we typically teach about movements and the work of exemplary practitioners (Gandhi, MLK, etc.), as well as the theories of Gene Sharp. Things quickly become controversial, however, when deciding whether or not to explore the question, "Can violence ever be a legitimate means of changing social structures?" Some programs teach only strategies of active nonviolence and attempt to provide the strongest case for why all other means are wrong. This sometimes leads to charges of bias or naiveté, from realist international relations scholars, scholars of third world revolutions, or those who study the complex relationships of the civil rights movement, for example, the contrast between MLK and Malcolm X. The moral development literature, in my view, supports a curriculum that encourages robust and ethical debate about all means of making just social change (i.e., ends justify means; orthodox and radical versions of just war theory; violence only against property and/or agents of the state; and active non-violence). These must be examined in ethical and philosophical terms, and in terms of the factual consequences of those choices, viz. types of leadership thrown up by the use of different methods, human and material costs, record of successes/failures, and empirical pre/post measure of inequality and other justices. Finally we must have our students confront the question of where they locate themselves relative to this question about means and ends, and we must provide them frequent opportunities to begin to articulate their moral justifications for their positions.

Before closing let me just say that there is a natural bias, even resistance, in some JPS quarters to this topic of moral development—for it smacks too much of liberal individualism and models of change which rely upon an uncritical hope that all people once educated will embrace the good. To this I respond that those of us who teach as a form of justice promotion are in fact engaged in a project of individual conscientization and therefore we should have a deep awareness about what that entails. Some pedagogies may also achieve other things, for instance when students do a research project that helps a community document the need to further restrict the use of lead paint in rental properties. However even in these instances the pedagogical goal of JPS courses is not primarily to have students learn about the harmful effects of led paint. It is to deepen their understanding of how power operates and about the hardships and constraints that poor people face. In a JPS program, it is even appropriate to have the learning goals extend to such things as: (1) growing students' empathy for other people as well as a sense of themselves as a moral agent; (2) critically examining when and how to take appropriate action; and (3) enhancing students' sense of efficacy to affect change, as well as their commitment to change harmful environments.

In summary the moral development literature can be helpful for informing us about *how to teach* students about building social movements and for figuring out how to tap into people's moral energy. It also can help us to think more deeply about Paulo Freire's method, or about why Ernesto Cardinal's work with Nicaraguan Christian base communities was effective. It also leads us to think differently about creating other strategies for creating a more just and peaceful world, and about how to engage people to take on these tasks.

References

Blasi, A. 1984. Bridging moral cognition and moral action: A critical review of the literature. *Psychological Bulletin* 88:593-637.
—. 1995. Moral understanding and the moral personality: The process of moral integration in *Handbook of moral behavior and development: Vol. 1 Theory,* eds., W. Kurtines and J.L. Gewirtz, 229-253. Hillsdale, NY: Lawrence Erlbaum.
Colby, A. and W. Damon. 2002. *Some do care: Contemporary lives of moral commitment.* New York: the Free Press, Macmillan, Inc.

Eisenberg, N. 1996. In search of the good heart, in *The developmental psychologists: Research adventures across the life span*, 89-104. New York: McGraw-Hill.

Eisenberg, N., and R. A. Fabes. 1998. Prosocial development. In *Handbook of child psychology: Vol. E Social, emotional and personality development.* 5th ed., eds., W. Damon and N. Eisenberg, 701-779. New York: John Wiley.

Foucault, M. 1980. Power/Knowledge: Selected interviews & other writings 1972-1977, edited and translated by Colin Gordon et al. New York: Pantheon Books.

Gibbs, J. C. 2003. Moral development & reality: Beyond the theories of Kohlberg and Hoffman. Thousand Oaks: Sage Publications.

Giesbrecht, N, and L. Walker. 2000. Ego development and the construction of the moral self, *Journal of College Student Development* 41: 157-171.

Gruber, H.E. 1993.Creativity in the moral domain: Ought implies can implies create, *Creativity Research Journal*, 6:3-15.

Hekman, S. J. 1995. *Moral voices, moral selves: Carol Gilligan and feminist moral theory.* University Park, PA: The Pennsylvania State University Press.

Hoffman, M.L. 2000. *Empathy and moral development: Implications for caring and justice.* Cambridge, UK: Cambridge University Press.

Kelman, H.C. 1958. Compliance, identification, and internalization: Three processes of attitude change, *Journal of Conflict Resolution* 2: 51-60.

—. 1973. Violence without restraint: Reflections on the dehumanization of victims and victimizers, *Journal of Social Issues*, 29:25-61.

Kelman, H.C., and V.R.M. Baron. 1968. Determinants of modes of resolving inconsistency dilemmas: A functional analysis, *Theories of Cognitive Consistency: A Sourcebook* ed., R.P. Abelson, et al., 670-683. Chicago: Rand McNally.

Kelman, H.C., and V.L. Hamilton. 1989. *Crimes of obedience: Toward a social psychology of authority and responsibility.* New Haven CT: Yale University Press.

Killen, M., N. G. Margie and S. Sinno. 2006. Morality in the context of intergroup relationships, in *Handbook of Moral Development*, eds., Melanie Killen and Judith Smetana, 155-183. Mahwah NJ and London: Lawrence Erlbaum Associates, Publishers.

Kuhn, T. S. 1970. *The structure of scientific revolutions,* 2nd Ed., Chicago: University of Chicago Press.

Mayhew, M. J., and Patricia King. 2008. How curricular content and pedagogical strategies affect moral reasoning development in college students, *Journal of Moral Education* 37:1 (March):17-40.

Maccoby, E.E. 1980. *Social development: Psychological growth and the parent-child relationship.* New York: Harcourt, 1980.

Moshman, D. Cognitive development beyond childhood, *Handbook of child psychology: Vol. 2. Cognition, perception, and language,* 5th ed., 947-978. New York: John Wiley.

Piaget, J. 1965 (1932). *Moral judgment of the child.* Trans., M. Gabain. New York: Free Press.

Reardon, B. 1989. Pedagogical approaches to peace studies, in *Peace and world order studies: A curriculum guided,* 5th ed., eds., Daniel C. Thomas and Michael T. Klare, 20-27, Boulder: Westview Press.

Rest, J. R., and D. Narvaez, eds. 1994. *Moral development in the professions: Psychology and applied ethics.* Hillsdale NJ: Erlbaum.

Rest, J. R. et al. 1999. *Postconventional moral thinking: a Neo-Kohlbergian approach.* Mahwah, NJ: Erlbaum.

Rostan, S. 2005. Understanding extraordinary moral behavior in children and adolescents, in *Education, arts, and morality: Creative journeys,* ed., Doris B. Wallace, 103-120. New York: Kluwer Academic/Plenum Publishers, Path in Psychology Series.

Ryan, W. 1972. *Blaming the victim.* New York: Vintage Press.

Turiel, E. 1998. The development of morality. In *Handbook of child psychology: Vol. 3. Social, emotional, and personality development,* 5th ed., 863-932. New York: John Wiley.

Walker, L. J. 2006. Gender and morality., In *Handbook of moral development,* eds., Melanie Killen and Judith Smetana, 155-183. Mahwah NJ and London: Lawrence Erlbaum Associates, Publishers.

—. 2004. Gus in the gap: Bridging the judgment-action gap in moral functioning, in *Moral development, self, and identity,* eds., Daniel K. Lapsley and Darcia Narvaez, 1-20. Mahwah NJ: Lawrence Erlbaum Associates, Publisher.

Walker, L. J, et al., 1995. Reasoning about morality and real-life moral problems. In *Morality in everyday life: Developmental perspectives,* eds., Melanie Killen and Daniel Hart, 371-407. Cambridge: Cambridge University Press.

PART II:

SOCIETY AND CULTURE

Peace is a phenomenon that, when successfully promoted and sustained, finds itself located in all aspects of society. Conversely, its absence is likewise reflected in our social and cultural institutions, and this tends to be self-perpetuating in the sense of creating a world that not only lacks peace but also views it as impractical or even impossible as well. Addressing both the critical and constructive elements of this eventuality, the authors in this section focus upon issues ranging from sports and music to media and criminal justice. By casting a light on practices of oppression as well as causes for hope, these chapters combine in their impact and import to suggest that the quest to attain a culture of peace is not merely desirable, but rather, it is essential.

CHAPTER SEVEN

SPORT-BASED PEACE INITIATIVES: PLAYING FOR PEACE

ROBERT E. BAKER AND CRAIG ESHERICK

In this chapter, we will demonstrate the power of sport in building a culture of peace. Sport is a very potent vehicle, having significant economic influence. It can also be used to address a myriad of social objectives. Sport is a very valuable method for nations and cultures to build relationships, and for individuals within diverse cultures to engage with one another. Pierre de Coubertin, the founder of the modern Olympic Games, had this in mind when he described his vision for this world sporting event:

> Should this institution prosper-as I am persuaded, all civilized nations abiding, that it will-it may be a potent, if indirect, factor in securing universal peace. Wars break out because nations misunderstand each other. We shall not have peace until the prejudices which now separate the different races shall have been outlived. To attain this end, what better means than to bring the youth of all countries periodically together for amicable trials of muscular strength and agility? The Olympic Games, with the ancients, controlled athletics and promoted peace. Is it not visionary to look to them for similar benefactions in the future? (Mandell 1976,72)

This gathering of diverse athletes from every nation in the world, to live in an Olympic Village, to compete against each other in many individual and team events, embodies the sport-based interpersonal engagement that is crucial to building cultures of peace.

Theoretical Framework Supporting Sport-Based Peace Initiatives

Interpersonal interactions and intergroup interventions are central to facilitating peace and resolving conflicts (Kuriansky 2007). Referred to as the *public peace process,* an effective peace process must address all levels of society and develop in multiple arenas (Broome and Hatay 2006, 637). "While governments negotiate around interests and issues, citizens play a crucial role in changing behavior and relationships, for it is in the public political arena...that issues are reframed, comparable interests recognized, perceptions changed, fears allayed..." (Chufrin and Saunders 1993, 158). A broader theory of diplomatic negotiation, described as "multi-track diplomacy," calls for "sustained action by citizens outside government to change the fundamental relationship between groups in conflict (Chufrin and Saunders 2006, 156; McDonald 1991; Saunders 1985). Lederach (1995, 214) criticized "the trickle down approach that dominates international diplomacy and that assumes that the key to peace is negotiations at the top level," going on to conclude that peacemaking is, "embedded in the development and transformation of relationships over time... the peace process must address the grassroots level, the military, the national leaders..."

Beer and Nohria (2000) delineate the direction of organizational change through Theory E and Theory O. They suggest that Theory E, or top down, change might have a more immediate economic upside, but may not have sustainability, while Theory O may be more costly but yield longer term results. In distinguishing top down and bottom up change initiatives, Beer and Nohria suggest balancing the direction of change.

While top-down peace initiatives are common and receive both resources and attention, the middle-out and bottom-up approaches are essential in humanizing the stakeholders, building mutual understanding, enhancing accuracy in the historical interpretations, and even uniting past enemies. This concept of global liberalism being supported by local populism can make a difference in the peace process (Ben-Porat 2007). But, change is a long term process (Simpson, Hamber, and Scott 2001). This process toward peace utilizing sport as a vehicle must be sensitive to specific cultures, and acknowledge the differences and similarities of local populations (Lyras 2008).

The forced contact between groups that live segregated lives has been shown to lessen hostility between these groups, break down stereotypes, and engender more tolerant attitudes. The interactive contact also brings new knowledge, which serves to remove the element of fear associated with lack of personal experience and contact with another group (Allport 1954). The very nature of team sports and competition creates close physical proximity among teammates and opponents.

Allport's (1954) contact hypothesis supports the mechanisms at work in sport-based peace initiatives. The crux of the matter appears to be that contact must be meaningful, interactive, and not superficial in order to be effective in fostering change.

Only the type of contact that leads people to do things together is likely to result in changed attitudes. The principle is clearly illustrated in the multi-ethnic athletic team. Here the goal is all-important; the ethnic composition of the team is irrelevant. It is the cooperative striving for the goal that engenders solidarity. So too, in factories, neighborhoods, housing units, schools, common participation and common interests are more effective than the bare fact of equal-status contact (Allport1954, 276).

Thus, diverse groups that yield equal contributors to common goals, and require individuals to have interactive contact and build interdependent relationships in pursuit of those goals, are likely to be successful in enhancing intergroup understanding and contributing to a culture of peace. "The effect is greatly enhanced if this contact is sanctioned by institutional supports (i.e. by law, custom or local atmosphere), and provided it is of a sort that leads to the perception of common interests and common humanity between members of the two groups" (Allport 1954, 281). Since sport is a setting in which common interests are clear and mutual contributions are essential to success, diverse groups engaged in sport can, through individual members' interactive contact, enhance peace building efforts.

Sport can, within this framework, be a valuable mechanism in fostering peace and social justice. This proclamation of the utility of sport for the enhancement of individual and collective understanding compels the query: Why is sport useful?

The Social Impact of Sport

As a social institution, sport can influence society on a large scale (Coakley 2007). Yet, on a local level, sport is an arena for individual engagement and exchange. Therefore, the enhancement of peace initiatives can be bolstered both in and through sport. Sport's economic, social, and political implications are evident, and will be addressed for their utility in supporting peace-building efforts through sport.

Sport is a valuable contributor to the global economy, and a significant component of the United States' GDP, ranking in the top ten segments of the U.S. economy, as an estimated $425 to $450 billion dollar industry in America (Fort 2003; Pitts and Stotlar 2002; Plunkett Research Ltd 2008; Sports Business Journal 2008). Whether manufacturing and selling sporting goods, conducting and televising sport competitions, constructing and using sport facilities, generating sponsorship and endorsement deals, or providing other sport-related services, sport is a major economic force. The majority of sponsorship agreements, which provide economic and other benefits beyond the scope of sport, remain sport-related (Daniels et al 2007). Television networks reap huge rewards from the airing of sporting events. The majority of TV's most-watched programming is sport related (Neilsen Wire; Variety). In the U.S., the 24 hour sport network, a relatively recent historical phenomenon, has morphed from a single ESPN channel to multiple networks, including ESPN2, ESPNU, CSTV(CBS College), Fox Sports and virtually every cable company having a 24 hour sports network of their own. In 2009, two stadia, each with construction costs exceeding a billion dollars, will house the Dallas Cowboys and the NY Yankees (Farmer 2008; Fernandez 2008; Mosier 2008). In many cases, sport facilities are subsidized by public funds. In the U.S., education and sport coexist, with public funds frequently diverted to support school-based athletics programs. The point being that the power of the social institution of sport generates huge economic investment, which creates opportunity for extensive social impact. Whether that opportunity is realized or not is dependent upon the conduct of sport.

Sport is pervasive not only in the government-supported societal fabric, but throughout societies (Parks et al. 2007). For example, the influence of sport as a change agent can be seen through the American movie industry, which has depicted both positive and negative impacts of sport in films such as *Hoosiers, Field of Dreams, Jerry Maguire, Blue Chips, The Program, Radio, On Any Given Sunday, Hoop Dreams*, and many more. Many of these films have captured the notion of sport as an agent for social change and as a community builder. The following film adaptations of actual events reveal the influence of sport in culture. The film *Remember the Titans* portrayed how that high school football team and its coach taught the segregated community of Alexandria, Virginia how diverse student-athletes could work together in pursuit of a common goal. The movie *Glory Road* chronicled an historic season of Texas Western University. A small school competing for a national championship, Texas Western was the first predominantly white Division I school to play an all African American lineup. Texas Western concluded its magical season by beating an All-White team from perennial powerhouse Kentucky in the 1966 NCAA Championship. The film *The*

Express reflected on the life and football career of star running back Ernie Davis at Syracuse University. Despite the prevailing treatment of African-Americans at the time in the US, Davis' ability to overcome many hurdles displays how sport touched many lives and imparted many lessons in community and race relations. Of international scope, the film *Kicking It* explores the lives of homeless soccer players. In examining the role of the sport in the lives of these homeless athletes, the film documents sport's influence upon changes that occur in the players' lives.

Without question, sport's "enormous popularity, coupled with its ability to reach across social, political, and economic divides, makes sport one of the few institutions that can serve as a catalyst for change" (Parks et al 2007, 410). Bill Bradley (1998, 110), an All American basketball player at Princeton, a Rhodes Scholar (at Oxford), a professional basketball player with the New York Knicks, a 3-term United States Senator and Presidential candidate, frames the incredible power of sport:

> Sports are an important part of many people's lives, both as pursuit and as pastime. They can influence people in subtle ways, helping shape their ideas about how life works and about what is acceptable behavior. When professional baseball and basketball decided on racial desegregation in the late 1940's and early 1950's, it had a far-reaching impact on society. Once the taboo of separateness was challenged on the fields of millions of American's dreams, children began to ask their parents questions and adults increasingly found the old ways indefensible. What had seemed impossible began to change. If desegregation worked in sports, why shouldn't it work in the rest of American life? The heroes in this racial drama are well known: Branch Rickey of the Brooklyn Dodgers, Bill Veeck of the Cleveland Indians, Ned Irish of the New York Knicks-all of them executives who saw the future; Jackie Robinson, Larry Doby, Nat "Sweetwater" Clifton-black players who lived the experience and in so doing exposed the hollowness and falseness of racial stereotypes.

Bradley (1998, 76, 79) also observed the impact of the sport that he played and its ability to educate its participants and influence beyond the end lines of its court:

> Basketball, perhaps above all other sports, affords a unique perspective on a fundamental moral issue of our times: the need for racial unity...You can't play on a team with African Americans for very long and fail to recognize the stupidity of our national obsession with race. The right path is really very simple: Give respect to teammates of a different race, treat them fairly, disagree with them honestly, enjoy their friendship, explore your common humanity, share your thoughts about one another candidly, work together for a common goal, help one another achieve it. No

destructive lies. No ridiculous fears. No debilitating anger. Why of all places in America, is that ideal closest to being achieved on a basketball court? I believe it's because the community of a team is so close that you have to talk with one another; the travel is so constant that you have to interact with one another; the competition is so intense that you have to challenge one another; the game is so fluid that you have to depend on one another; the high and the low moments are so frequent that you learn to share them; the season is so long that it brings you to mutual acceptance. That is not to say that no racists have ever survived a multiracial team experience with their prejudices intact, but my guess is that the numbers are few.

Clearly, both individual and collective benefit can be garnered through sport. As a social institution, sport has the power to influence society. As Nelson Mandela stated, "Sport has the power to change the world. It has the power to unite people in a way that little else does" (Indicorp).

Sport and Power

Wolf (1990) delineated four modes of power. In his model, power can be viewed as a personal attribute akin to Nietzsche's concept of individual capability. Power can be influential in establishing the form and direction of interpersonal relations, useful in interaction as a transactional or transformation agent. Power can be employed at the organizational level to establish control of the environment in a tactical manner. Or, structural power can shape the settings of power play on a large scale. Thus, utilizing Wolf's framework of power, sport can and has been associated with every mode outlined.

Individual capacity, both physical and intellectual, can be affected by sport, advancing an individual's personal power. On an individual level, sport can enhance health and wellness, as well as individual self-esteem (Weinberg and Gould 2003). Sport impacts our identity and sense of humanity (Hums and Moorman 2006). Of course, in peace building efforts, it is the social capacities of sport that garner our attention. Given that interpersonal interactions are central to bottom-up and middle-out peace initiatives, sport's use in establishing the parameters of intergroup interaction can be crucial. Take, for example, the 1971 T.C. Williams High School Titans (*Remember the Titans*). The undefeated Virginia State High School Football Champions led the city of Alexandria, Virginia, which was in the throes of racial strife, to cast aside racial divisions and find common ground on a football field. On an interpersonal level, the interaction of coaches, team members and common citizens alike, in combination with their wider impacts upon the city collectively, demonstrated that peace and understanding could be enhanced both within and through sport. Individual engagement and exchange can clearly be fostered within the sport arena. However, broader exchanges can be fostered through sport as well.

Government Support of Sport:
Political and Cultural Implications

Governments frequently utilize sport as a tactical measure to further their national interests. In fact, sport has many social uses for governments, both internally and externally. Internally, governments have long employed sport to enhance the lives of their citizens. For example, local governments use sport and recreation programs to teach community, to connect dissimilar socio-economic groups, and to engage youngsters and adults alike in productive activities that reinforce the qualities of good citizenship. State governments in the United States have a large sports apparatus, supporting school competitions, rules education, professional development, and even budgetary support for state schools from the elementary to the collegiate level. States spend a portion of their budget on coach's salaries, sport administrator salaries, and the infrastructure necessary to support recreational, interscholastic, and intercollegiate competition. Additionally, public funds are frequently diverted in support of professional sports through tax exemptions or funding of the construction of stadia. In other political systems, elite sport is subsidized directly through the government coffers. For example, the Australian Institute of Sport was established and funded by the government to train elite athletes. Specialist training academies were built and those athletes identified as "elite" were given government subsidies too. Great Britain modeled their elite program after the Australian model. UK Sport was funded by the National Lottery and one of its stated goals was to win gold medals (Bergsgard et al 2007).

Governments also utilize sport to consolidate their own power. It has been suggested that sport appeases the masses, as witnessed in the Roman Empire. The blood sport spectacles of the Colosseum attracted hundreds of thousands of citizens to the entertaining diversion for free (Kyle 1998). This Roman model for spectator sport may serve as an impetus for our modern day mega-events. Relative to external interests, modern governments attempt to stir national pride and promote themselves through their association with sport prowess and mega-events. The popularity of the Olympics and the worldwide media attention given to this event creates high stakes. For example, in the 1936 Olympics, Nazi leader Adolf Hitler attempted to show the world the superiority of the Aryan race and the advances of the Third Reich. Shirer (1960, 232) noted that, "The signs Juden unerwuenscht (Jews not welcome) were quietly hauled down from the shops...the country put on its best behavior. No previous games had seen such a spectacular organization nor such a lavish display of entertainment." However, Jesse Owens, the great African-American sprinter, tarnished Hitler's Olympic vision by winning 4 gold medals. Before this Olympics, there was a debate within the African American community. Should Owens and other black athletes participate, or should they boycott the Olympics to oppose Hitler's racism and religious bigotry (Dyerson 2006, 117)? The call to participate was grounded in the belief that a victory by an African American athlete would be a huge symbolic victory against Nazi racism. Given sports' significant influence on public opinion and national reputation, that which could be used by Hitler could also be used against his regime. Clearly, the choice to participate made a statement through sport. While it yielded Owens no immediate benefit in a racially divided America, he was posthumously awarded the Congressional Medal of Honor in 1990 (Garner 1999).

Despite attempts by the IOC to preserve the Olympics from world politics, the power of sport has prevailed, resulting in many other attempts to politicize this event for tactical purposes (Hums and MacLean 2009). In 1956, several countries boycotted the Melbourne Olympics in protest over the Soviet invasion of Hungary and the United States' involvement in the Suez crisis. Millions witnessed the Israeli-Palestinian conflict alarmingly played out at the 1972 Munich Olympics. That same Olympics saw a controversial gold medal basketball game between the United States and the Soviet Union that reflected their Cold War struggles. The Montreal Olympics in 1976 saw a boycott by many African nations, protesting apartheid after a New Zealand rugby team toured South Africa. The US voted to boycott the 1980 Moscow Summer Olympics to protest the Soviet invasion of Afghanistan. Also in 1980, the Winter Olympics in Lake Placid saw the 'miracle on ice' as the US hockey team defeated the Soviet Union. With the Olympics held in Los Angeles in 1984, the USSR and other Eastern Bloc nations boycotted in return for the 1980 Moscow boycott. Political statements surrounding this sport mega-event clearly illuminate the power of sport. Protests have been held at nearly all modern Olympics. For example, the bombing in 1996 in Atlanta, local protests in 2000 in Sydney, and the many Tibetan protests affiliated with the 2008 Beijing Games. These Beijing Games were immensely important to China (Gottwald and Duggan 2008). The country spent over $40 billion in preparation for the Olympics (Pravda 2008). These Games were considered an international coming of age for China, an introduction to the world, wherein they would not only display their sport prowess to the sporting public, but they would also present their country to the world through this sporting event. More people watched the Beijing Olympics via TV than any sporting event in the history of the world (Huffington Post 2008).

In addition to its tactical utility, sport enjoys structural power in an ever-more global society (Wolf 1990). Sport literally provides the field of play, complete with accepted rules and procedures, for global interface. More than three decades prior to the Beijing Games, China and the United States engaged in 'ping pong diplomacy,' which yielded the start of normalized relations between the two countries (Kissinger 1979, 709). This initiative illustrates the convergence of the interpersonal, tactical, and structural power of sport. While at a tournament in Japan on April 4, 1971, Glenn Cowan, a member of the US table tennis team, joined the Chinese team on a sightseeing excursion to a Japanese pearl farm (Ibid). Cowan gave one of the Chinese players a t-shirt and in return received a handkerchief. Two days later, the United States team was invited to visit China. The team visited China on April 14, 1971, where they were welcomed by the Premier Chou Enlai (Kissinger 1979, 710). This truly historic visit evolved from sport, the only arena where these two countries had contact, and led the two governments to engage in necessary dialog. By February of 1972, President Nixon visited China where he pledged to end 30 years of hostility and move to normalize relations. By the end of the decade, full diplomatic exchanges had taken place (Schulzinger 1984, 296-297).

Through mega-events such as the Olympics, World Cup, Paralympic Games and other interpersonal sport interactions, countries and individuals around the world have come to recognize the positive benefits of sport, such as promoting community and peace (United Nations). Recognition of sport's utility inspired the modern Olympic movement, which began in Athens in 1896 (Hums and MacLean 2009). These Olympics have been dwarfed many times over by the recent Olympic Games and other mega-events; however, their aims previously articulated by Coubertin resonate to this day.

The governing body of the world Olympic movement is the International Olympic Committee (IOC). This organization is based in Lausanne, Switzerland and is currently under the direction of President Jacques Rogge (International Olympic Committee). The IOC hopes to "contribute to building a peaceful and better world by educating youth through sport practiced without discrimination of any kind and in the Olympic spirit, which requires mutual understanding with a spirit of friendship, solidarity, and fair play" (Hums and MacLean 2009, 250). The IOC has advanced its own interests alongside that of world peace, promoting human rights and tolerance globally. Believing change occurs both in and through sport, the IOC (2004) stated "The practice of sport is a human right." By assisting deprived areas in fielding teams, the IOC has committed resources to support international development efforts through sport (Hums and MacLean 2009). Illustrating the immense power of sport in the global community, the Olympics attracts over 10,500 participants from 200+ countries and 4.7 billion spectators and viewers from around the world (Huffington Post; IOC; United Press International). Likewise, developmental impacts can be manifested through other mega-events. For example, through a program sponsored by theWorld Cup and FIFA, ten soccer facilities will be constructed in Africa before the 2010 World Cup begins in South Africa.

The United Nations (UN) has also recognized the value of sport to bring people together and contribute to peacebuilding and community building. A UN Resolution in November of 2003 established the year 2005 as the International Year of Sport and Physical Education (IYSPE 2005). The purpose was to "...highlight the significant role that sport can play in accelerating progress towards the achievement of the Millennium Development Goals by 2015 and to add strong impetus to efforts to better integrate sport into the development agenda as well as into efforts to achieve lasting peace" (United Nations). The IYSPE yielded two conclusions by the UN: a) "Sport as a universal language has been found to bridge social, religious, racial and gender divides, hence contributing to lasting peace."; and, b) "The United Nations has proved it has the ability to help Governments and communities harness the positive aspects of sport and channel them in a coordinated way by highlighting and encouraging the use of sport in international development programmes and projects" (United Nations). The UN goes on to highlight the power of sport:

> Access to and participation in sport and physical education provide an opportunity to experience social and moral inclusion for populations otherwise marginalized by social, cultural or religious barriers caused by gender, disability, or other forms of discrimination. Sport and physical education can represent an area to experience equality, freedom and a dignifying means for empowerment. The freedom and control over one's body experienced in the practice of sport is particularly valuable for girls

and women, for people living in conflict areas, for people recovering from trauma… (United Nations).

The UN program also acknowledges the nature of sport in building community and peace in the many diverse areas where sport programs have been introduced, stating, "The Office of the United Nations High Commissioner for Refugees (UNHCR) has long been using the power of sport in its programmes to foster refugee integration and to ensure tolerance and understanding between the communities" (United Nations).

Using Sport for Individual and Collective Benefit

Many instances of the utility of sport in the promotion and preservation of peace involve both individual and collective benefits. To be expected, individual and collective inputs produce both individual and collective results. While not always aligned, individual benefits can be amassed concurrently with collective benefits. Collective benefits can evolve from individual contributions. Or, individual members of the collective can benefit from collective programs, thus the purpose of many sport-based peace initiatives. A variety of stakeholders, representing individual and collective interests alike, are engaged in sport ventures. If conducted toward the aims of peace, and founded on the principles of bottom-up, interactive contact-driven, institutionalized sport-based programs, the ventures can successfully contribute to the establishment of cultures of peace. A variety of sport-based vehicles and methods are possible in these efforts. For example, both for-profit and non-profit organizations provide a vehicle through which sport is employed in promoting peace and resolving conflicts.

Corporate Sport and Social Responsibility

Given the power, and the social and economic magnitude of sport, many for-profit sport organizations acknowledge their responsibility toward greater society. Whether a professional league, a franchise, a sport management or marketing agency, a media outlet, or a local sport enterprise, the role of the sport industry in promoting social responsibility parallels the growth of this concept in non-sport industries as well. For example, in a broad sense, the National Basketball Association (NBA) has impacted international peace and development opportunities through its Basketball without Borders program (Means & Nauright 2007). Akin to its role in other profitable industries, corporate social responsibility (CSR) has grown in importance in the sport industry as well, with significant pressure to engage (Babiak & Wolfe 2006; Walker 2008). Like many sport companies, Nike has established and enumerated its CSR goals, and many companies, such as Coca-Cola, reap public relations and other rewards through their commitment to CSR programs (Cregan 2008; Snell 2007). Additionally, governmental involvement in CSR has increased simultaneously as sports have demonstrated their value in CSR (Albareda et al 2007; Misener & Mason 2008; Smith & Westerbeek 2007). There is currently no conclusive evidence of the short or long term impacts of the economic downturn on CSR programs in sport, or in other economic segments. However, it appears that once the commitment to CSR has manifested itself, it becomes ingrained in the corporate culture. Therefore, as a supplement to public funding, CSR might serve as an important source of support for peace initiatives through sport-based private enterprises.

Non-Profit Organizations

Non-profit sport-related organizations often engage in the management of sport education and competition. For example, the YMCA, the YWCA, Boys and Girls Clubs of America, the Catholic Youth Organization and the Jewish Community Centers all operate youth sports teams, youth sports clinics, and youth sports leagues and competitions. These non-profits assist local populations in providing community building opportunities for their local citizens. The YMCA and YWCA combined have over 40 million members worldwide (Hums and MacLean 2009). Their clubs welcome all ages, races, abilities and incomes. No one is turned away for inability to pay. The majority of the Y's activities revolve around sports, including sports instruction and league competition. Individual youths are brought together on the playing field, often yielding the results Senator Bradley observed, increased understanding and mutual respect. This approach builds community from the bottom up.

The Amateur Athletic Union (AAU) is another non-profit organization established in the US whose purpose results in individual development and community building. From the bottom-up and middle-out, the AAU is responsible for the promotion of specific sports and the organization of local and national competitions. Additionally, through the moral development of individual participants, the AAU promotes the building of local and national community. The AAU was formed in 1888 and has had a long history of administering sport in the U.S. While its operations touch every corner of the U.S., the AAU is headquartered in Orlando, Florida in partnership with the Disney Corporation (Hums and MacLean 2009). While national in scope, the impact of its operations is felt more directly at the local level. The AAU mission statement confirms its commitment to employing sport in the development of character and citizenship:

> To offer amateur sports programs through a volunteer base for all people to have the physical, mental, and moral development of amateur athletes and to promote good sportsmanship and good citizenship (Amateur Athletic Union).

The aforementioned non-profit organizations reflect the power that many believe sports has to build community and to affect social change. The organizations mentioned and many others like them (e.g. Boys and Girls Clubs, CYO, JCC, Police Recreation Dept, etc.) have used sport not just as exercise, as recreational entertainment, or as a competitive outlet, but as a means to build community, to embrace people from all walks of life, and to break down barriers built in society.

Specific Peace Initiatives

Examining the use of football (soccer) as a tool for peace building, Cwik (2008) maintained that soccer has improved the lives of refugees in divided communities, helped to reintegrate former child combatants, and provided peace education. Having had experience in Cambodia, Namibia, Trinidad, and with the U. N. Institute for Disarmament Research, Cwik observed successful sport-related programs in Palestine/Israel, Bosnia, Cyprus, Pakistan, Rwanda, Ivory Coast and Bangladesh. These grassroots programs reach local communities where conflict has been felt directly. The large numbers of young people in many conflict areas make sport-related peace initiatives ideal as entry points to enhance communication. For example, soccer and/or basketball leagues can be run year round. If run properly, these programs can bring rivals together toward productive ends, as Cwik (2008, 2) observed, "the development of a positive relationship starts with the willingness to try and cooperate, and proceeds with the realization that a common interest is shared with 'the other' be it the love of a sport or the desire to see your village rebuilt."

In like spirit, Peace Players International (PPI) is engaging individuals and communities through the establishment of local sport-based peace initiatives. PPI founders Sean and Brendan Tuohey are using basketball to unite opposing factions in places like Northern Ireland, Israel, the West Bank, Cyprus, and South Africa (Peace Players International). They even set up shop in post-Katrina New Orleans, to help that community heal from a devastating hurricane. After a high school and college basketball career, older brother Sean traveled to Ireland to play in the professional ranks. There he witnessed first hand the historical tension between Protestants and Catholics in Belfast, Northern Ireland. Recognizing that people could be drawn together around a simple game, the idea for PPI was hatched (Ibid). The brothers established their first PPI programs in Belfast and, then in Durban, South Africa, using basketball to break down barriers. They organize clinics, tournaments, and leagues in communities where for generations kids from clashing sides barely spoke.

Peace Players International has brought together more than 40,000 children from among the most intractable enemies on the planet (Peace Players International). Utilizing connections with community leaders, teachers, and organizers, PPI coaches teach teamwork, discipline and perseverance. As players learn these values through the vehicle of basketball, they also learn to trust one another as PPI begins to teach tolerance. Palestinian and Israeli children become teammates, white and black South Africans compete with and against each other, Catholics and Protestants share a common goal, and soon Greeks and Turks will join together as teammates on the island of Cyprus. After each day on the court, these children go home to their families and tell the story of that day's game. Whether a win or a loss, they played on the same court, together. As their sport experiences begin to break down long-standing walls, to enhance mutual understanding and respect, and perhaps to begin the long process toward peace, so too do these stories help their families. From the bottom up, PPI is harnessing the power of sport to bring about positive change in the world. This global initiative is executed locally through the game of basketball.

Through their Israeli-Palestinian operation, Peace Players International organizes teams of young basketball players, both Israelis and young Palestinians, who play and practice together. They are coached by an American who plays on a professional team in Israel. Observing that "Israelis and Palestinians share this tiny space in the world, but don't actually talk to or know each other," this managing director uses sport to try and get youngsters to talk to each other, hoping that if relationships emerge despite the enormous historical, religious, economic, and cultural divide, their parents and neighborhoods might see some hope (Ford 2006). On organized social outings, these teammates share meals together. They take in the occasional professional basketball game too. Using this PPI model, the idea is to create meaningful bonds that can hopefully break down preconceptions, destroy stereotypes, and maybe even create friendships that can withstand conflict (Ford 2006). In a similar PPI effort, centered in the West Bank city of Tul Karem, the program director runs a clinic for college physical education majors at Khadori College. After he is finished teaching the coaches, he and some of the trainees run a clinic and league for 50 youngsters down the street from the college. While Peace Player's efforts do meet local resistance, volunteer coaches see the value of the interaction spurred through the sport of basketball, as one notes, "I have good relations with the Palestinians. I buy vegetables from them. I talk to them in the city. Arabs and Jews have to introduce themselves to each other to achieve peace. Hundreds of peoples lives can be changed. I believe this program can make a difference. I would do anything for it" (Ford 2006). This PPI program epitomizes the impact of a bottom-up peace initiative (Racioppi and Sullivan-See 2007).

A quarter of the way around the globe, PeacePlayers is involved in breaking down barriers in another land with a sordid history of conflict, Northern Ireland (Friend 2007). Akin to the coaches in Israel and Palestine, PPI coaches attempt to bridge the chasm that separates Catholics from Protestants. Peace Players arranged a competition between (Catholic) Holy Cross and (Protestant) Wheatfield schools. The 10 year old girls played basketball, and ate pizza together after the game. This grassroots attempt at peacebuilding has as its starting point the creation of dialogue, "an ancient Greek word composed of dia (meaning through or across) and logos (meaning the word or reason). Broken down into its linguistic roots, dialogue implies a sense of creating meaning through talking or reasoning together, making intergroup contact effective in reducing prejudice" (Bloome and Hatay 2006, 630-631). This dialogue opens up communication and can lead to a more trusting relationship between two groups in conflict (Bloome and Hatay 2006,).

At its core, PPI is a grassroots organization that encourages dialogue, interaction, and engagement in a non-threatening environment. Their chosen environment is a basketball court. However, PPI is not the only organization that is using sport as a keystone in peace building. Trevor Ringland and Hugo MacNeill co-founded Peace International (Friend 2007). This organization utilized rugby to promote reconciliation in Northern Ireland. Ringland also started One Small Step, an organization that encouraged Catholics to play 'Protestant sports' like cricket, and conversely, encouraged Protestants to play Gaelic football. The use of sport in the peace process is revealed in Ringland's philosophy "...you hammer away at it...drip, drip, drip and take little steps toward peace. Drip, drip, drip" (Friend 2007, 3).

Another group that utilizes basketball to build community is Full Court Peace, founded by Dave Cullen and Michael Evans. Their mission is to "use team basketball to cultivate and inspire enduring friendships between teenagers from rivaling communities in war-torn regions of the world" (Full Court Peace). They form teams composed equally of Catholic and Protestant basketball players from high schools in Northern Ireland. Traveling to the U.S. in 2008, they were provided opportunities to meet new friends while bonding together as they played basketball on the road. Cullen, a veteran of peace efforts in Northern Ireland, won ESPN's 2007 Arthur Ashe Courage Award for his efforts to build community between Catholics and Protestants (Full Court Peace).

The International Foundation for Education and Self Help (IFESH) was founded by Leon Sullivan 25 years ago and makes use of basketball to reach young people in Nigeria (IFESH). One of IFESH's programs is Basketball for Peace. Youngsters receive basketball skills training. Once relationships have been established through sports, these young people also receive training in conflict mitigation, as well as dressmaking, electronics, hairdressing, auto mechanics and/or welding (Ibid). The administrators and coaches work to prevent conflict while teaching very useful job skills. Basketball for Peace has created 30 peace clubs and 72 peace zones. Along with basketball and job skill education, IFESH introduces civic education, voter education, and leadership training, making Basketball for Peace that much more effective in building community in Nigeria (Ibid).

Mercy Corps, Nike, the Sudanese Ministry of Culture, and Grassroots Soccer have initiated a program called 'Sports for Peace and Life' in southern Sudan. This program has reached 7000 youngsters between the ages of 13 and 24 (Mercy Corps). They use soccer to help introduce Aids/HIV education to these young people. Peace building and life skills are also introduced in a structured teaching environment using the sport of soccer to attract male participants (Martin 2007). The sport of volleyball has been used for the girls in this region, who don't play soccer (Mercy Corps). In Mongolia, Mercy Corps has established a basketball program, and they have added soccer programs in Liberia and Peru (Ibid).

England's University of Brighton, aided by the Israeli Football Association, spearheads Football4Peace, which began in the Arab village of Ibilin in Galilee with 100 youths aged 10-14 (Football4Peace). Since 2001, they have grown steadily to over 1000 participants, Arab and Israeli alike. They use soccer to teach values and principles that can break down barriers and build community in Israel and Palestine (Ibid). They train coaches not only in soccer methods, but also in conflict resolution techniques. The organization insures that each team is equally mixed with Arabs and Israelis. They try to alternate practices in each community so that each group can literally see how the other half lives. The belief is that these youngsters are the future leaders of their communities. Perhaps a dialogue can be created between children in a way that has not succeeded with adults (Football4Peace; Sugden 2006).

These grassroots peace initiatives are mirrored in a program initiated by then-Secretary of State Colin Powell called CultureConnect. The Department sent four former college basketball players around the globe, to conduct basketball clinics, visit schools, and speak with young people "about sports, educational and social issues" (Deaner 2004, 36). Like other coaches on the front lines of the peace initiatives, these young men are out to break down barriers, to overcome stereotypes, and to try to make friends of old enemies. They are US Government employees attempting to utilize sport to foster better relations among ordinary citizens around the globe. CultureConnect expanded to include baseball, conducting baseball clinics in the countries of Venezuela and Columbia, creating grassroots connections in these two South American countries (U. S. Department of State).

Summary and Conclusion

Many organizations around the world recognize that sport has unique characteristics that permit it to bridge divides of class, race, religion, ethnicity, national citizenship and gender. This universality of team sports with common rules, like basketball and soccer, literally compel teammates and opponents to interact in close quarters and to communicate, making participation easy, even if the participants don't speak the same language. The game becomes the language of teamwork, through sharing the ball, anticipating a teammate's movements, or making a perfect pass that leads to a score. As each individual's success impacts the whole team, most players experience the joy of a teammate's accomplishment in a very profound yet simple way. They recognize teammates for their work toward a common goal in sport, ignoring where their teammates are from. In sport, a player is not Israeli, not rich, not Muslim, not black. The player is your teammate working together to score for your team. It is not coincidental that United States President Barak Obama played team sports. He saw the power of sport playing soccer in Indonesia and basketball in the U. S., and attests to the lessons learned both in and through sport (Obama 2004; Wolff 2009).

When not managed properly, sport can be used to divide communities, to express xenophobia, to express domination. Sport can be used to advance political interests of governments. Individuals can misuse the competitiveness of sport to incite violence. However, groups like PeacePlayers, Football4Peace, Mercy Corps, and others utilize the power of sports to bring people together. These organizations commonly employ a formula for the successful use of sport in peace building: 1) Hire coaches that have an expertise in a team sport; 2) Provide these coaches training in conflict resolution and the language of peace and community building; 3) Form teams that are equally divided between the groups you are trying to bring together; 4) Constantly emphasize the values of sportsmanship, teamwork, exercise, hard work, and civility in developing relationships through sport; and 5) Provide social outlets for each team so that opportunities for individual and group dialogue can be created.

We have sought here to lay a foundation with specific implications for those charged with the responsibility of managing sport for purposes of promoting peace and human rights. These initiatives are not self sustaining financially. However, having demonstrated the ability of sport to bridge divides, it is imperative for the growth of bottom up peace initiatives to garner financial support through community, corporate, and governmental investment. Large scale private and public funding efforts will foster the utility of sport as an agent of cultural change. By facilitating the funding of sport-based peace initiatives, demonstrable gains are currently being made at the grassroots level. The support of sport-based programs conducted in alignment with the foundational concepts of Allport (1954), Beer and Norhia (2000), and Wolf (1990) will have positive results, initially at the local level. Thus, individual participants in sport-based peace initiatives are the foundations for broader cultural change. Just as a forest evolves from many individual trees, cultural change occurs through its individual members. When taken collectively, all of these sport-based efforts will yield broader impact in building a culture of peace.

References

Albareda, L., J. M. Lozano, A. Tencati, A. Midttun, and F. Perrini. 2008. The changing role of governments in corporate social responsibility: drivers and responses. *Business Ethics: A European Review* 4, 347-363.

Allport, G. W. 1954. *The Nature of Prejudice*. Reading, MA:Addison-Wesley Publishing Company.

Amateur Athletic Union. *Mission Statement*. http://www.aausports.org.

Babiak, K. and R. Wolfe. 2006. More Than Just a Game? Corporate Social Responsibility and Super Bowl XL. *Sport Marketing Quarterly* 4, 214.

Beer, M. and N. Nohria. 2000. *Breaking the code of change*. Boston, MA: Harvard Business School Press.

Ben-Porat, G. 2007. *Global Liberalism, Local Populism: Peace and Conflict in Israel/Palestine and Northern Ireland*. Syracuse, NY: Syracuse University Press.

Bergsgard, N. A., B. Houlihan, P. Mangset, S. I. Nodland, H. Rommetvedt. 2007. *Sport Policy: A comparative analysis of stability and change*. Oxford: Elsevier.

Bradley, B.1998. *Values of the Game*. New York: Artisan.

Broome, B. J. and A. J. Hatay. 2006. Building Peace in Divided Societies. In *The Sage Handbook of Conflict Communication*, ed. John G. Oetzel and Stella Ting-Toomey, 627-662. Thousand Oaks: SAGE Publications.

Chufrin, G.I. and H.H. Saunders. 1993. A Public Peace Process. *Negotiation Journal* 2. 155-177.

Coakley, J. J. 2007. *Sport in Society: Issues & Controversies, 9*[th] *ed*. New York, NY: McGraw-Hill.

Cregan, R. 2008. Rewards of being a good sport. *Brand Strategy* 223, 54-55.

Cwik, L. A. 2008.Football as a Tool for Peacebuilding. *Peace Prints, South Asian Journal of Peacebuilding* 1 (Spring), http://www.wiscomp.org/pp-vi/Leszek_Cwik.pdg

Daniels, M., R. E. Baker, K. Backman, and S. Backman. 2007. What Sponsors Want. *International Journal of Sport Management* 2, 131-146.

Deaner, N. 2004. Dribbling, Dunk and Dialogue. *State Magazine*: US Department of State. December.

Dyerson, M. 2006. Jesse Owens: Leading an in modern American tales of racial progress and limits. In *Out of the Shadows: A biographical history of African American* Athletes, ed. David K Wiggins. Fayetteville, AR: The University of Arkansas Press.

Farmer, S. 2008. Sky is the limit for new Dallas Cowboys stadium. *Los Angeles Times*.October 1. Sports section.

Fernandez, M.. 2008. Fans in Mourning as Sun Sets on the Old Yankee Stadium. *The New York Times*, September 22. Sports section.

Football4Peace. http://www.football4peace.org.uk/

Ford, C. M. 2006. Hooping with the Enemy. *espn.com* (Aug. 15), http://sports.espn.go.com/espn/eticket/story?page=playingforpeace (accessed January 20, 2009).

—. 2006. Peace and Hoops: Basketball as a Role Player in Sustainable Peacebuilding. *Williamette Law Review* 42. 709-736.

Fort, R. P. 2003. *Sports Economics.* Upper Saddle River, NJ: Prentice Hall.

Friend, T.. 2007. Hate is a waste of time. *espn.com* (July 10), http://sports.espn.go.com/espn/print?id=2930860&type=Story&imag (accessed January 20, 2009).

FullCourtPeace. http://www.fullcourtpeace.org

Garner, J.. 1999. *And the Crowd Goes Wild.* Naperville: Sourcebooks, Inc.

Gottwald, J., and N. Duggan. 2008. China's economic development and the Beijing Olympics. *International Journal of the History of Sport* 3. 339-354.

Hums, M. A. and A. M. Moorman. 2006. Sport as a human right: The status of sport organizations. Presented at the annual conference of the Sport and Recreation Law Association. March, Albequerque, NM

Hums, M. A. and J. C. MacLean. 2009. *Governance and Policy in Sport Organizations, 2nd ed.* Scottsdale: Holcomb Hathaway Publishers.

Indicorps. 2009. *Galvanize a Sport Culture.* http://apply.indicorps.org/ProjectInformation.php?prjId=76   (accessed February 16, 2009).

International Foundation for Education and Self Help. *Basketball for Peace.* http://www.ifesh.org/content.php?section=program&info_id=193.

International Olympic Committee. http://www.olympic.org

—. 2004. *Olympic Charter.* Lausanne, Switzerland.

Kissinger, H. A. 1979 *The White House Years.* Boston: Little, Brown and Co.

Kuriansky, J.. 2007. Beyond bullets and bombs: *Grassroots peacebuilding between Israelis and Palestinians.* Portsmouth, NH: Praeger Publishers.

Kyle, D. G. 1998. *Spectacles of death in ancient Rome.* New York, NY: Routledge.

Lederach, J.P. 1995. Conflict transformation in protracted internal conflicts: The case for a comprehensive framework. In *Conflict Transformation* ed. K. Rupeshinghe. 201-222. London: Macmillan.

Lyras, A.. 2008. Organizational change theory: Sport for peace and development. *The Chronicle of Kinesiology and Physical Education in Higher Education* 2, 14-16.

Mandell, R. D. 1976 *The First Modern Olympics.* Berkley: University of California Press.

Martin, C.. 2007. Sports for Peace and Life. Mercy Corps, (Aug. 15), http://www.mercycorps.org (accessed January 28, 2009).

McDonald, J.W. 1991. Further exploration of track two diplomacy. In *Timing the de-escalation of international conflicts,* ed. L. Kriesberg and S.J. Thorson. 201-220. New York, NY: Syracuse University Press.

McIntosh, P. 2004 Telling America's Story: Powell Honors State Department Culture Connect Ambassadors. *America.gov, U.S. Department of State,* (Dec. 15), http://www.america.gov/st.washfile-english/2004/December/20041 (accessed January 10, 2009).

Means, J., and J. Nauright. 2007. Going global: The NBA sets its sights on Africa. *International Journal of Sports Marketing and Sponsorship* 1, 40-50.

Mercy Corps. http://www.mercycorps.org.

Misener, L. and D. S. Mason. 2008. Urban Regimes and the Sporting Events Agenda: A Cross-National Comparison of Civic Development Strategies. *Journal of Sport Management* 5, 603.

Mosier, J.. 2008. New Dallas Cowboys Stadium is set to join Federal Green Program. *Dallas Morning News,* October 17. Sports section.

Neilsen Wire. 2008. *Tops In 2008: Top TV programs, single telecasts.* (December 12). http://blog.nielsen.com/nielsenwire/consumer/tops-in-2008-top-tv-programs-single-   telecasts/ (accessed Janaury 29, 2009).

Obama, B.. 2004. *Dreams of my father: A story of race and inheritance.* New York, NY: Crown Publishers.

Parks, J. B., Jerome Quarterman and Lucie Thibault. 2007. *Contemporary Sport Management, 3rd ed.* Champaign, IL: Human Kinetics.

Peace Players International. http://www.peaceplayers.org/dsp.about.aspx#overview

Pitts, B., and D. Stotlar. 2002. *Fundamentals of sports marketing.* Morgantown, WV: Fitness Information Technology

Plunklett Research Ltd. 2009. *Sports Industry Trends.* http://www.plunkettresearch.com/Industries/Sports/tabid/209/Default.a spx (accessed February 16, 2009).

Pravda. 2008. *Beijing Olympics to cost China 44 billion dollars.* (June 8). http://english.pravda.ru/sports/games/06-08-2008/106003-beijing_olympics-0 (accessed January 23, 2009).

Racioppi, L. and K. Sullivan-See. 2007. Grassroots Peace Building, *Peace and Change,* no. 3. 362-365.

Ross, M. H.. 2007. *Cultural Contestation in Ethnic Conflict.* Cambridge: Cambridge University Press.

Sabine, G. H. 1960.*A History of Political Theory.* New York: Holt, Rinehart and Winston.

Saunders, H.H. 1985. We need a larger theory of negotiation: The importance of prenegotiation phases. *Negotation Journal* 3. 249-262.

Schulzinger, R. D. 1984 *American Diplomacy in the 20th Century*. Oxford: Oxford University Press.

Sedberry, M.. 2008 James Cleveland "Jesse" Owens: First American in Olympic track and field history to win four gold medals. In *Pioneers* ed. Richard Lapchick, 424-426. Morgantown, WV: Fitness Information Technology.

Shirer, W. L. 1960. *The Rise and Fall of the Third Reich*. New York: Simon and Schuster.

Simpson, G., B. Hamber, and N. Scott. 2001. Future challenges to policy-making in countries in transition. Presentation to the workshop Comparative Experiences of Policy Making and Implementation in Countries in Transition, *F*ebruary 6-7, Derry/Londonderry Northern Ireland.

Smith, A. C. T. and H. M. Westerbeek, 2007. Sport as a Vehicle for Deploying Corporate Social Responsibility. *Journal of Corporate Citizenship* 25, 43-54.

Snell, P.. 2007. Nike reveals CSR targets for 2011. *Supply Management* 12, 7.

Sports Business Journal. 2008. *About us: The sports industry*. Street and Smith. http://www.sportsbusinessjournal.com/index.cfm?fuseaction=page.feat ure&featureId=43

Sugden, J.. 2006. Teaching and Playing Sport for Conflict Resolution and Co-existence in Israel. *International Review for Sociology of Sport* 2, 221-240.

United Nations. 2005. *International Year of Sport and Physical Education*. http://www.un.org/sport (accessed January 5, 2009).

—. http://www.un.org

United Press International. 2008. *4.7 billion viewers watched Olympics*. http://www.upi.com/2008_Olympics/News/UPI-59411220725670/ (accessed March 25, 2009).

U.S. Department of State. 2004. *New CultureConnect Amabassador Bernie Williams visits Venezuela and Columbia*. (February 11), http://america.gov/st/washfile-Variety. *Top 100 TV shows of all time*. http://www.variety.com/index.asp?layout=chart_pass&charttype=chart _topshowsalltimeenglish/2004/December (accessed December 22, 2008).

Walker, M. B. 2008. Assessing the influence of corporate social responsibility on consumer attitudes in the sport industry. *Dissertation Abstracts International Section A: Humanities and Social Sciences*, no9-A, 3959.

Weinberg, R. W., and Daniel Gould. 2003. Foundations of sport & exercise psychology. Champaign, IL: Human Kinetics Publishers.

Wolff, A.. 2009. The audacity of hoops. *Sports Illustrated.* January 19.

Wolf, E. R. 1990. Facing power: Old insights, new questions. *American Anthropologist.* 586-596.

Xulu, N.. 2008. Learning to play the game. *The Times*, (October 1). http://www.thetimes.co.za/PrintArticle.aspx?ID=853737   (accessed December 12, 2008).

CHAPTER EIGHT

MINDFULNESS AS ARMOR, COMPASSION AS WEAPON: KEEPING THE PEACE WITH MINDFULNESS PRACTICES FOR POLICE OFFICERS

MICHAEL J. DEVALVE AND CARY D. ADKINSON

"Breathing in, I know that mindfulness is the path to peace.
Breathing out, I know that peace is the path to mindfulness.
Breathing in, I know that peace is the path to justice.
Breathing out, I know that justice is the path to peace.
Breathing in, I know my duty is to provide safety & protection to all
beings.
Breathing out, I am humbled and honored by my duty as a peace officer.
Breathing in, I choose mindfulness as my armor & compassion as my
weapon.
Breathing out, I aspire to bring love and understanding to all I serve."
—Lamp Transmission Gatha, Cheri Maples, January 9, 2008

Early on New Year's Day 2009, in Oakland, California, Oscar Grant was fatally shot by a Bay Area Rapid Transit (BART) police officer, while lying on the train station floor in the custody of another police officer (CNN 2009). The shooting likely is not an example of hate-motivated violence occurring under color of law, all too common in the past. Instead, the officer who shot Grant is said to have claimed that he intended to reach for his taser pistol (apparently mounted in a cross-draw position), but grabbed his sidearm instead; under calmer circumstances a rather difficult mistake to make.

Less than three weeks later, in his inaugural address, President Barack Obama reminded his listeners that although the son of a man who most likely would not have been served by a Memphis, Tennessee, soda jerk 60 years ago can now assume the mantle of President of the United States, he observes that much remains to be done toward the creation of what he refers to as a "new era of peace," both at home and abroad. The benediction of Reverend Joseph Lowery, however, asks considerably more of us than President Obama's message, calling hearers to choose love over hate, tolerance over intolerance, and inclusion over exclusion. What is certain, what was probably intended by the two speakers, but what may well have been missed by more than a few members of their audience, is that in essence, their messages were the same.

We would like to be able to say that the history of beating tanks into tractors has been led by those charged with the daily implementation of justice in America. Sadly, though, the relationship between many communities and criminal justice agencies sworn to serve them has been lukewarm at best, with relatively few exceptions (Barlow and Barlow 2000). Worse, the past eight decades are studded with examples of outright brutality and warmaking on the part of justice professionals and justice organizations, against those who would seek no more than to make their claim on the promise of equality, made to all by America's founding fathers.

If we are to take President Obama at his word, that old rhetoric is passé, and the cynic has nowhere to hide; if "what works" is the controlling question, then indeed justice organizations have a great deal of work ahead if they are to maintain their credibility and legitimacy. But it should never be overlooked that justice organizations may be the most natural context for a concerted effort at the creation of a culture of peace. Indeed, police officers fall under a broader category of individuals charged with the maintenance of peace (meaning quiet): peace officers. What may appear to some to be merely linguistic synchronicity is, in point of fact, a finger pointing to the moon. A reorientation of the view of peace is necessary in this regard, it is certain, but such a reorientation is not without precedent and foundation (see, e.g., DeValve and Adkinson 2008).

It is our position that justice organizations, and in particular the police, can and should be at the forefront of the creation of a culture of positive peace (see, e.g., Barash and Webel 2002, for a description of the meaning of positive peace). The reorientation of managerial attention called for by problem-oriented policing (POP) (e.g., Goldstein 1990) has received considerable support from police agencies (even if just in rhetorical terms), and has been viewed by academics and policymakers as an effective orientation to ameliorating problems surrounding crime, despite the fact that the empirical literature regarding POP is small and equivocal (Bichler and Gaines 2005; Eck 2003). The shortcomings observed regarding POP, though, may well be attributable to an implementation gap between the vision of its coiner, Herman Goldstein, and the actual practice in the field. What is missing from implementation, however, is a desideratum; Goldstein challenged police officers and agencies to transcend the traditional reliance upon legal authority, and to find creative, nonparadigmatic solutions to local criminogenic problems that are particular to the areas of interest. We have argued elsewhere (DeValve and Adkinson 2008) that this challenge is closely akin to a special case of the First and Second Noble Truths: deep, profound understanding of suffering (*dukkha*) being central to discovering the path to ending that suffering. Who, better than the police, is in the position to view the depth of suffering in a community, and, with insight gained through concerted contemplation, to help transform it?

In the process of serving the community, however, individual police officers need to take every opportunity to protect themselves from harm. Harms come not only from physical attack, but as we shall illustrate, from numerous stressors related to the job. Nietzsche (1990, aphorism 146) has said that when one stares into the abyss, the abyss stares back. In the normal course of their jobs, the police are exposed to people often at the lowest points of their lives. They are asked to take considerable risks to their own personal safety, and not infrequently feel that the communities they serve are indifferent at best, and even occasionally hostile. Dealing with non-officers has been identified as an empirically discernable source of stress (Newman and Rucker-Reed 2004). Moreover, another identified source of stress is the police organization itself (Newman and Rucker-Reed 2004).

The purpose of this chapter is to provide a technology that, through its diligent use by police officers and agencies, will foster the cultivation of a culture of peace in two ways: first, by aiding officers to become instruments of positive peace, and not merely instruments of order maintenance, and second, by helping to protect officers from harms that are a natural part of their jobs. The technology to which we refer is mindful practice (e.g., sitting and walking meditation) and the fruits of that practice, and compassion in particular. When officers first attend "the academy" they are most often unaware of what they will be "really doing" as a police officer. At the end of the academy they have practiced the skills and incorporated the knowledge learned so that when they are placed in the field with a field-training officer they are able to respond to a limited degree. Over time, the responses they practice become ingrained. This is how the paradigm shift of incorporation of mindfulness and compassion must also be integrated into the police job. It will take time, but as the officer becomes more knowledgeable and practiced about meditation, the effects of incorporating the new skills will be more evident and helpful to society and themselves.

We will, in the furtherance of our stated aims, defend mindfulness and compassion as central to successful interpersonal interaction. We will then discuss briefly the bodies of literature on mindfulness and compassion, as well as the current state of the empirical evidence regarding the benefits of compassion-generative mindfulness practice. We will then discuss the nature of police work, highlighting the harms police officers experience as part of their jobs. Following, we shall illustrate how compassion-generative mindful practice can help officers create a culture of peace, both in terms of the rendering of their services to the community, and the rendering of services to themselves. Finally, we will offer suggestions to police executives as to how to implement compassion-generative mindful practice in their departments.

Why Mindfulness and Compassion?

Mindfulness, by its very nature, assumes attentiveness to one's emotional states so that these states do not result in psychological and/or physical harm to oneself and/or others. So to understand mindfulness, we must first understand what emotions are, how they work, and how we might learn (if possible) to exert conscious influence over them on a moment to moment basis. Boyatzis and McKee (2005) provide a useful definition of "emotional intelligence" in their work on leadership theory. To be an effective leader, they argue, a person must regularly display a high level of competence both managing their own emotions (personal competence) and in positively nurturing the emotions of others (social competence). Personal competence consists of self-awareness and self-management, whereas social competence refers to social awareness and relationship management. Inherent within these concepts is the importance of mindfulness training for emotional awareness and management; however, a clear understanding of what emotions are and how they work is necessary for the successful cultivation of mindfulness. When we look into the actual physiological process whereby emotions arise and affect our behavior we begin to see why dedicated mindfulness training is absolutely essential for achieving a high level of emotional intelligence.

Research conducted by Ekman (The Dalai Lama and Ekman 2008) confirms that emotions are in a very basic sense the antithesis of mindfulness. Emotions, it seems, supersede conscious, rational, and "mindful" thinking. This makes perfect sense in an evolutionary context.

Fear, anger, and the desire for self-preservation arose as adaptations for dealing with the predatory dangers of the Paleolithic environment. Human physiology, therefore, represents a bias toward quick, intense emotional reactions when human beings are confronted by a perceived physical and/or social threat (Goleman 2005). According to Ekman, three defining characteristics of emotions are (a) they can be triggered automatically in a fraction of a second, (b) they can arise intuitively and instinctively below the level of conscious awareness, and (c) they can often have disastrous consequences for ourselves and others because they can be triggered so instantaneously and automatically. Specifically, these consequences become so disastrous because they can result in what Goleman (2005) describes as an "emotional hijacking." When confronted by intense and chronic stress that lead to intense emotional reactions, pathways in the human brain responsible for "higher order" thinking such as rationality and "cost-benefit analysis" can be momentarily overridden by our emotional and instinctive pathways, resulting in those all too familiar moments where we "lose it emotionally" or our emotions "get the better of us". So we must forever balance on the edge of a double-edged emotional sword: because emotions must act so quickly, instinctively, and powerfully, we may often be at the whim of emotional reactions that do us more harm than good.

Mindfulness and Compassion: Habits to Open the Heart

Before we can commence with an overview of mindfulness practices, it is appropriate for us to clarify what, exactly, is meant by mindfulness. We must also make clear what we mean by compassion. The first portion of this section will endeavor to clarify these two vital constructs for our use.

Mindfulness

Most often the term mindfulness is used to denote a state of being where one is experiencing bare attention (e.g., Shapiro, Oman, Thoresen, Plante and Flinders 2008), when an individual's full consciousness is directed to events occurring in the present moment (e.g., Hanh 1975, Mace 2008). Bare attention is the term used to describe the cognitive backdrop against which human thought and emotion are projected. Kornfield (2008) likens bare attention to a blank movie screen, upon which feelings and experiences are projected. The movie is not the screen and vice versa. The Sanskrit *smrti* is commonly translated as "mindfulness," but others (Nhat

Hanh 2008) have enlarged upon the meaning, indicating that a more literal translation is "that which can be remembered," which underscores the preexisting capacity in all beings to witness their bare attention, and to be fully attentive to the present moment.

Brown and Ryan (2003) indicate that mindfulness can be seen as a function of two consciousness states: awareness and attention. Other common aspects of mindfulness are receptivity to experience (Kostanski and Hassed 2008; Langer 1989; Nhat Hanh 1975) and the idea that mindfulness is a practice, a process and a path, and less a thing acquired. Many treatments of mindfulness also recognize a distinction between the deep, restful state of bare awareness one experiences while in a meditative state, and the ability to keep a sense of awareness and full attention about one's self while moving through one's day. With continued meditative practice, the "permeation" of mindfulness often occurs; mindfulness ceases to be limited to the meditation cushion, and becomes a regular part of more domains of daily activity (Mace 2008). In research conducted in 2006, Mace (2008, 40) identified empirically three central attributes of mindfulness: inclusive awareness, retaining a sense of self, and in-touch-ness with one's body. Five other attributes were uncovered as well: (1) focused attention on the present; (2) a sense of equanimity attendant to the present-focus; (3) an end to efforts to control one's experience; (4) the awareness of a distinction between thoughts and feelings, and the self, that thoughts and feelings can occur and pass without influencing bare awareness, and; (5) the ability to be comfortable with spontaneity during regular activity. But what may be the most important aspect of mindfulness is that both the meditative and workaday mindfulness states are linked with a powerful sense of wellbeing, equanimity, joy and compassion (Brantley 2007; Kabatt-Zinn 1990; Kostanski and Hassed 2008; Mace 2008; Nhat Hanh 1975; 2005b).

Compassion

Like other constructs with great potency, compassion has been leveraged, utilized, dissected and manipulated by a host of authors, each with her own purpose. Linguistically, compassion means literally "feeling-with." There is considerable richness in the construct, and confusion among its students, however, which is not evidenced etymologically. The scope of this chapter does not permit a complete enumeration of all of the aspects of compassion, but the reader is invited to consider the following statements. One can recognize the feelings of others because of their own experience (empathy); one may feel badly for one who is in pain, and act to alleviate that pain (i.e., an act of compassion). George Will has intimated that compassion is an emotion that obliges the subject to do whatever it takes to feel better (c.f. Garber 2004, 17). Compassion has been described as a "moral theory in vogue" (c.f. Garber 2004, 17), and as the very engine of enlightenment (Dalai Lama 2001, 91). Compassion has been viewed as an illegitimate basis for policy (Arendt 1965, 90) and, in the guise of empathy, seen as instructive in understanding key court decisions (Henderson 1987, 1577). There is compassion fatigue, self-compassion (e.g., Neff 2003), and compassionate conservatism; and there is a not-inconsiderable debate as to whether the last is an oxymoron. Both major political parties in the United States have made claims to being more compassionate than their opposite number, from Clinton's "I feel your pain" to George W. Bush's rallying of "the armies of compassion" (see Garber 2004, 24).

Using the works cited above, Table I presents common themes among views of compassionate interaction, in rough temporal order. Western and Eastern perspectives on compassion differ considerably, but still tend to follow the structure presented in Table I.

Clinically, compassion is a dyadic interaction where, through the affective state of the subject and the behavior that results therefrom, both subject and object experience a positive change in affect. Such a perspective, though accurate, is denuded of its power and importance; this description is likely to fall fully away when, while you are reading this chapter, you see over the top of the book someone trip and fall awkwardly, hurting themselves. The unconsidered urge you have to jump to his aid is the spark of compassion. Compassion must be seen as the human experience of becoming acutely aware of the suffering of another (or others), fueled by a deep awareness of inter-existence among all beings and the agape love that results, expressed in mindful action intended to transform the suffering experienced by both.

Table I: Anatomical Elements of a Dyadic Compassionate Interaction

Attribute	Variables
1. *Subject/object relations*: Compassionate interactions can be conceptualized as dyadic interactions between the subject (feeler) and object (recipient) of compassionate action, even if the object is all humanity, or the self.	*Equality or inequality*: The subject is perceived, in some Western treatments, to be in a position of greater social status, and thus able to help the object (e.g., Garber 2004, 23). Eastern treatments (e.g., Nhat Hanh 2007) tend to eschew "equality complexes."
2. *Subject's affective roots*: The mainspring of the emotional experience of compassion varies across authors, and particularly between Eastern and Western treatments.	*Affective states*: self-interest, interbeing, reflex. Some Western psychological treatments (see, e.g., Bierhoff 2005, 151) have focused on the innateness of prosocial and compassionate action, whereas Eastern discourses (e.g., Dalai Lama 2002; Nhat Hanh 1975; 2005b) have tended to focus on the cultivation of the ability to extend compassion to all beings, regardless of innate ability.
3. *Subsequent action*: compassion requires a behavioral manifestation; many, from both Eastern and Western traditions view compassion as existing at an action/reflection (reflex?) nexus.	*Action variables*: When action is guided by unexamined self-interest, there is no clear relation between the action and transformation of suffering. When action is guided by mindfulness, the results of the action are more likely to offer effective healing and transformation.
4. *New affective state in subject*: After the intervention of the subject, a new affective state is generated in the subject.	*New Affective states*: States that have been mentioned include indignation, self-satisfaction, equanimity, and generalized well-being.
5. *New condition for object*: The action rendered by the subject should produce some meaningful change for the object.	*Action variables*: When action is guided by unexamined self-interest, there is no clear relation between the action and transformation of suffering. When action is guided by mindfulness, the results of the action are more likely to offer effective healing and transformation.

Returning to President Obama's address (2009), he reminded his audience that "the success of our economy has always depended not just on the size of our gross domestic product, but on the reach of our prosperity; on our ability to extend opportunity to every willing heart—not out of charity, but because it is the surest route to our common good." Here, he illustrates a crucial component of compassion—connectedness among all humans, or interbeing (e.g., Nhat Hanh 1975; 2005b; 2007). Compassion in Nhat Hanh's sense and, to a degree as illustrated in President Obama's inaugural address, recognizes that all humans are not merely alike, or feel the same things, or are one family, but are meaningfully indistinguishable from each other. The recognition of interbeing is at the core of a policing predicated upon mindful and compassionate service. If one is to be a protector or service provider to another, does he not also need to feel connected to that being in order to remember *why* he needs to help them—especially as the "other" is yelling at him, crying, and likely experiencing some sort of turmoil?

Benefits of Compassion-Generative Mindful Practices (CGMP)

This section will review empirical literature on the benefits accrued by those engaging in types of mindful practices. The literature is small but growing, and rigorous empirical work in the area of mindfulness is relatively limited. Still, evidence so far is encouraging. It is the perspective of the authors, though, that the gap between the rich benefits of mindful practices and empirical evidence thereof speaks as much about shortcomings in the current state of the art in social research as it does about the objective merit of mindfulness. Probably the benefits of mindfulness are more apparent to those who practice actively; many of the fruits of practice experienced by the authors would be difficult to quantify under even the most ideal circumstances.

Mindfulness interventions should not be seen as a therapeutic tool to be used to intervene in crises (e.g., Kostanski and Hassed 2008). Its use for psychotherapy is more prophylactic in nature, in that patients should seek to develop the specific set of skills, living every moment in the present, constantly aware of their thoughts, feelings and surroundings, but not vigilant. In this manner, they may be able to fend off future bouts with depression, anxiety, suicide ideation, *inter alia*. Indeed, one needn't be sick or in chronic pain to benefit from mindful practices. For instance, college students at a Jesuit university in California were randomly assigned to two different mindfulness-based programs (MBSR and the

"Eight Point Program"), and to a control (Shapiro et al., 2008). Students in both mindfulness-based programs evidenced increased mindfulness, and this mindfulness appeared to decrease stressful thinking.

Much of the empirical work in the area on mindfulness has focused on the program developed by Kabat-Zinn (1990), called Mindfulness-Based Stress Reduction (MBSR), or derivations thereof (i.e., mindfulness-based cognitive therapy - MBCT). Mindfulness practice has been found to aid patients with anxiety, panic and agoraphobia disorders (Kabat-Zinn, Massion, Kristeller, Peterson, Fletcher, Pbert, Lenderking, and Santorelli, 1992), to decrease anxiety among female cardiac patients (Tacon, McComb, Caldera, and Randolph 2003), to improve sleep, and diminish stress and mood difficulties among cancer patients (Carlson and Garland 2005). Mindfulness meditation has also shown to be promising for patients with more than three bouts with depression (Ramel, Goldin, Carmona, and McQuaid 2004).

Evidence exists that mindfulness meditation may offer the potential to capitalize on human neuroplasticity. Davidson and his colleagues (2003) found that mindfulness meditation practice was linked with increased activity in subjects' anterior left prefrontal cortexes, an area associated with positive emotional experiences. Additionally, as compared to control, meditating subjects exhibited a more robust response to an influenza vaccine. Meditation may even have the potential to thicken cortical tissues (see Mace 2008, 30). Continual practice of learned skills appears to be crucial for continued benefits to accrue (Mason and Hargreaves 2001), however.

Stress and the Nature of Police Work

A cursory inspection of the basic nature of police work reveals that stress is often inherent to the characteristics that define the role of police in contemporary society. Bohm and Haley (2007) suggest that there are four primary characteristics of police work that are inherently stressful: (1) quick decision making, (2) the independent nature of police work, where individual officers rarely, if ever, perform their duties under the direct auspices of a supervisor, (3) "dirty work," or the unpleasant and distasteful elements police officers must expose themselves to simply to carry out the obligatory functions of their job, and (4) danger. These findings are echoed by Violanti and Aron (1995), who found that police stressors can basically be divided into two distinct, but not necessarily mutually exclusive, categories: (1) organizational/administrative stressors (e.g., shift work, excessive paperwork, going up for promotion, inadequate supervisory support) and (2) stressors inherent to the nature of police work (e.g., killing someone in the line of duty, the possibility of physical injury, witnessing the effects of domestic violence and child abuse). Perhaps the most important way these two categories overlap to exacerbate the destructive effects of police stress is that officers are often propelled into the most stressful life-threatening situations at a moment's notice after long periods of boring routine. Such extremes can wreak havoc with officers sympathetic and parasympathic nervous systems, which can trigger emotional trauma and severe immunological compromise (Grossman and Christensen 2007).

What may also be highly damaging psychologically for many officers is the realization that, despite one's best effort over the course of one's career, the likelihood of making even a small impact on crime is extremely small. The reality for nearly all police officers at retirement is that crime in their communities likely will be no less serious a problem than when they began their careers. This apparent lack of efficacy may be linked to depression and burnout (see, e.g., Roberg, Novak and Cordner 2002).

Harms Attendant to the Police Job

Not counting the 72 police officers killed as a result of the attack on the World Trade Center on September 11, 2001, an average of 55 police officers have been killed feloniously each year for the past ten years (Federal Bureau of Investigation 2009). In 2007, 57 officers were killed feloniously; the deadliest state for police officers in 2007 was Texas, where nine officers were feloniously killed. In 2007, more than 59,200 officers were assaulted nationwide, and more than 25 percent of these assaults resulted in injury (Federal Bureau of Investigation 2009). Nationwide in 2007, an officer had better than a one-in-ten chance of being assaulted, though a considerably lower chance of being injured. Although not all officers shared the same level of risk in 2007 (rural police officers were involved in assaults less frequently than officers in larger cities, and this trend is typical), the risk of assault or death is very real for all police officers, regardless of jurisdiction size.

Taken from an email conversation with one of the authors on 1/28/2009, consider also the experiences of Cheri Maples, dharma teacher in the lineage of Thich Nhat Hanh and former police officer, currently engaged in consulting with police departments and justice professionals: "…I have known several police officers that have taken another person's life in the line of duty. Even when it has been without question in order to save another's life, I have never seen a police officer recover from taking another's life. Actually, I've seen few police officers recover from the effects of their job— period" (Maples 2009). Even if the likelihood of being violently attacked are somewhat exaggerated by many officers, the risks of the job are very real, and the consequences of violence are profound.

Stress among Police and Its Consequences

The trauma from assault or injury, and the risk of assault, injury or death are only two among several, and may well not be among the most significant, sources of stress and eventual harm suffered by police as a result of their job (Newman and Rucker-Reed 2004). This section will present some of the evidence on police stressors and the consequent damage done to officers.

Stress, generally. The existence of a relatively uniform amount of state-type stress among police officers was investigated by some of the earlier projects on police stress and, taken together, the evidence can be seen as equivocal. One particularly notable study seemed to point to the possibility that the richer source of stress for police stemmed from (a) the police organization itself (e.g., shift work) (Storch and Panzarella 1996; Violanti and Aaron 1995), and (b) dealing with non-cops; the latter category including dealing with citizens and the court system, as well as the fear of being injured, and less an accurate assessment of the likelihood of injury (Storch and Panzarella 1996). Police officers may perceive the job to be more potentially dangerous that it is in reality (Newman and Rucker-Reed 2004, 632). Moreover, Storch and Panzarella's evidence seemed to indicate that, through the use of a standardized state (situational)-trait (long-term) anxiety inventory, police officers as a group had a relatively low level of state-trait anxiety, as compared to, for example, high school students (Storch and Panzarella 1996, 105).

Work that just predates that of Storch and Panzarella, however, examined coping strategies among police officers, relative to the coping strategies of their spouses (Beehr, Johnson, and Nieva 1995), and found evidence that a rugged individualist tendency among officers was related to unhealthy coping strategies, like drinking and burnout (exhaustion and depersonalization). An interesting finding is that negative coping strategies (drinking, suicide, and divorce) were negatively associated with emotion-focused coping (i.e., dealing with the emotional aspects of the stress experienced). Paying attention to officers' and their spouses' emotions, as encouraged in mindful practice, were effective at reducing the reliance upon destructive coping technologies (Beehr et al. 1995). Although Beehr, et al. did not employ a validated measure of state-trait stress comparable to that of other studies, their results support the argument that however abstractly stressful police work may be, some choose unhealthy avenues for stress abatement, which can have serious consequences for officers, their families, and the citizens they serve.

Expanding on the organization as a source of stressors is the work of Laufersweiler-Dwyer and Dwyer (2000). They found that organizational *policies and structures* were the most potent source of stress for officers, including inadequate support from supervisors, ineffective communication and questionable policies. Shift-work has also been found to be a source of stress for officers (e.g., Charles, Burchfiel, Fekedulegn, Vila, Hartley, Slaven, Mnatsakanova, and Violanti 2007; Vila and Kenney, 2002). One obvious course of action to address these sources of stress is to "de-militarize" (e.g., Kraska and Cubellis 1997) police organizations. Although the 24-hour nature of the police requires officers to staff patrols round the clock, mindfulness-generated and empirically tested creative policies might well reduce the impact of shift-work.

Demographic variables among officers appear to have little impact on whether they are more prone to stress and its damaging effects (e.g., Storch and Panzarella 1996, Newman and Rucker-Reed 2004), although some research (Violanti and Aaron 1995) has identified non-trivial differences among officers at different experience levels; officers with more time on the force evidenced significantly higher stressors than officers with less time.

Consequences of prolonged stress. In terms of the actual damage wrought by stress, somatic complaints like headaches and digestive difficulties are common, and may constitute a first sign of more serious health difficulties, like weight loss or gain, insomnia, lethargy, and muddy thinking (e.g., Colbert 2003, 7). Eventually, diseases like cardiopulmonary disease, high blood pressure and stroke may manifest, if the stress is not managed.

These negative consequences are a result of the continued release of so-called stress hormones adrenaline and cortisol. Adrenaline causes an increase in blood pressure and heart rate, as well as capillary constriction. In short bursts, adrenaline is helpful in managing physical crises, but long-term release of adrenaline due to stress keeps blood pressure high, with attendant consequences. Also, long-term cortisol release has been linked to several negative consequences, including decreased bone density, diminished muscle mass, and impaired immuno-response (Colbert 2003, 17) which may lead to the onset of cancer (Colbert 2003). Violanti and his colleagues (2007) found that in officers with severe PTSD indicators, cortisol levels tended to remain high over the course of the observation period, whereas officers with few or moderate PTSD tended to evidence a more normal cortisol pattern.

Somatic complaints, from headaches to cancer, are not the only expressions of unmanaged stress. Emotional harms, including suicide and divorce have roots in unmindful stress-coping as well. Violanti (2004) found that when PTSD and alcoholism are comorbid in police officers, the likelihood of suicide ideation increases nearly tenfold.

One particularly interesting study (Euwema, Kop, and Bakker 2004) found evidence indicating that increased levels of burnout, resulting from a mismatch between work demands and benefits (akin to the organizational stressors discussed above), may be linked to *decreased* dominance and possibly *more effective* conflict management. The letting-go that may accompany burnout can be achieved in ways that do not require emotional and physical damage to officers—specifically, mindfulness practices.

As with all beings, stress is experienced by each individual officer differently, according to their abilities and predispositions. Also, there are forms of stress that are helpful and healthy (called eustress), and forms of stress that are damaging (called distress) (see, e.g., Roberg, et al., 2005 463). The aim, then, cannot be to eliminate stress from the police workplace, but to develop the capacity of each officer to handle the stresses they experience in productive, healthy and edifying ways, and to modify the work environment so that unnecessary distress is eliminated.

Taken together, the evidence indicates that police stress is a not-infrequent syndrome; PTSD, obesity, divorce, poor coping skills, cynicism, burnout, and exhaustion may all feed on each other, fueling a downward spiral (e.g., Burke and Mikkelsen 2007; Charles, Burchfiel, Fekedulegn, Vila, Hartley, Slaven, Mnatsakanova, and Violanti 2007; Charles, Burchfiel, Fekedulegn, Andrew, Violanti, and Vila 2007; Martinussen, Richardsen, and Burke 2007; Roberts and Levenson 2001; Vila and Kenney 2002), potentially resulting in decreased job effectiveness, serious and life-threatening medical conditions, like heart disease, stroke and cancer.

CGMP and the Police Job

We have traced the literature that illustrates the harms attendant to police work: depression, anxiety, PTSD, among others, as well as the somatic manifestations of these negative affective states, from headaches, and unhealthy weight change, to bone and muscle loss to cancer. We have also examined the evidence of the effectiveness of mindfulness meditation; mindful practice has been shown to be effective at reducing the likelihood of future bouts of depression, anxiety and PTSD, as well as mitigating the onset of somatic symptoms.

Compassionate action, to the Western ear, is often confused with a "goo-goo" softness (Garber, 2004, 16), and perhaps a low level of intellectual rigor as well. It is often a difficult case to make for justice organizations and businesses alike that compassionate action can be beneficial to the bottom line (e.g., Boyatzis and McKee 2005). Although there is increasing reason to doubt the existence of a monolithic police culture (Paoline 2003), police cultures historically have been marked by three attributes: an orientation to fighting crime, conflict with those in charge, and considerable intragroup loyalty coupled with considerable intergroup mistrust (e.g., Moon 2006, 706); even with the more diverse and representative contexts of many police departments today, it is likely remnants of the more traditional police culture remain. Each of the above mentioned attributes is likely to have a negative impact on the acceptance of mindful practice in a department, especially if implemented through the command structure.

Because of the possibility that mindfulness trainings may be resisted by police cultures that have been notoriously insular and resistant to change and innovation, it might be helpful to frame the discussion by grounding CGMP firmly in the realm of affective neuroscience and its implications for personal and professional satisfaction in police work. Goleman's (2005) work on "emotional intelligence" offers one such avenue by focusing on the scientific study of emotions, specifically how emotions are processed and interpreted neurologically and the implications this has for social behavior. As previously discussed, "mindfulness" as a concept may be somewhat vague as a basis for encouraging behavioral change, but when couched in terms of its scientifically verifiable effects on (a) emotional health, (b) physiological health, and (c) decision-making, we adopt a significantly more rigorous vantage point from which to proclaim the benefits of mindfulness training for the law enforcement professions.

More than just a good idea, the implementation of CGMP may be one of the most useful technologies in the effort to render a more effective justice system. Wang (2005) speaks of compassion as species-preservative behavior, rooted in an awareness of one-ness with all beings. Nhat Hanh's (e.g., 2005a) term "interbeing" crystalizes the importance of continuing efforts to dissolve the false distinction between the police and those they serve. Nhat Hanh (2007) tells his students that through confident and diligent practice (e.g., sitting and walking meditation), mindfulness will allow compassion to take deeper root in practitioners, ultimately culminating in insights into the nature of existence, including impermanence, non-self, and interbeing. As the authors have argued elsewhere (DeValve and Adkinson 2008), the insights that come from CGMP can be highly useful in the process of responding to crime and harm conditions, after the fashion indicated by its author (Goldstein 1990).

CGMP

CGMP consists of a collaboratively-managed curriculum of meditation training, substantive program offerings, and policy recommendations woven into all aspects of training and work. The curriculum shall be designed to teach officers the requisite skills to reinforce officers' awareness of the place of solitude in each of them, as well as to offer course content intended to support mindfulness in the police job. It also intends to modify the organizational culture in such a way that mindfulness becomes ingrained in all aspects of organizational functioning. In implementation, CGMP would involve a training component at pre-service academy, as well as in-service trainings; both pre-service and in-service academy programs would offer both meditation and relaxation training as well as the substantive content discussed below. Additionally, there would be reinforcement of mindfulness practice in roll-calls, and encouragement to practice in the field as appropriate. Finally, there would be policies and programs intended to cultivate a culture of mindful thought, speech and action. A program of CGMP implemented in a police department would have to have the following characteristics: (1) it needs to be repetitive across the entire organization, and throughout each officers' career; (2) police executives must themselves be fully engaged in the practice, and; (3) it cannot be standardized and applied "off-the-shelf" to any police department; it must be tailored to each department's needs and context, and grafted into the department in such a way that it can modify its "organizational DNA" (e.g., Sawatsky 2009).

The meditation practice can take a number of forms, but most commonly would involve a period of sitting meditation (perhaps fifteen or twenty minutes long) and walking meditation. Mindfulness and insight meditation techniques will be combined to fit the needs of participants. For example, participants will be taught to cultivate an awareness of bare attention (one-point concentration), and then introduced to the process of analytical observation in one session, then taken on a guided relaxation meditation the next. Community being essential to long-term success, along with the meditation portion CGMP involves regular debriefings and discussions on experiences, where participants would have the chance to discuss their practices as well as their experiences in applying what they learn to their jobs.

In terms of course content to be offered to participants, collaborative discussions on the role of faith and belief in participants' lives and jobs, the science of emotional intelligence, mindful (resonant) leadership, organizational decision making, "warrior science", human diversity, and cultural criminology will be offered. Policies and programs will be devised and recommended on an individual departmental basis, but may include mindfulness-based critical incident stress debriefing, "cops on cushions" meditation groups, and mindfulness-based critical incident in-service programs.

The Importance of Being Earnestly Mindful

Generally, there are several benefits of mindful practice offered by a variety of authors from a variety of traditions and perspectives. Our purpose here is to offer a comprehensive treatment of each of the major avenues of inquiry into mindfulness so that police departments can progress toward instituting CGMP as part of academy curricula with a sound sense of the state of current knowledge as to its benefits.

Earlier it was stated that CGMP can benefit police departments' daily practical efforts to serve their communities in two ways: by providing the foundation for compassion as a guide for police-citizen interaction and transformation of the misery witnessed by police in the natural course of their jobs, and by providing officers a powerful tool for protecting themselves from many of the harms associated with their work. The reader should note that in this section we will present both arguments in favor of CGMP together, as they are inextricably interconnected.

Practical Implications of Mindfulness Training for Police

Research by a variety of leading scholars in the growing field of behavioral medicine support the assertion that mindfulness and compassion can be a powerful force in law enforcement efforts to promote peace and justice in our communities (Goleman 1997). These researchers have identified six "wholesome" emotions (positive states of mind) that seem to have scientifically verifiable positive benefits on human physiology and psychology: (1) equanimity, a state of calmness, (2) optimism, (3) confidence, (4) social connectedness, or "friendliness," (5) joy, or deep happiness, and (6) loving-kindness. This contrasts with four major afflictive mind states: (1) anger, (2) depression (e.g., sadness, self-pity, and hopelessness), (3) fear (e.g., anxiety, agitation, and stress), and (4) repression or denial. Unfortunately, the afflictive mind states seem to be disproportionately nurtured by the defining characteristics of police work. This is especially tragic because this comes at the cost of the wholesome emotions, which are critical for the cultivation of compassion and therefore peaceful interactions between police and the communities they serve.

Personal Benefits

The officer's most immediate obligation is to his or her own personal mental and physical health. Without tending to himself first, an officer cannot be effective in his effort to help others. Research indicates that our neurological and immunological systems are intimately linked in a symbiotic process called "psychoneuroimmunology" (Brown 1997) where wholesome mind states increase the body's resistance to illness and disease while afflictive mind states compromise our immunological functioning.

Brown (1997) highlights a wide variety of demonstrable ways that meditative practice can supplement medical science. The positive health benefits associated with meditative practice include reduced risk of heart disease, stroke, hypertension, and other cardiovascular ailments. Such advantages are compounded by attendant improvements in immunosuppressant response. People who have learned to monitor and reduce their levels of stress exhibit marked increases in white blood cell production, clotting, and healing after injury and surgery. Pain tolerance and alleviation also seem to be directly affected by dedicated mindfulness practice. Headaches, asthma, hypertension, and chronic pain all seem to be particularly ameliorated by simple, yet persistent, conscious attention.

Even more encouraging, these benefits do not seem to be restricted to physical well-being. Perhaps most importantly, mindfulness training encourages officers to develop emotional balance and affective coping skills for dealing with the harsh realities of police work (and life in general, for that matter). A vocation that regularly elicits fear, cynicism, sadness, anger, and apathy can lead to a host of psychologically-related problems. Suicide, depression, domestic and interpersonal relationship problems, high turnover, ethical lapses and outright corruption, drug and alcohol abuse, risk-taking behavior, post-traumatic stress disorder (PTSD), and existential despair are the major pitfalls facing officers who have not mastered techniques for generating emotional quiescence. Fortunately, all of these tragic outcomes can be addressed through mindful attention to our destructive emotions. Research examining the emotional benefits of mindfulness practice on such contrasting populations as prisoners and elementary school children all report similar results. The coping skills and emotional awareness generated by systematic mindfulness practice address the root causes of destructive selfish and interpersonal behavior, thereby improving one's ability to deal with life's upsets and injuries optimistically, constructively, and compassionately (Goleman 2004).

Practical Professional Benefits

Law enforcement officers unaware of the physiological mechanisms and create a limbic *quid pro quo* in every social interaction are literally at the mercy of the powerful afflictive emotions. They are expected to remain calm and to act justly with Solomon-like wisdom (e.g., Bayley and Bittner 1989), despite the fact that the majority of the people they interact with are likely to be highly contagious with the equivalent of emotional typhus. Failure to inoculate themselves against such affective virulence can lead to a plethora of negative professional consequences. The more agitated an officer becomes, the less she is able to calm others and gain compliance from citizens. Escalation of aggression is one of the most serious problems resulting from unmindful policing, and potentially one of the most easily avoidable with dedicated mindful practice. The wholesome mind states nurtured by mindfulness training are all invaluable for providing officers with the mental fortitude necessarily to skillfully disarm others with compassionate action.

Sometimes, however, all the compassion and mindfulness in the world cannot pacify those in the grip of the most intense afflictive emotions. Therefore, another benefit of mindfulness practice is its potential to save lives during critical incidents. At a moment's notice, officers may be faced with a life-or-death situation in which their sense of emotional control determines the outcome. Grossman and Christensen (2007) survey the research examining the physiological and psychological consequences of combat on soldiers and domestic police and conclude that one of the main reasons these professions are so stressful is because they force human beings to regularly confront the "universal human phobia" of life-or-death combat. These findings are supported by Klinger (2004) in a study of officers who have been involved in deadly force encounters. Anger, emotional detachment, PTSD, and existential angst plague officers from all walks of life who have faced death and/or seriously injured or killed another human being in the line of duty. A groundbreaking study conducted by Strozzi-Heckler (2007), however, suggests that mindfulness training may significantly improve law enforcement officers' performance during critical incidents. Using a combination of meditation practice and martial arts training in Aikido, Strozzi-Heckler found that 85% of special forces soldiers participating in the program experienced an increase in their ability to manage stress and shock, 100% reported an increase in their ability to marshal their mental and emotional resources, 65% indicated an improved ability to coordinate their mind, body, and emotions, and 70% reported they were able to solidify key values such as accountability for their actions (p. 309).

The horrific shooting of Oscar Grant provides a near-ideal example of the importance of mindful practice for police officers. Oscar Grant may well be the most recent victim of police mindlessness. Currently he is, to be sure, its most recognized victim. Shipley and Baranski (2002) assessed the impact of visuo-motor behavioral rehearsal (VMBR) on officers' management of a simulated critical incident. VMBR is a program that utilizes relaxation, visualization and performance-related imagery (Shipley and Baranski 2002, 72), closely akin to mindfulness meditation. Results indicated that officers who participated in the VMBR training not only experienced significantly less stress during the critical incident simulation, but also performed more effectively in the simulation.

Consider also with regard to the Grant/BART shooting the subsequent police-community dynamics. A number of protests followed on the heels of the shooting, evidencing a level of animus toward the police on the part of a historically marginalized community. If the BART police had been actively cultivating a relationship of trust with its communities, it is likely that the level of scandal and anger would be considerably lower. Instead of a sense of anger and indignation, coupled with loss on the part of the African-American community, and a sense of fear and embattled-ness on the part of the BART police, there would be a collective sense of loss, and concern to transform the pain resulting from the incident into something of value.

Evidence exists that in one large southern police department, calls for service involving property crimes (and not domestic complaints, traffic stops or violent crimes) were related with the most use of force by police officers, relative to suspect resistance (MacDonald, Manz, Alpert and Dunham 2003). This finding is thought to be related to officers' relaxed expectations upon arriving at a call for a property complaint, as compared to heightened expectations of conflict when responding to calls regarding domestic disputes, violent crimes, or while conducting traffic stops. This finding highlights the importance of officer expectations on the results of police-citizen encounters. Officers must take the time to understand themselves and their expectations when responding to any call for service. Officers who have taken the time to be fully present with themselves (through a sustained mindfulness meditation practice, for example), to understand their consciousness and its constructs, as well as their surroundings will be able to have the capacity to offer themselves fully to their department and their community, but in a way that is edifying and not self-sacrificing. The insights gained from mindful police service likely will be useful in developing creative and effective strategies for transforming community problems. When police are called upon to resolve conflicts, the establishment of a command presence may be inimical to success (e.g., Euwema, et al. 2004). This is not to argue that a command presence has no value, but merely to point out that officers need to be sufficiently aware and reflective to understand different approaches are more likely to succeed in different contexts.

Guidance for Police Executives

Jon Kabat-Zinn (1990, 141) tells patients participating in his Mindfulness-Based Stress Reduction program, "you don't have to like it, you just have to do it," which will sound familiar to individuals who have attended police officer academies. Mindfulness is, like mastering the penal law or crafting a command personality, a capacity or skill that requires long-term cultivation. Kabat-Zinn's sentiment applies to police executives as well. Perhaps the single most important aspect of instituting CGMP in a department is leading through example. Leading from the front with regard to mindful practice is effective in at least two ways: first, officers will see that the effort toward increased mindfulness is not a passing fad, but is something behind which the leadership stands fully enough to commit their own time to it. Second, there is what Gilbert (2005) refers to as contagion: others will see the practitioner's power and serenity, and seek to achieve the same motion-at-rest well-being for themselves.

Police executives who develop a mindfulness practice likely will recognize aspects of their organization that are stress-productive for their officers (like poor communication and obtuse, Byzantine policies typical of quasi-military organizations), and most likely will act to diminish or eliminate those sources of stress. Our recommendation, then, is to allow executives' own mindfulness practices, and that of subordinates to freely develop suggestions for organizational improvement. Including officers in the process of organizational improvement will have the additional benefit of granting them a voice, and thereby, legitimacy (DeValve 2008).

Adkinson (2008) argues that the awesome power and authority that law enforcement officers possess obligates them to wield this power with a grave and solemn sense of responsibility. Because stress can have such deleterious effects on police effectiveness and professionalism, we argue that officers have a deep obligation to hone their emotional resources so that they become a help, instead of a hindrance, to law enforcement practice. So, despite the challenges that intense mindfulness training poses, officers can take heart knowing that research suggests such efforts will pay significant dividends for themselves, their agencies, and society in general.

References

Adkinson, C. D. 2008. *The Amazing Spider-Man* and the evolution of the Comics Code: A case study in Cultural Criminology. *Journal of Criminal Justice and Popular Culture* 15 (3): 1-21.

Arendt, H. 1965. *On revolution.* New York: Viking.

Barash, D. P., and C. P. Webel 2002. *Peace and conflict studies.* Thousand Oaks, CA: Sage.

Barlow, D. E., and M. H. Barlow. 2002. *Police in a multicultural society.* Long Grove, IL: Waveland.

Bayley, D. H., and B. Egon. 1989. Learning the skills of policing. In *Critical issues in policing: Contemporary readings*, ed. R. G. Dunham, and G. P. Alpert (87-110). Prospect Heights, IL: Waveland.

Beehr, T. A., L. B. Johnson, and R. Nieva . 1995. Occupational stress: Coping of police and their spouses. *Journal of Organizational Behavior* 16 (1): 3-25.

Bichler, G., and L. Gaines. 2005. An examination of police officers' insights into problem identification and problem solving. *Crime and Delinquency* 51 (1): 53-74.

Bierhoff, H.W. 2005. The psychology of compassion and prosocial behavior. In *Compassion: Conceptualisations, research, and use in psychotherapy.*, ed. P. Gilbert, Paul (148-167). New York: Routledge.

Bohm, R. M., and K. N. Haley. 2007. *Introduction to criminal justice* 4th ed. New York: McGraw-Hill.

Boyatzis, R., and A. McKee. 2005. *Resonant leadership.* Cambridge, MA: Harvard Business School Press.

Brantley, J. 2007. *Calming your anxious mind: How mindfulness and compassion can free you from anxiety, fear and panic*, 2nd ed. Oakland, CA: New Harbinger.

Brown, D. 2003. Behavioral medicine. In *Healing emotions: Conversations with the Dalai Lama on mindfulness, emotions, and health*, ed. Daniel Goleman (145-164). Boston, MA: Shambhala.

Brown, K. W., and R. M Ryan. 2003. The benefits of being present: Mindfulness and its role in psychological well-being. *Journal of Personality and Social Psychology* 84 (4): 822-848.

Carlson, L. E., and S. N. Garland. 2005. Impact of mindfulness-based stress reduction (MBSR) on sleep, mood, stress and fatigue symptoms in cancer outpatients. *International Journal of Behavioral Medicine* 12 (4): 278-285.

Charles, L. E., C. M Burchfiel., D.Fekedulegn , M. E.Andrew, , J. M. Violanti, , and B. Vila. 2007. Obesity and sleep: the Buffalo Police health study. *Policing: An International Journal of Police Strategies and Management* 30 (2): 203-214.

Charles, L. E., C. M.Burchfiel, , D.Fekedulegn, B.Vila, T. A Hartley., J.Slaven, and A. Mnatsakanova. 2007. Shift work and sleep: the Buffalo Police health study. *Policing: An International Journal of Police Strategies and Management* 30 (2): 215-227.

CNN. 2009. "Spokesman: Officer in subway shooting has resigned". http://www.cnn.com/2009/CRIME/01/07/BART.shooting/index.html?iref=newssearch. (accessed January 28, 2009).

Colbert, D. 2003. *Deadly emotions: Understand the mind-body-spirit connection that can heal or destroy you*. Nashville, TN: Thomas Nelson.

Dalai L., 2001. *An open heart: Practicing compassion in everyday life*. Boston: Little, Brown.

Dalai L., and P.Ekman. 2008. *Emotional awareness: Overcoming the obstacles to psychological balance and compassion*. New York: Henry Holt and Company.

Davidson, R. J., J.Kabat-Zinn, J.Schumacher, M. Rosenkranz, D.Muller, S. F. Santorelli, F.Urbanowski, A.Harrington, K.Bonus, J. F.Sheridan. 2003. Alterations in brain and immune function produced by mindfulness meditation. *Psychosomatic Medicine* 65: 564-570.

DeValve, M. J. 2008. *Purpose, power, justice and marginality: Key prerequisites for diversity at the Texas Department of Criminal Justice*. Saarbrucken, Germany: VDM Verlag.

DeValve, M. J., and C. D. Adkinson. 2008. Mindfulness, compassion, and the police in America: An essay of hope. *Human Architecture* 6 (3): 99-104.

Euwema, M. C., N.Kop, A. and B. Bakker. 2004. The behaviour of police officers in conflict situations: How burnout and reduced dominance contribute to better outcomes. *Work & Stress* 18 (1): 23-38.

Federal Bureau of Investigation. 2009. "Law enforcement officers killed & assaulted". http://www.fbi.gov/ucr/killed/2007/index.html. (Accessed January 28, 2009).

Garber, M. 2004. Compassion. In. *Compassion: The culture and politics of an emotion,* ed. L.. Berlant (15-28). New York: Routledge.

Gilbert, P. 2005. Compassion and cruelty: A biopsychosocial approach. In *Compassion: Conceptualisations, research, and use in psychotherapy,* ed. P. Gilbert (9-74). New York: Routledge.

Goleman, D. ed. 2003. *Healing emotions: Conversations with the Dalai Lama on mindfulness, emotions, and health.* Boston, MA: Shambhala.

Goleman, D. 2004. *Destructive emotions: How can we overcome them?* Ed. Daniel Goleman. New York: Bantam.

—. 2006. *Emotional intelligence: Why it can matter more than IQ.* New York: Bantam.

Goleman, D., R.Boyatzis, and A. McKee. 2004. *Primal leadership: Learning to lead with emotional intelligence.* Boston, MA: Harvard Business School.

Goldstein, H. 1990. *Problem-oriented policing.* Boston: McGraw-Hill.

Grossman, D., and L.W.Christensen. 2007. *On combat: The psychology and physiology of deadly conflict in war and peace.* United States: Warrior Science Publications.

Henderson, L. N. 1987. Legality and empathy. *85 Mich. L. Rev. 1574.*

Kabat-Zinn, J. 1990. *Full catastrophe living: Using the wisdom of your body and mind to face stress, pain and illness.* New York: Bantam Dell.

Kabat-Zinn, Jon, A. O. Massion., J. Kristeller, L .G..Peterson, K. E Fletcher., L..Pbert, W. R. Lenderking., and S. F. Santorelli. 1992. Effectiveness of a meditation-based stress reduction program in the treatment of anxiety disorders. *The American Journal of Psychiatry* 149 (7): 936-943.

Klinger, D. 2004. *Into the kill zone: A cop's eye view of deadly force.* San Francisco, CA: Jossey-Bass.

Kornfield, J. 2008. *The wise heart: A guide to the universal teachings of Buddhist psychology.* New York: Bantam.

Kostanski, M., and C. Hassed. 2008. Mindfulness as a concept and a process. *Australian Psychology* 43 (1): 15-21.

Kraska, P. B., and L. J Cubellis. 1997. Militarizing Mayberry: Making sense of American paramilitary policing. *Justice Quarterly* 14 (4): 607-629.

Langer, E. 1989. *Mindfulness*. Cambridge, MA: Da Capo.

Laufersweiler-Dwyer, D. L, and R. G. Dwyer. 2000. Profiling those impacted by organizational stressors at the macro, intermediate and micro levels of several police agencies. *The Justice Professional* 12: 443-469.

MacDonald, J. M., P. W Manz., G. P., Alpert and R. G. Dunham. 2003. Police use of force: Examining the relationship between calls for service and the balance of police force and suspect resistance. *Journal of Criminal Justice* 31: 119-127.

Mace, C. 2008. *Mindfulness and mental health: Therapy, theory and science*. New York: Routledge.

Martinussen, M., A. M., Richardsen, and R. J.Burke. 2007. Job demands, job resources, and burnout among police officers. *Journal of Criminal Justice* 35: 239-249.

Mason, O., and I. Hargreaves. 2001. A qualitative study of mindfulness-based cognitive therapy for depression. *British Journal of Medical Psychology* 74: 197-212.

Moon, B. 2006. The influence of organizational socialization on police officers' acceptance of community policing. *Policing: An International Journal of Police Strategies and Management* 29 (4), 704-722.

Newman, D.W., and M.L. Rucker-Reed. 2004. Police stress, state-trait anxiety, and stressors among U.S. Marshals. *Journal of Criminal Justice* 32: 631-641.

Nietzsche, F. 1990. *Beyond good and evil*. New York: Penguin.

Nhat Hanh, T. 1975. *The miracle of mindfulness: An introduction to the practice of meditation*. Boston: Beacon.

—. 2005a. *Keeping the peace: Mindfulness and public service*. Berkeley, CA: Parallax.

—. 2005b. *Being peace*. Berkeley, CA: Parallax

—. 2007. *The art of power*. New York: HarperCollins.

—. 2008. Personal communication: Dharma talk, 5 May, 2008, Hanoi, Vietnam.

Obama, B. 2009. Inaugural speech. http://www.npr.org/templates/story/story.php?storyId=99590481 (accessed January 21, 2009)

Paoline III, E. 2003. Taking stock: Toward a richer understanding of police culture. *Journal of Criminal Justice* 31: 199-214.

Ramel, W, P. Goldin, R., P. E. Carmona, and J. R.McQuaid. 2004. The effects of mindfulness meditation on cognitive processes and affect in patients with past depression. *Cognitive Therapy and Research* 28 (4): 433-455.

Roberg, R., K. Novak, and G. Cordner. 2005. *Police & society* 3rd ed. Los Angeles: Roxbury.

Sawatsky, J. 2009. The ethic of traditional communities and the spirit of healing justice. Philadelphia: Jessica Kingsley.

Storch, J. E., and R. Panzarella. 1996. Police stress: State-trait anxiety in relation to occupational and personal stressors. *Journal of Criminal Justice* 24 (2): 99-107.

Shapiro, S. L., D.Oman, C. E. Thoresen, T. G. Plante, and T. Flinders. 2008. Cultivating mindfulness: Effects on well-being. *Journal of Clinical Psychology* 64 (7): 840-862.

Shipley, P., and J. V. Baranski 2002. Police officer performance under stress: A pilot study on the effects of visuo-motor behavioral rehearsal. *International Journal of Stress Management* 9 (2): 71-80.

Strozzi-Heckler, R. 2007. *In search of the warrior spirit: Teaching awareness disciplines to the military.* Berkeley, CA: Blue Snake.

Swanson, C. R., L. Territo, and R. W. Taylor 2005. *Police administration: Structures, processes, and behavior.* Upper Saddle River, NJ: Pearson.

Tacon, A., M., J. McComb, Y. Caldera, and P. Randoplh. 2003. Mindfulness, meditation, anxiety reduction, and heart disease: A pilot study. *Family & Community Health* 26 (1): 25-33.

Vila, B., and D. J. Kenney. 2002. Tired cops: The prevalence and potential consequences of police fatigue. *NIJ Journal* 248: 16-21.

Violanti, J. M. 2004. Predictors of police suicide ideation. *Suicide and Life-Threatening Behavior* 34 (3): 277-283.

Violanti, J. M., Aaron, Fred. 1995. Police stressors: Variations in perceptions among police personnel. *Journal of Criminal Justice* 23 (3): 287-294.

Violanti, J. M., M. Andrew, C. M. Burchfiel , T. A, Hartley. L. E. Charles, and D. B. Miller. 2007. Post-traumatic stress symptoms and cortisol patterns among police officers. *Policing: An International Journal of Police Strategies and Management* 30 (2): 189-202.

Wang, S. 2005. "A conceptual framework for integrating research related to the physiology of compassion and the wisdom of Buddhist teachings". In *Compassion: Conceptualisations, research, and use in psychotherapy,* ed. P. Gilbert (75-120). New York: Routledge.

CHAPTER NINE

PROMOTING PEACE PROFESSIONALS IN THE U.S. MEDIA

TOM H. HASTINGS

All our dignity consists, then, of thought. By it we must elevate ourselves, and not by space or time, which we cannot fill. Let us work, then, to think well—this is the principle of morality.
—Todd Gitlin (2006, 124).

People who are expected to know more and more about less and less—and moreover, to publish their findings to fewer and fewer—are not likely to conduct their education in public or, for that matter, to give a fig about the general reader.
—Sanford Pinsker (1995, 14)

Source and Significance of the Problem

From a peace perspective, there is a nest of problems. Beginning with the largest: we are at war, which is just as problematic for our field of Peace Studies and Conflict Resolution as metastasizing cancer would be to a cancer researcher. The policy repair—peace—is obvious; the long-term fix is that we humans remove war from our menu of options. First we must acknowledge the debate about the necessity of the very existence of the public intellectual, the person who helps by "filling the gap between the academic elite and the educated public" (Parsi & Geraghty 2004, 17). The distinctions between the intellectuals inside and outside the academy (Grafton 2001) are irrelevant to this inquiry; the necessity of disseminating critical discourse into a democracy is the concern here.

Our second problem: peace professionals are missing from the national discourse. We might not have gone to war if peace professors and other peace professionals had been a serious voice in our national discussion in 2002 and early 2003. Where were these voices? Why were they silent?

Peace-oriented professors do not often speak or write publicly for the mainstream media, and thus cannot be a part of the national debate about anything. What are some of the obstacles and deterrents?

Local business and partisan political figures will, at times, apply pressure to the institution if a professor is speaking out. The arguments for nonviolent methods of conflict resolution are seldom uncontroversial. Adjuncts, fixed-term and even tenure-track professors are at more risk, and at some institutions even tenure is a thin protection from determined partisans who aim to silence professors. Hence, self-censoring is natural. We are "weak, a prey to various temptations: above all, the temptation to make a living" (Brantlinger 2003, 122).

Rational choices relate to a complex set of factors; if peace professors can be convinced that the choice to participate in public discourse will gain much (some for them, some for their profession, some for society) and that the risks can be minimized, the tipping point toward choosing involvement can be a part of promoting, passing, and implementing this policy. Solution: see that peace analysts with credentials gain voice. It can work. The presence of the public intellectuals in the national discourse in the fight for freedom in Central and Eastern Europe was so valuable that they were entrusted with the spirit of aspiration of their peoples and in some cases even have gone on to govern since the Velvet Revolution (Skąpska 2002).

Like cancer, war is a major human problem, a killer, and even more preventable, especially if the geopolitical motivations could be understood by the citizenry, rather than the usual dissembling about motive (Byrne 2005). If the field of Peace and Conflict Studies is primarily responsible for stopping even one war every century, that will be vindication of all our efforts. If we shorten wars by bringing findings on peace processes to our policymakers and those who elect them, we will have achieved an enormous good. Those who study peace need to know how to convince policymakers that peace is not weak, nor appeasement, nor surrender, nor shirking, nor shrinking. "Those who used nonviolent action in our stories did not come to make peace. They came to fight" (Ackerman and DuVall 2000, 5). Constructive conflict management achieves the most gain with the least pain. "Revolutionary war," wrote public peace intellectual Simone Weil in 1933, "is the grave of revolution" (Weil 1994, 250). Similarly, war for installed democracy is inimical to its putative goal. While peace intellectuals may deconstruct war causes and correlatives in ex-post exegesis, a public peace intellectual comes to grips with the conflicts that "arise between an intellectual's commitment to the public interest, against the interests of professional knowledge. A clear decision in favour of the former, made without compromising the latter, distinguishes what we may call the 'public intellectual'" (Lane 2005, 73). Intellectuals "who attempt to influence social and political events and reality directly with their ideas" (Chametzky 2004, 211) require encouragement (Smyth and Hattam 2000).

When can a peace culture inform a war culture? Critical discussion of peace is counterintuitive in the U.S.; we live in a war culture. Communication from public peace scholars promoting alternatives is more than simple education, it is intercultural communication (Jandt 2004). The theories of andragogy—how adults learn—suggest that concrete ideas with utility generate the greatest learning (Daniels and Walker 2001; Jones and Brinkert 2008). In a society bloodied and impoverished by war, peace professionals have a teachable moment. It is time to approach the general public about Afghanistan, Iran, Venezuela, and any other extant or potential hot conflict as well as military spending; war weariness, military pollution, the connections to domestic violence, and a broken economy. A new U.S. administration offer peace analysts a real set of opportunities to shape policy by educating a more receptive public.

Demonstrating peace analysis competencies publicly right now might also help alter the perception of the need for peace education. Indeed, basic educational decisions might be affected by peace educators promoting peace solutions and education. As Marshall and Gerstl-Pepin (2005) point out, more feminist, nurturing curricula would alter the teaching of "history, literature, and science" (91), and the same is true, and overlapping, with peace education. Viewing education as a gestalt approach to engagement helps us expect to enhance our educative value by such participation (Phillips and Soltis 2004). Certainly we engage in the most collaborative learning from the painted porch of praxis, or, as Freire (2000, 137) noted, we learn to swim not in the library but in the pool.

We also have a significant efficiency issue with the lack of voices for peace. Many conflict scholars warn against closing off the search for solutions quickly, before we have heard from all the parties (Fisher and Ury 1991; Umbreit 1995; Daniels and Walker 2001). This is patently true for our search for good conflict management policy. He who controls the process controls the alternatives under consideration and thus the basic outcome, as discourse analysis shows (Marshall and Gerstl-Pepin 2005). If there are peaceful conflict management processes that can avoid destructive conflict, but we never learn of them, that is gross inefficiency to all except the war-profiting elite who control the agenda. Soldiers, innocent civilians abroad, taxpayers, drivers who pay more for fuel, victims of the opportunity costs, and the environment all take the hit. This is expedient for only that elite class of war profiteers and absolutely fails all the benchmarks for efficiency in every other aspect.

While some disparage academics who take a public scholar approach (Posner 2003), we are currently in a culture giving uninformed consent to war, and at least we can inform. Kozol (1991) documents a clear sense of disproportionate exposure to the risks of war amongst poor youth; let us give them and their parents the tools needed to elect policymakers who have learned how to avoid that injustice.

Johan Galtung (2002) is optimistic that the public intellectuals who serve the war system—people he will not honor with the title public intellectual—are the intelligentsia, and they are on the wane as societies gradually watch alternative media become important.

> What will the future look like when this dialectic moves some more steps on, into the great puzzle of history? My bet would be that the days of think tanks for State or Capital or big factories for the mass production of future intelligentsia are counted. The alternative model already crops up all over the world, the Internet cafe'. Equip them with dialogue facilities for group learning and the future looks brighter. In short: Intellectuals all over the world unite; you have only your intelligentsia to lose! (68)

While peace professionals are both academics and analysts, we might wish to consider our peace commitment in the light of rightwing think tanks and the funding that has enabled them to seize a significant portion of the public discourse. One side—the war side—has most of the money; the other side has most of the people power. Fowler (2004) observes that "the powerful have more influence on policy agendas than do the disempowered" (185), but power can be money and guns, or it can be relationships and unity of people (Sharp 1973; Cortright 2006). With commitment and an extra effort, we can match the output and presence of the war-promoting academics who are employed by institutes that favor war.

We can, of course, dare hope that our work helps transform the intelligentsia. Jonathan Lane (2005) describes how Daniel Ellsberg made that conversion, moving from his position as an intellectual architect of the Vietnam War to one who revealed to the American people " a clear and chilling pattern: from 1945 until 1968, American presidents had escalated their commitment to the war," (75) even after it became obvious it could not be won.

Research and Academic Publishing versus Public Scholarship

"Meeting the civic mission is part of the assessment criteria for review of tenure."
—Dr. Carolyn Carr

What disincentivizes peace professors from playing a public role? There is little encouragement for peace and conflict studies professors to engage in public commentary; institutions often discourage or even punish professors who do express a challenger message. Local partisan political figures will, at times, apply negative pressure to the institution if a professor is speaking out. The arguments for nonviolent methods of conflict resolution are seldom uncontroversial. At some institutions even tenure is a thin protection from determined partisans who aim to silence professors.

Ahearne (2006) describes some of those risks. He stresses that public intellectuals must not only be able to work on the policy alternatives under broad consideration, but must be able to offer a counter-agenda with entirely new alternatives. Public intellectuals rarely blend neatly into the policy world (Epstein 2000). They are reluctant to get involved, are seen as abrasive once they do. Indeed, public intellectuals often validate their reluctance, since they can rarely see that their contributions have any policy effect. In particular, Ahearne examines these questions through the prism of France since the founding of the Fifth Republic in 1958. The insights are often applicable to the paucity of public intellectual involvement in the U.S. Our peace lenses can rarely fix on the *rara avis* of the public peace intellectual in flight—those lenses can be the action research "meant to be a double-sided process of research, self research and education directed at individual empowerment and collective empowerment and/or emancipation" (Boog 2003, 426).

A few do bring a specialized, highly informed corpus of information into the public discourse. Allahwala and Keil (2005) introduce us to the World Social Forum, a grassroots gathering held simultaneously to the World Economic Forum, the latter for the elites, the former for the masses. More than 120,000 people from around the world participated in person in 2005 in Porto Alegre, Brazil, and the gathering featured a number of public intellectuals whose allegiance and analysis is clearly to the challenger groups, clearly toward peace and economic justice. While academics often seem to serve the interests of the elites—if only by sequestering their fine minds in ivory towers—the public intellectuals who have helped power the World Social Forum have been instrumental in the development of "the other superpower," that is, the coalition of nongovernmental groups that can achieve results and policy change from the bottom-up. Social learning theory is critical to this process. (Lave 1996; Illeris 2003).

Peace cannot be left to the generals; "it must be part and parcel of the democratic process" (Boyce and O'Donnell 2007, 276), and therefore requires analysis that is tuned to democracy. Policy comes about via politics (Sroufe 1995) and the distinction helps locate policy goals and process in realism. That realism involves recognizing opportunity and understanding the resource mobilization required to use the existing structures (e.g., "religious, educational, and occupational") to assist any challenger message and movement (Zunes, Kurtz and Asher 1999, 304).

Rational choices relate to a complex set of factors (Boyd, Crowson and van Geel 1995); if our professors can be convinced that the choice to participate in public discourse will gain (some for them, some for their profession, some for society) and that the risks can be minimized, then the tipping point toward choosing involvement can be a part of promoting and implementing a new level of peace professional civic engagement. This may relate to institutional theory and the deep understanding of how our educational institutions are changing and how they can become more positive influences (Rowan and Miskel 1999; Boyer 2002). This is toward changing the paradigm of how the politics of education happens; at present it is entirely explicable by, and follows the principles of, political science (Wong 1995). The very methods advocated in our field of Peace and Conflict Studies are a part of that potential shift (Galtung 2004). It would make a great deal of sense, as the resources invested in our professors really represent a public good that cannot properly be left to the market. "These public goods are indivisible and nonexclusive" (Cochran and Malone 2005, 19).

McCutcheon (2005) is the curmudgeon who encourages public intellectuals to reconsider, and understand how much their intellectual content will be attenuated when they enter public discourse. He writes of the ways in which public intellectuals in his field—religion—must simplify and dumb down concepts and historical interpretation in order to make their points understandable in the public arena. McCutcheon only examines Bush challengers, and in particular, Bruce Lincoln, who had expressed great reluctance toward the entire phenomenon of public intellectualism prior to the Bush administration. McCutcheon's insights hold public scholars quite accountable for the quality and integrity of their work.

Anthropologist Carla Freeman (2000) acknowledges the drawbacks for her discipline but believes the quality of scholarship relies upon discipline and that doesn't vanish as a result of engaging in public scholarship unless a person is drifting from the discipline. In short, she holds the "both/and" possibility, not either/or. Asian scholar David Kelly (2006) is less sanguine, merely pointing to the reciprocity of the diminution of scholarship once it becomes public and the elevated education of the public—positing a bit of a meeting-in-the-middle analysis. David Goa (2005), a religion professor, notes that Muslim head covering, destruction of Buddhist statues, Danish editorial cartoons, President Bush's public religious proclamations and many more issues are simply inadequately thought through without the scholars' contributions.

Some might argue that scholars don't have to "go public" in order to make a difference; indeed, they chose a life of making a deep difference in the quality of education for each student in whatever institution they teach. But higher levels of education in the classroom may not translate into a more educated electorate, and if an educator is presenting an alternative, challenger body of information to a handful of students every year, that is not the same as offering current analysis and options that can save us from destructive conflict. Ideas of education and independent thinking are often incorrect assumptions. Green, Preston, and Janmaat (2006) ask and present data and interpretation on some of these key questions that illuminate the idea of the value of public scholarship. Does social cohesion relate to education? If so, how? These authors attack the extant theories of some of the most important researchers, from Putnam to Piaget. They do so quantitatively, using massive amounts of data gathered cross-nationally under the rubric of World Values. Each chapter analyzes another section of related data on another aspect of the overarching topic of education as it plays into a society and governance either more or less oppressive or democratic or conflictual or harmonious.

The scholarly work is private in one sense and rightly public in another. Or, as one university mottos: "Let knowledge serve the city." If all concerned actors are not heard, the chance for peace and democracy wanes (Cousens and Kumar 2001). May and Mumby (2005) note that learning about how organizations communicate is not "a 'canon' per se but, rather…a struggle for competing ideas" (265). Our society is not able to take advantage of the actual potential competition in a marketplace with such a paucity and narrow range.

A constant and evolving rightwing series of initiatives tends to silence academic voices with a gender, race and peace analysis (Cohen 2008). There are at least three right-wing websites focused on attacking peace professors. They are all founded by former Marxist, now-Neocon, David Horowitz and are all militaristic, essentializing, and engage in little other than ad hominem attack. The list of targeted professors includes two basic strands: peace professors and professors from the Middle East.

Another problem is the reticence of most mainstream media to print peace-oriented commentary. The blood-brain barrier between editorial and advertising (or ownership) may be ideologically robust, but may be porous and irrelevant at times in real life. Self-censoring editors and reporters who are often well educated in journalistic ethics are still small cogs in the vast corporate media and usually do not wish to risk career security any more than do employed professors.

Finally, Hall (1992) notes that another serious barrier to getting the voices of peace into the mainstream media is that any ethical or moral challenge to those in power is viewed askance by the masses of Americans.

We Shall Overcome (We Hope)

Issues of conflict are clearly primary for peace scholars; our contribution is known as constructive conflict (Kriesberg 2007). Traditional statecraft has produced a great deal of destructive conflict and there is an unbroken line of those who engage in orchestrating that destruction and thinking about it, in modern times from von Clausewitz through Kissinger, Albright, Bush and Cheney. Peace researchers explore alternatives to that model, and look at power differently. We consider the latent power of the people in any society and in fact look particularly hard at how "powerless" peoples have swept aside oppressors. We also find power in professional conflict resolution that adheres to principles of inclusion, empathy, generosity and agreements based on fairness that all stakeholders ultimately approve. This is the new realism.

What we are finding nowadays in public policy is that our definition of self-interest is changing, and so our basic philosophy vis-à-vis policy change—which is largely about conflict—is shifting as well. We used to focus on adversarial conflict with a nod to the smoky cloakroom personal relationships that were always associated with corrupt mutual backscratching pork. The attention now is on collaborative learning— moving our educational models into another arena and improving upon them in both. "Cognitive psychology, today's dominant theory, emphasizes the social nature of learning and the fact that human being 'construct' their own knowledge as they learn" (Fowler 2004, 175). The peace goal is to move that collaboration from the backrooms and boardrooms to public conversation so that the public becomes an informed party.

It is already happening in the parallel field of environmental policy problem-solving. Agranoff and McGuire (2003) take the synthesis of theories from Daniels and Walker (2001) and study many cases, "framed from many theoretical and applied management perspectives" (20). They note well that collaboration now (at last) needs no justification in policy management, especially since the trend is toward "prominence of knowledge as a factor in social and economic production, while land, labor, and capital are becoming secondary factors," (25) putting collaborative public management "on the front lines of the transformation from the traditional concept of bureaucracy" (38).

Strategy and Tactics: The Day the Earth Stood Still

> In the councils of government, we must guard against the acquisition of unwarranted influence, whether sought or unsought, by the military-industrial complex. The potential for the disastrous rise of misplaced power exists and will persist. We must never let the weight of this combination endanger our liberties or democratic processes. We should take nothing for granted.—Dwight D. Eisenhower, Farewell Address, 1961

Marshall and Gerstl-Pepin (2005) give hope from the notion of punctuated equilibrium; that is, society is ripe, at times, for a massive policy shift. This need not take decades. Like surfers, we need to anticipate the waves of public sentiment so we can both amplify and ride them toward an analysis that will place much higher value on dialog, nonviolence and collaborative learning problem-solving. The Bush-Obama shift signals this, with more emphasis on outreach (e.g. the 2009 historic Nowruz greeting to the people of Iran).

Louis Kriesberg (2007) points to the need to take the initiative. Help people develop strong identity with your challenger peace message and then take swift action in the moment when minds are being made up, appealing to that peace identity in people. This sets up the "rally round the flag" support for the challenge before the war seizes that advantage (188). Peace scholars ought to be strenuously working to develop that identity with an insistence that the U.S. stay out of war with Iran, for example. This, and our efforts to reverse U.S. military commitment to occupying Afghanistan, are our next big opportunities to affect public policy. With economic, historical and psychological evidentiary triangulation, we can make a cogent, even dispositive argument (Mintrom 2003).

Historically, the stakeholder coalition to work against violent conflict has been largely limited to anticonscriptionalists, religious objectors, anti-militarists, anti-imperialists, internationalists, and generally those with an ideological commitment to nonviolence (Leon-Guerra 2005). Adding to this coalition by appealing to international norms and law as they affect policy (Malone and Khong 2003) or through economic or sociological or medical argument, is our function. Public peace scholars can help build this coalition from a historic minority to a sustainable majority. This is similar to the Habermas (1994) concept of public sphere, where citizens decide how to govern within a "metaphorical space" (Marshall and Gerstl-Pepin 2005, 84). Peace education should change the master narrative; the op-ed is precisely where the writer constructs a new framework (Treadwell and Treadwell 2005).

> It could be argued from the perspective of other national intellectual traditions that the term "public intellectual" is redundant. In the United States, however, where intellectual life was early institutionalized as professional academic life, the "public intellectual" indexes a well-understood set of issues about how intellectual life should be practiced, and it directs our specific attention to the intersections of the academic and journalistic fields. —Eleanor Townsley (2006, 39)

What are the draws and dangers of public intellectualism in general? Jonathan Lane is himself a public intellectual with a background both in the academy and as a journalist, so his scholarly analysis (2005) of two works—a memoir of Daniel Ellsberg's spectacular revelation of the lies that were indispensable in the architecture of the Vietnam War and Richard Posner's 2003 book on the decline of the public intellectual—was written as someone with a foot in both worlds. He looks at the role of the insider intellectual—Ellsberg in this case—who sees the problem with lack of public scrutiny (a nation lied to enters and then descends further and further into an unjust and unwinnable war), and the clear necessity of his specific public role. The broader role of the public intellectual who has authority beyond the specific is problematic and Lane also examines that.

> We must distinguish two different roles for the intellectual, [even though] these often go together: the intellectual in search of truth and the intellectual in search of power. The former is, perhaps, most similar to the artist. The latter is a quite different type and is possibly the main constituent of the "new class" in all countries, irrespective of their political systems.—Johan Galtung (Galtung 2002, 65)

Those in power almost always fear the challenger in search of the truth and almost always try to employ the intellectual in search of personal power within a system that rewards intellectual justification of the status quo. While Jules Chametsky (2004) believes the public intellectual to be a relatively new substantive phenomenon with individual pioneers ("Certainly Voltaire was one, and Diderot and the Encyclopedists who aimed with reason to combat superstition and religious obscurantism were others" (211)), this dynamic on an individual level probably even precedes Socrates, the exemplar of the public intellectual who paid with everything for his unwillingness to seek or even abide unjust power. On the other hand, Aristotle was in some ways an early member of the intelligentsia—declarations to the contrary (Ozick 1995) notwithstanding—declaring with great xenophobia and jingoism that the only just war was one fought against non-Hellenes. The Bishop of Hippo, St. Augustine, was the first successful Christian intelligentsia to favor using the military, providing them with the Just War doctrine that excused everything the Holy Roman Empire was doing while invalidating challenges to it. Augustine lived; Socrates died. The public intellectual who challenges war will do so risking opprobrium and vindictiveness of the war system—a system that ignores the waning peace movement in its discontinuity between wars and rejects it forcefully as it waxes in times of war (Young 2000).

Judith André, in her 2005 review of Martha Nussbaum's 2004 book, *Hiding from humanity: Disgust, shame, and the law*, notes some of the other constraints upon those who might consider attempting to be public intellectuals:

> Nussbaum is one of our few contemporary public intellectuals: grounded in traditional academic disciplines (in her case, both philosophy and the classics), she is never confined to their boundaries; well read in many fields, she writes accessibly for the general educated public. (Nussbaum holds a primary appointment at the Law School of the University of Chicago, but is also on the faculty of its Philosophy Department and Divinity School.) There are risks in such a role, the risks of eclecticism and superficiality, but the role is an important one (52).

Part of the point is to inform those masses who really want peace but don't know how to argue for it. When public intellectuals stand alone they are weak and ineffective. Transforming a Don Quixote into a political force is, in some ways, a matter of simple numbers. One intellectual arguing publicly is a crackpot. Ten are dissidents. One hundred are the reasoned voice of a movement and a thousand help lead that movement to victory. Tom Hayden notes that "the Machiavellians are few, and

multitudes are diverse" (2007, 216). The constraints fall away as the
power ratio shifts.

Part of this power equation and willingness to go out on a limb
revolves around the need to start that positive feedback loop from research
to public expression and approbation and the resultant increase in
research—if that can be achieved. For instance, utilizing the 2005 study by
Karatnycky as robust, peer-reviewed research that reveals the advantages
of waging conflict with nonviolence is a way to encourage further research
and dissemination of that peace research. It offers much more positive
proof that these methods work better than shooting and bombing, which is
going to tend to strengthen our peace curricula and ability to present
alternatives cogently. Or, from the qualitative side, the 1998 edited Smith-
Christopher compilation of nonviolence in religious traditions can help us
overcome the Muslim-as-violent-religious-warrior image. Of course,
overcoming our own self-image as a violent people who are obligated to
police the world is another key. Looking toward the examples of conflict
leadership elsewhere can help us with this task (Kriesberg 2007).

Who Has Done Public Peace Scholarship?

There are hundreds of public peace scholars. Select examples include
Mohandas K. Gandhi (Juergensmeyer 2005), Edward Said (Zeleza 2005),
Todd Gitlin 2004), George Lakoff (2004), Phyllis Bennis (2003), Steve
Breyman (2001), John Paul Lederach (1997), Staughton Lynd (1997),
Betty Reardon (1988), and many more have taken their intellectual
findings to the public. Colman McCarthy is the best-known (and perhaps
the only) one who made the journey in reverse: he spent 28 years as a
syndicated columnist and gradually moved into the classroom to teach
peace in his 'retirement' (McCarthy 2002, *xi*).

Identifying the latent pool of public peace scholars will provide paths
to research about the potential for more public peace scholarship. There
are more than 400 professors in the U.S. who belong to the Peace and
Justice Studies Association and many more who teach related courses in
various fields. There are many hundreds of peace professionals who work
in positions as disparate as analysts, activists, democracy capacity-
builders, humanitarian aid workers and many more. Almost none wanted
the Iraq war to happen, yet were not heard above the din of the drivers to
war.

Conclusion

Our war system is in need of a peace analysis, and peace professionals are positioned to make a significant contribution to that process. This notion, if implemented, would help us consolidate and improve our model of civic engagement as an organization and as individual professors. It would serve to help legitimate the field and make it relevant to more than simple well wishers and navel-gazers. While the downsides to public scholarship must be acknowledged, they clearly do not outweigh the obligation and opportunity (Halwani 2002) before us today. This chapter proposes a modest agenda to foster this process, but one that is worthy of the field of potential public peace intellectuals in a time of unjust war.

References

Ackerman, P., and J. DuVall. 2000. *A force more powerful: A century of nonviolent conflict*. New York: St. Martin's Press.

Agranoff, R. and M. McGuire. 2003. *Collaborative public management: New strategies for local governments*. Washington DC: Georgetown Press.

Ahearne, J. 2006. Notes from a French perspective. *International Journal of Cultural Policy* 12 (1):1-15.

Allahwala, A. and R. Keil. 2005. "Introduction to a Debate on the World Social Forum," *International Journal of Urban and Regional Research* 29 (2):409-416.

André, J. 2005. "Disgust, Dignity, and a Public Intellectual," *Criminal Justice Ethics* 24 (1):52-57.

Barash, D. P., ed. 2000. *Approaches to peace: A reader in peace studies*. New York: Oxford University Press.

Bennis, P.. 2003. *Before and after: US foreign policy and the war on terrorism*. New York: Olive Branch Press.

Boog, B. W. M. 2003. The emancipatory character of action research, its history and the present state of the art. *Journal of Community & Applied Social Psychology* 13 (6):426-438.

Boyce, J. K. and M. O'Donnell, Eds. 2007. *Peace and the public purse: Economic policies for postwar statebuilding*. Boulder, CO: Lynne Rienner Publishers.

Boyd, W. L., R. L. Crowson, and T. van Geel, T. 1995. Rational choice theory and the politics of education: Promise and limitations. In *The study of educational politics: The 1994 commemorative yearbook of the Politics of Education Association (1969-1994)*, eds. J.D. Scribner and D.H. Layton and Politics of Education Association (127-145). Washington, DC: Falmer Press..

Boyer, W. H. 2002. *Education for the twenty-first century*. San Francisco: Caddo Gap Press.

Brantlinger, P. 2003. Professors and public intellectuals in the information age. *Shofar: An Interdisciplinary Journal of Jewish Studies* 2 *(*3):122.

Breyman, S.. 2001. *Why movements matter: The West German peace movement and U.S. arms control policy*. Albany NY: State University of New York Press.

Byrne, E. F. 2005. The 2003 U.S. invasion of Iraq: Militarism in the service of geopolitics." In *Justice and violence: Political violence, pacifism and cultural transformation,* eds. A. Eickelmann, E. Nelson, and T. Lansford (pp.). Burlington, VT: Ashgate.

Carr, C.. 2007, May 2. In-class observation, Portland State University.

—. 2007, May 15. Personal conversation.

Chametzky, J.. 2004. Public intellectuals - now and then. *Melus 29(* 3):211-226.

Cochran, C. L. and E. F. Malone. 2005. *Public policy: Perspectives and choices* 3rd ed.. Boulder, CO: Lynne Rienner.

Cohen, P.. 2008. Conservatives try new tack on campuses. Nytimes.com. September 22.

Cortright, D.. 2006. *Gandhi and beyond: Nonviolence for an age of terrorism*. Boulder, CO: Paradigm Publishers.

Cousens, E. M., and C. Kumar, C., Eds. 2001. *Peacebuilding as politics: Cultivating peace in fragile societies.* Boulder, CO: Lynne Rienner.

Daniels, S. E., and G. B. Walker. 2001. *Working through environmental conflict: The collaborative learning approach*. Westport, CT: Praeger.

Eisenhower, D. D. 1961. Farewell address. http://coursesa.matrix.msu.edu/~hst306/documents/indust.html.

Epstein, J. 2000. Intellectuals—Public and Otherwise. *Commentary*, 109 (5):46-49.

Fisher, R., and W. Ury. 1991. *Getting to yes: Negotiating agreement without giving in..* 2nd ed. New York: Penguin Books.

Fowler, F. C. 2004. *Policy studies for educational leaders: An introduction*. 2nd ed. Upper Saddle River, NJ: Pearson Prentice Hall.

Freire, P. 2000. *Pedagogy of the oppressed*. New York: The Continuum International Publishing Group Inc.

Freeman, C. 2000. Comments. *Current Anthropology 41*(2):181-182.

Galtung, J. 2002. The role of the intellectual II—This time as other-criticism. *Higher Education in Europe 27* (1):65-68.

—. 2004. *Transcend and transform: An introduction to conflict work.* Boulder, CO: Paradigm Publishers.

Gitlin, T. 2006. The necessity of public intellectuals. *Raritan 26* (1):123-136.

Goa, D. 2005. Editorial introduction. *Material Religion. 1 (*2):251-252.

Grafton, A.. 2001. The public intellectual and the American University. *American Scholar 70* (4):41.

Green, A., J. Preston, and J. G. Janmaat. 2006. *Education, equality and social cohesion: A comparative analysis.* New York: Palgrave Macmillan.

Hall, M. K. 1992. CALCAV and religious opposition to the Vietnam War. In *Give peace a chance: Exploring the Vietnam antiwar movement,* eds. M. Small and W. D. Hoover. Syracuse, NY: Syracuse University Press.

Halwani, R.. 2002. Introduction to the Philosopher as Public Intellectual. *Metaphilosophy* 33 (5):495-501.

Hayden, T.. 2007. *Ending the war in Iraq.* New York, NY: Akashic Books.

Horowitz websites:
http://www.horowitzfreedomcenter.org/;
http://www.frontpagemag.com/;
http://www.studentsforacademicfreedom.org;
http://www.discoverthenetworks.org/IndividualDesc.asp?type=aca

Illeris, K.. 2003. Towards a contemporary and comprehensive theory of learning. *International Journal of Lifelong Education* 22 (4):396-406.

Jandt, F. E. 2004. *An introduction to intercultural communication: Identities in a global community.* 4th ed. Thousand Oaks, CA: Sage Publications.

Jones, T. S. and R. Brinkert. 2008. *Conflict coaching: Conflict management strategies and skills for the individual.* Thousand Oaks, CA: Sage Publications.

Juergensmeyer, M. 2005. *Gandhi's way: A handbook of conflict resolution.* Berkeley. CA: University of California Press.

Karatnycky, A. 2005. *How freedom is won: From civic resistance to durable democracy.* New York, NY: Freedom House.

Kelly, D. 2006. Citizen movements and China's public intellectuals in the Hu-Wen era. *Pacific Affairs 79* (2):183-204.

Kozol, J. 1991. *Savage inequalities: Children in America's schools.* New York: Crown Publishers.

Kriesberg, L.. 2007. *Constructive conflicts: From escalation to resolution.* Lanham, MD: Rowman and Littlefield.

Lakoff, G. 2004. *Don't think of an elephant: Know your values and frame the debate*. White River Junction, VT: Chelsea Green Publishing.

Lane, J. 2005. Loyalty, democracy and the public intellectual. *Minerva: A Review of Science, Learning and Policy,* 43 (1): 73-85.

Lave, J. 1996. Teaching, as learning, in practice. *Mind, Culture & Activity* 3 (3):149-164.

Lederach, J. P. 1997. *Building peace: Sustainable reconciliation in divided societies*. Washington, DC: United States Institute of Peace Press.

Leon-Guerrero, A. 2005. *Social problems: Community, policy, and social action*. Thousand Oaks, CA: Pine Forge Press.

Lynd, S. 1997. *Living inside our hope: A steadfast radical's thoughts on rebuilding the movement*. Ithaca, NY: Cornell University Press.

Malone, D. M., and Y. F. Khong, Y. F., eds. 2003. *Unilateralism and U. S. foreign policy: International perspectives*. Boulder, CO: Lynne Rienner Publishers, Inc.

Marshall, C., and C. Gerstl-Pepin. 2005. *Re-framing educational politics for social justice*. Boston: Pearson Education, Inc.

May, S. and Mumby, D. K., eds. 2005. *Engaging organizational communication: Theory and research, multiple perspectives*. Thousand Oaks, CA: Sage Publications.

McCarthy, C. 2002. *I'd rather teach peace*. Maryknoll NY: Orbis Books.

McCutcheon, R. T. 2005. Affinities, Benefits, and Costs: The ABCS of Good Scholars Gone Public. *Method and Theory in the Study of Religion* 17(1):27-43.

Mintrom, M. 2003. *People skills for policy analysts*. Washington DC: Georgetown University Press.

Ozick, C. 1995. Public and private intellectuals. *American Scholar 64* (3): 353.

Parsi, K. P., and K. E. Geraghty. 2004. The Bioethicist as Public Intellectual. *The American Journal of Bioethics 4* (1):W17-W23.

Phillips, D.C., and Jonas F. Soltis. 2004. *Perspectives on learning*. 4th ed. New York: Teachers College Press.

Pinsker, S. 1995. The public intellectual as beleaguered celebrity. *Academic Questions* 8 (4):14-17.

Posner, R. A. 2003. *Public intellectuals: A study of decline*. Cambridge MA: Harvard University Press.

Reardon, B. A., ed. 1988. *Comprehensive peace education: Educating for global responsibility*. New York: Teachers College Press.

Reuters. 2007, May 20. Carter criticizes Bush and Blair on war in Iraq. www.nytimes.com/.

Rowan, B. and C. G. Miskel. 1999. Institutional theory and the study of educational organizations. In *Handbook of Research on Educational Administration : A Project of the American Educational Research Association.* 2nd ed. eds. J. Murphy and K. S. Louis. San Francisco (359-383). Jossey-Bass Publishers.

Sharp, G. 1973. *The politics of nonviolent action: Part one: Power and struggle.* Boston: Porter Sargent Publishers.

Skąpska, G. 2002. Beyond Arrogance and Subordination to the 'System': On Public Intellectual, Power, Morality, and Law. *Law & Society Review* 36 (1):45-50.

Smith-Christopher, D. L., ed. 2007. *Subverting hatred: The challenge of nonviolence in religious traditions.* 2nd ed. Maryknoll, NY: Orbis Books.

Smyth, J., and R. Hattam. 2000. Intellectual as Hustler: Researching against the grain of the market. *British Educational Research Journal* 26 (2):157-175.

Sroufe, G. 1995. Politics of education at the federal level. In *The study of educational politics: The 1994 Commemorative Yearbook of the Politics of Education Association (1969-1994)*, eds. J.D. Scribner and D.H. Layton and Politics of Education Association (75-88). Washington, DC: Falmer Press.

Townsley, E. 2006. The public intellectual trope in the United States. *American Sociologist 37* (3):39-66.

Treadwell, D., and J. B. Treadwell. 2005. *Public relations writing: Principles in practice.* 2nd ed. Thousand Oaks, CA: Sage Publications.

Umbreit, M. S. 1995. *Mediating interpersonal conflict: A pathway to peace.* West Concord, MN: CPI Publishing.

Weil, S. 1994. Simone Weil: Revolutionary war. In *Peace/mir: An anthology of historic alternatives to war,* ed. C. Chatfield and R. Ilukhina (250-252). Syracuse, NY: Syracuse University Press. Originally published in *Reflections on war* in 1933.

Wong, K.K. 1995. The politics of education: From political science to multidisciplinary inquiry. In *The study of educational politics: The 1994 commemorative yearbook of the Politics of Education Association (1969-1994)*, eds. J.D. Scribner and D.H. Layton and Politics of Education Association (127-145). Washington, DC: Falmer Press.

Young, N. N. 1999. Peace movements in history. In *Approaches to peace: A reader in peace studies*, ed. David P. Barash (228-236). New York: Oxford University Press.

Zeleza, P. T. 2005. The politics and poetics of exile: Edward Said in Africa. *Research in African Literatures 36* (3):1-22.

Zunes, S., L. R. Kurtz, and S. B. Asher. 1999. *Nonviolent social movements: A geographical perspective.* Malden, MA: Blackwell Publishers.

CHAPTER TEN

PIANOS FOR PEACE:
A CONVERSATION

PEARL HUNT

On February 15, 2003, at least 35,000 people from all walks of life marched in the streets of Vancouver, British Columbia as part of the *International Day of Action* to say *No to War on Iraq*. The Vancouver contingency was part of more than 50 million who marched in over 600 events on five continents around the world. Bruce Child, former Australian Senator and a co-convenor of the *Walk Against the War Coalition*, declared on the Evatt Foundation Web site: "We are looking at the largest protest in world history: a stunning manifestation of globalization from below." It was certainly a day for the history books—a day where millions connected on a multinational plane to promote peace. Consequently, on February 17, 2003, *The New York Times* declared "...there may still be two superpowers on the planet: the United States and world public opinion."

The weather in Vancouver on that February day was damp and cool; the sun trying at times to break through the clouds. The peace march began at Library Square and proceeded through the downtown core to the Art Gallery (the former Vancouver Court House) where speakers spoke and musicians played for several more hours. The marchers eventually dispersed leaving the courthouse steps stone silent. In response to this march, I wrote a piano composition entitled *Pianos for Peace*, not only to celebrate the "power of the people", but also to connect myself and my piano students to the marches. Even though we weren't able to attend in person, making music created a metaphysical space that enabled us to become part of the march in spirit.

What is it about music that makes it such a powerful force of engagement, connection and transformation? The dynamics of music as transformative and the pervasiveness of music as social/historical representations of culture indicate that music continues to be a major component of social change. Yet, how music operates within a theoretical critical context is seldom discussed. Musician and scholar, George Lewis, introducing Pasler's (2008) *Writing Through Music,* acknowledges that:

> In contrast to previous eras, the work of many of the best known public intellectuals of our time seem distanced from musical considerations, and from new and experimental music in particular. As a result the practice of culturally and philosophically theorizing contemporary nonliterary, nonvisual texts tends to become marginalized and devalued in the public sphere —- not because music scholars are not producing these works but, perhaps, simply because it is somehow assumed that music has little to teach us about the critical issues of our time, (Lewis 2008, vii).

A Conversation trough Disciplines

This chapter then, attempts to begin a *conversation* whereby we look seriously at music's abilities to inform, intervene in and articulate critical social justice praxis. Using a conversation, rather than an argument, to negotiate differences is an idea that cultural theorist, Kwame Anthony Appiah, promotes in *Cosmopolisms* (2006). "Cosmopolitanism begins with the simple idea that in the human community, as in national communities, we need to develop habits of coexistence: conversation in its older meaning, of living together, association" (Appiah 2006, xix).

In many ways Appiah's model of conversation echoes that of Paulo Freire's (1970) formative work on the dialogic mode articulated in *Pedagogy of the Oppressed.* "Founding itself upon love, humility and faith, dialogue becomes a horizontal relationship of which mutual trust between dialoguers is the logical consequence. Trust is established by dialogue" (Freire 1970, 79-80). Drawing on Freire's dialogic model, peace educator Betty Reardon (1988) in her pioneering text, *Comprehensive Peace Education: Educating for Global Responsibility,* also acknowledges the benefits of conversation as a tool for establishing trust. Reardon suggests a collective community based approach to conversation that "connotes a community of inquirers, sharing questions and insights, mutually responsible for creating the knowledge necessary to the changes our common values impel us to seek" (Reardon 1988, 49). Conversation in this capacity becomes both pedagogy and a mode of peacemaking.

Jack Mezirow (2000) in *Learning as Transformation: Critical Perspectives on a Theory in Progress,* suggests that academia presents an ideal model for "reflective discourse." However, academia is still structured on a monastic (patriarchal) "culture of polarized argumentation in which reality is dichotomized and in which winning an argument seems to be more important than understanding different ways of thinking and reaching consensus" (Mezirow 2000, 64). Because of the essentially competitive nature of academia, introducing the idea of *conversation* versus *argument* in this discussion can open up possibilities within the questions that we ask and can potentially better serve transformative learning, educational praxis and social change.

Grossberg (1997), regarding the formulation of questions, additionally reiterates the elitist atmosphere of academia: "The elitism of the intellectual comes not merely from our assumption that we already know the answers but even more, from our assumption that we already know the questions" (Grossberg 1997, 389). So, in order to open up this conversation, I am implementing what Pasler refers to as *question spaces*. Question spaces operate somewhat differently than questions. Whereas questions tend to be oriented in a given direction and motivated by a linear force, question spaces allows what can be learned by chance. "To the extent that the exploration of such spaces unveils interaction and networks of connection between people, practices, and art works, question spaces allow for multiple linearities, nonlinearities, and simultaneities" (Pasler 2008, 9). Question spaces then broaden our awareness of the vague, presupposed and implied involved in any question and more fully embraces the partial nature of understanding. Pasler suggests that such a method presumes that "understanding is not just an articulation, rediscovery or ascription of meaning through thought or discourse but is instead *"transformative, productive* of new meanings" (Pasler's italics p. 10). If being accountable to complexity is necessary for transformative learning, then question spaces can provide the open terrain for this inquiry of music and social justice praxis with the understanding that the questions themselves are always already partial and incomplete. Since social justice praxis involves the articulation of theory and action, a conversation/dialogue that encourages thinking critically about music and its relationship to critical pedagogy could inform/become a model of social justice praxis.

What Is Music, Anyway?

Musician and scholar, John Cage, in his *Autobiographical Statement,* articulates his process of making music: "My favorite music is the music I haven't yet heard. I don't hear the music I write. I write in order to hear the music I haven't yet heard!" (Cage 1990, 75). Cage's revolutionary utilization of sound/noisescapes pushed the boundaries not only of how music is created but also of what actually constitutes music. For the purpose of this discussion, I am offering a very broad definition of music as it is used in music making. My definition includes: musical instrumentation, composition, songs, sampling, lyrics, and vocalizing. Yet, music is more than its acoustics; it also operates within and upon emotional paradigms. Perhaps, a definition that most closely describes music, a word Cage himself used to describe music's affect, is "*accord* suggesting a connection, a relationship, a being-in-accord with others, with what is, with what happens" (2008, 176).

Neuroscientist and musician Daniel J. Levitin (2008) in his latest popular writing, *The World in Six Songs: How the Musical Brain Created Human Nature,* recognizes the centrality of music as it comes to define humans through generations of evolution:

> Music, I argue is not simply a distraction or a pastime, but a core element of our identity as a species, an activity that paved the way for more complex behaviors such as language, large-scale cooperative undertakings, and passing down of important information from one generation to the next (Levin 2008, 3).

The centrality and pervasiveness of music in our everyday lives can be viewed (or heard as the case may be) as expressions of our identity and tactics for social change. David Huron notes there is no known culture now or anytime in the past that lacks music, and some of the oldest human-made artifacts found at archaeological sites are musical instruments. "Music is important in the daily lives of most people in the world, and has been throughout history" (Levitin 2008, 2). Indeed, examples of the centrality of music as a connective dynamic can be found throughout 20th century North American social/historical narratives of social change such as the protest song "Bread and Roses", which was inspired by a banner carried by a group of young female strikers during the 1912 walkout in the textile district of Lawrence, Massachusetts. The banner's slogan, "We want bread and roses, too" moved poet James Oppenheim to write "Bread and Roses", which was set to music by Caroline Kohlsaat and is still sung every March 8, on International Women's Day:

> As we come marching, marching, in the beauty of the day
> A million darkened kitchens, a thousand mill lofts gray
> Are touched with all the radiance that a sudden sun discloses
> For the people hear us singing, bread and roses, bread and roses.

Throughout the twentieth century the practice of "everyday" music was largely communal/collectively driven—around kitchen tables, front parlors, on the picket line and, in particular, through worship. One of the most popular and often sung anthems of social change we know today has its roots in a 1903 Baptist hymn written by the Reverent Charles Tindley entitled, "I'll Overcome Some Day." There are numerous other examples of social change songs such as Phil Ochs' (1965) *I Ain't Marching Anymore*, in response to the Vietnam War; Joni Michelle's (1972) *Big Yellow Taxi*, her response to the environmental degradation of southern California; Buffy St. Marie's (1964) *Universal Soldier*, which became the anthem for the peace movement in Canada during the 1980's and John Lennon's (1971) legendary peace song, *Imagine*. As we progress into the twenty-first century, music in the western world is more often accessed on a virtual site, such as You Tube, where performances of all the above songs can be found. One of the most remarkable, moving and innovative musical resources available through the internet is Playing for Change: Peace Through Music (www.playingforchange.com) - a multimedia movement created to connect, inspire and bring peace to the world through music.

If we can agree (or at least temporarily suspend judgment) on the centrality of music within our social/historical narrative, it is possible to imagine music as a tool to analyze contemporary critical issues whose importance cuts across fields—an analysis that invokes transdisciplinarity or interdisciplinary methods. Cultural theorists Arnold Shepperson and Keyan Tomaselli urge us to acknowledge that since concrete social problems ignore disciplinary fences, then solutions to these problems should also traverse disciplinary fences. "Transdisciplinarity acknowledges the specific insights of particular disciplines with the view to establishing their dialectical relations across specific social issues in an attempt to obtain a more integrated understanding of the human context in its multiple forms and dimensions" (Shepperson & Tomaselli 2004, 261).

Drawing on Cultural Studies

Building on the idea of using question spaces and a transdisciplinary approach to analysis, I want to now bring a cultural studies framework towards music and social justice pedagogy—a framework that is, as Grossberg (1997) suggests, "willing to take the risk of making connections, drawing lines, mapping articulations between domains, discourse and practices, to see what will work both theoretically and politically" (Grossberg 1997, 386). Cultural studies, according to Grossberg, starts where the people are, but "it does not assume that either they or we know the answers" (Grossberg 1997, 388). Cultural studies does assume a "reality that is constantly reworked by and only made available through cultural practices" (Grossberg 1997, 379).

How then do we define cultural practices and what constitutes cultural practices, as the construct of *culture* itself is a highly contested term? Because the very concept of culture is contextual and caught between social formation, everyday life, and representational practices, for our conversation I am suggesting we view culture as a *process* or as Raymond Williams (1958/1989) proposes "the community of process" and that cultural studies is, as Grossberg affirms, "the most human of all processes, the process of communication, which, it turns out, is the process of meaning and production" (Grossberg 1998, 73). This definition supports the idea that cultural studies provides an ideal framework to promote the idea of conversation. Cultural studies then is a process of communicating meanings through conversation, using many disciplines to articulate a way of making sense of the world. In short, "cultural studies is an attempt to answer the most basic question: *'What's Going On'* " (Grossberg 1998, 67). Grossberg's intentional use of Marvin's Gaye's (1971) title to his poignant protest album, *What's Going On,* demonstrates not only the pervasiveness of popular music as represented in popular culture, but also of how the lyrics of music become embedded in our *everyday language.* More importantly though, this example demonstrates how song lyrics emerge and evolve through history as a *dynamic* component of our everyday lives.

Tia DeNora (2003) in *Music in Everyday Life* notes that "we have very little sense of how music features within social process and next to no data on how real people actually press music into action in particular social spaces and temporal settings"(DeNora 2003, x). DeNora acknowledges this neglect is as common in the social sciences (with its cognitive bias) as in the arts and humanities (with their emphasis on text-objects). However, cultural studies appears to be one site that has, from time to time, taken up music as it pertains to identity formation and agency. For example, music as popular narrative of social/historical everyday representations is highlighted in Paul Willis's (1978) ethnography, *Profane Culture,* which conceives music as an active ingredient of social formation in the everyday lives of the working class 1960's British "bike boys" and middle class "hippies". Willis' study was one of the first critical ethnographies to investigate popular music in everyday life and was pioneering in its demonstration of how music does more than depict or embody values. It portrayed music as *active* and *dynamic.* "It signaled a shift in focus from [viewing music as] aesthetic objects and their content (static) to the cultural practices in and through which aesthetic materials were appropriated and used (dynamic) to produce social life" (DeNora 2003, 7). Music then can be characterized not only by sound but by *action*, and by *interaction* among makers of music in everyday practices.

Lee Hirsch's remarkable film, *Amandla! A Revolution in Four Part Harmony* (2002), demonstrates music making's liberating abilities during the apartheid period in South Africa as does Matt Mochary and Jeff Zimbalist film, *Favela Rising* (2005), which chronicles the formation of Afro-Reggae groups to provide music making as an alternative to street crime in the inner city slums (favelas) of Rio de Janeiro. These populist projects combine both documentary and music to illustrate how music making can and does influence social change through action and interaction.

The Role of Adult Education

In drawing further connections between cultural studies, music and critical theory, Raymond Williams (1989) notes that the origins of British cultural studies can be found in the informal and often marginalized field of adult education where music played a role in collaborative, collective community building:

> In the late 40's, people were doing courses in the visual arts, in music, in town planning, and the nature of community, the nature of settlement, in film, in press, in advertising, in radio: courses which if they had not taken place in that notably underprivileged sector of education [namely adult education] would have been acknowledged much earlier (1989, 154).

Grossberg (1997) and Wright (2004) also identify adult education as an original site of British cultural studies (upon which both Canada and the United States have largely modeled their versions of the historical origins of cultural studies). Although the origins of cultural studies are many and varied (see Wright 1998), the adult education movement was and continues to be a site of contestation, struggle and organization upon which social movements such as feminism, anti-racism and environmentalism mobilize. Budd Hall locates adult educators as major contributors to the theorizing of social movement learning because "the organizational or communicative mandate of all social movements is a necessarily educational concern" (Hall, 2004, 231). The legacy of social movement learning is similar to cultural studies' legacy as a site of continual contestation over class, race and gender. Hall notes that "social movement learning is located in the heart of contestations over class, political, racial, gender, and /or other differences, existing within the climate of contestation" (Hall 2004, 236).

One example where adult education, social movement learning, and peace education converge (and could even represent a site of origin for cultural studies in the United States) is the Highlander Research and Education Centre. Founded in the 1930's in Tennessee by Myles Horton and his wife Zilphia, Highlander's turbulent story of community organizing is socially connected to terrains of resistance through economic, racial, gender and environmental justice. The first integrated co-operative in the American South, Highlander was an initiator of non-violent workshops during the civil rights movement. Because of Horton's controversial stance in support of civil (voting) rights for all Americans, Horton was hounded for several decades by the F.B.I. and his property was eventually seized by the state of Tennessee in 1962. Then, Highlander's buildings mysteriously burnt to the ground. Myles Horton was not without hope: "You can destroy a place, but you can't destroy an idea" (Bledsoe 1969, 135).

Highlander rebuilt, this time outside of New Market Tennessee, and continues to provide community based, non-violent adult education. Part of Highlander's vitality has always been the inclusion of music as an active component of agency; music serving as a tool to promote collective identity and crucially as a tool for literacy. During the Civil Rights Movement of the 1950's and 1960's , Highlander played an instrumental role in the creation of *Citizenship Schools*—adult education based literacy teaching for African Americans, which utilized music as both a mnemonic device and a community building tool.

How Does Music Make Such a Connective Power with Words?

Long time Highlander supporter and folksinger Pete Seeger (2008) suggests music makes connections with words because of the way that medium and meaning combine in song, the combination of form and structure uniting with an emotional message.

> Musical force comes from a sense of form; whereas ordinary speech doesn't have quite that much organization. You can say what you mean, but similarly with painting or with cooking, or other arts, there is a form and design to music. And this becomes intriguing; it becomes something you can remember. Good music can leap over language barriers, and barriers of religion and politics (Seeger as quoted by Levitin 2008, 13).

Drawing again on the idea of question spaces and transdisciplinary analysis, I want to connect the role of adult education/ literacy with recent work in neuroscience. Music's ability to serve as a mnemonic device is, as neuroscience claims, most likely a product of evolution. Levitin acknowledges music's capacity as a highly efficient memory and transmission system in the following way: "Across history, song has been one of the primary ways in which life lessons are taught…well formed songs, combining musical and rhythmic redundancies with lyric message, facilitate both the encoding and transmission of important information" (Levitin 2008, 239). Recent neurological research has also pointed out that singing together releases oxytocin, a neurochemical now known to be involved in establishing bonds of trust between people, (Levitin 2008, 51). Why oxytocin is released when people sing together is probably related evolutionarily to the social bonding function of music and, as Freeman (1990) suggests, "most likely evolution may have selected those individuals who could settle disputes in nonviolent ways such as music-dance" (1990, 53).

It appears there is now some empirical evidence to substantiate music's capacity as a peacemaking and educational tool and that our ability to make music has provided this capacity in continuum for many milleniums. Levitin, referencing Ian Cross, remarks that ultimately music developed as a communicative medium optimally adapted for the management of social uncertainly. "The very thing that music lacks—external referents—makes it optimal for situations of uncertainly and one that conveys an *honest signal—a window into the true emotional and motivational state of the communicator"* (Levitin 2008, 145). It is music's capacity as a powerful communicative force binding us together through honest interactions that indicates the enormous potential for music to be utilized within education pedagogy as a tool for peace.

A Critical Theory of Peace

To proceed any further with this conversation we need to develop a framework for discussing peace as, once again, we encounter another highly contested term. I turn now to O'Sullivan, who in "Dimensions of Power: Education for Peace, Social Justice and Diversity," takes on the task of defining peace: "If peace could be paraphrased it would be as people affirming and experiencing connectedness empathetically. It has to be based on everyday living experience of people. It has to be done out of encountering each others' stories" (O'Sullivan 1999, 174). In many ways O'Sullivan's definition articulates a similar *dynamic process* with how we have defined music and that this *connectedness*—this *accord,* as our conversation suggests, is also experienced by encountering each others' stories through music and lyric.

Although cultural studies has shed light upon the complexities and performativity of song lyrics, this post structural focus on lyrics does not articulate the dynamic nature of music but rather treats lyrics as a separate and somewhat static component of music. More crucial to our conversation through is that the post structural turn in cultural studies has left little room for cultural workers whose intent in cultural practice is one of informing peace education through *experiential* social justice praxis. Currently, there are cultural practitioners and theorists who want to reposition cultural studies within the discourse of social justice praxis and human rights. For example, Keyan Tomaselli (2000) calls for a return to the social versus the textually based analysis of popular culture, informing cultural studies as performative inquiries utilizing participatory, community-based experiences in the field. Tomaselli and Arnold Shepperson (2004) in developing the construct of *dynamic justice*—the value ideas of freedom and life chances—challenge cultural studies to return to the basically moral project of inquiry into social justice and suggest that this inquiry have global reach. Their construct of dynamic justice reinforces the actions of transdisciplinarity, performativity and human rights and has implications for peace pedagogy whereby the goal of social justice is praxis, which, as Freire affirms, is "reflection and action upon the world in order to transform it" (Freire 1970, 33).

Making Music as a Pedagogy of Hope

One of Freire's major contributions to the field of peace education is the insight that both education and hope are a form of politics. Just as Freire believes that trust is essential for establishing dialogue, he also claims that dialogue cannot exist without hope, what Freire terms *radical hope.* Lesley Barlett further articulates the contribution of Freirean critical pedagogy towards the development of peace education:

> "Freire's philosophy thoroughly informs peace education pedagogy and practice …and provides the foundation of peace education's hope for a link between education and social transformation. His insistence on dialogue and his discussion of egalitarian relations provide the basis for peace education pedagogy" (Barlett 2008, 5).

Radical hope as critical pedagogy is further conceptualized by scholars such as Henry Giroux whose work is rooted in Freire's notion of radical hope. Giroux's concept of an ideal pedagogy illustrates how "moral and political agency coming together to inspire both a discourse of hope and a political project that takes seriously what it means to envision a better life and society" (Giroux 1988, 38). Diaz-Soto, again rooted in a Freirean analysis of power with the aim of consciousness raising, calls for "border crossing" and a reliance on "love as a paradigm" (Diaz-Soto 2005, 96).

An example of using music making to apply pedagogy of hope is the recent work in critical ethnography of Canadian educator and cultural theorist, Brett Lashua, (2006) who in "'Just Another Native?' Soundscapes, Chorasters, and Borderlands in Edmonton, Alberta, Canada," investigates how using rap music can give First Nations teenagers in Edmonton secondary schools a sense of place and identity formation within the context of their often alienating urban environment. Lashua's ethnography illustrate how his students, making music through rap lyrics, developed stories which became an education about "the self" and its relation to the world and to others in it. Paul Willis claims that "making messages and meaning in your own context and from materials you have appropriated is, in essence a form of education in the broadest sense" (Willis 1990, 137). Crucial to Willis' argument is the process of *making* versus *receiving* and why making music serves to further illustrate the potential for both inclusion and resistance in everyday lives. In terms of educational practices, both Willis and Lashau underscore the necessity of utilizing common/popular culture (and by extension music making) in relevant educational pedagogy.

> In so far as educational practices are still predicated on traditional liberal humanistic lines and on the assumed superiority of high art, they will become almost totally irrelevant to the real energies and interests of most young people and have no part in their identity formation. Common culture will, increasingly, undertake in its own ways, the role that education vacated...We need an altogether new approach to education" (Willis1990, 147).

In particular, twenty-first century music making in the western and affluent worlds is being made, disseminated and shared in the virtual worlds of *You Tube* and *My Space*. It is in these virtual sites that identities are explored (and in some cases exploited) producing a cultural dynamic process (or as William's (1981) refers to as a community of processes) unlike any we have witnessed before and it is in these sites that educators must begin to access the potential for pedagogy, or we will be left behind.

By filtering this conversation through a cultural studies framework as we develop a critical theory of peace that is based on dynamic justice and radical hope, we see that the sites of adult education and critical ethnography continue to operate as spaces whereby the dynamics of music making successfully promote connections between and among people to further collective social justice goals. In fact, it is in these two often marginalized fields where the most dynamic work can be found. There is also the escalating use of virtual space that indicates there are a broad range of opportunities, as yet unexplored, within more formal educational settings to incorporate music making and forms of popular culture as a core component of peace pedagogy.

A Final Point

In supporting an approach to education that incorporates popular cultural practices to advance peace pedagogy, I come to the final point of our conversation. Making music to promote peace makes sense because it is, among many other things, just plain fun. Levitin notes: "a principle of evolution is that, in general, if something feels good, evolution must have made it so—evolution must have provided a reward mechanism for synchronized movement and music-making, in the same way that evolution provided mechanisms of reward when we eat and have sex" (Levitin 2008, 54). Apparently, humans have been crossing borders and relating through their music making prior to languages being developed on into the present day. And, just as importantly, music, as I have tried to relay in this conversation, continues to function as an agent of hope.

Whether it interrogates our perception of time, helps us understand our past in the context of our present, or connects personal to communal identities through the dynamics of gender, sexuality, race, class and nation, music embodies and helps us understand human experiences (Pasler 2008, 4).

The preamble to the Constitution of UNESCO (United Nations Educational, Scientific and Cultural Organization) declares: "since wars begin in the minds of men, it is in the minds of men that the defenses of peace must be constructed." Given the evidence of music's peace building capacities, then constructing peace in the minds of men by promoting music making may be a good place to start.

Coda

Pianos for Peace is a series of three progressions (movements) that can be played in sequence or as a musical round whereby the sequences are repeated indefinitely. Because the sequences are interchangeable there is room to improvise throughout the composition and still find a progression in which to resolve the music. The music tells the story of people gathering for the march: at first just a few early birds, then building in momentum until the people move as a mass reaching a crescendo of actively and then gradually fades away—the *dynamics* of the music representing the *dynamics* of the march. *Pianos for Peace* can be played by two hands, or four hands, or six hands; one piano, two pianos or an infinite number of pianos. Playing the musical composition with my students allowed us to connect to the larger movement of the peace march—we felt less alone, in fact, even hopeful that our music making made a difference.

References

Appiah, K. A. 2006. *Cosmopolitanism: Ethics in a world of strangers.* New York: W.W. Norton and Company.

Barrett, L. 2008. Paulo Freire and peace education. *Encyclopedia of Peace Education,* http://www.tc.edu/centers/epe/PDF%20articles/Bartlett_ch5_22feb08.pdf (accessed November 11, 2008).

Bledsoe, T. 1969. *Or We'll all hang separately: The highlander idea.* Boston: Beacon Press.

Bread and Roses. 1912. James Oppenheim (lyrics) and Caroline Kohlsaat (music). Public Domain.

Cage, J. 1990. An Autobiographical statement. *Southwest Review* 76: 59-76.

DeNora, T. 2003. *Music in everyday life.* Cambridge, New York: Cambridge University Press.

Freeman, W. J. 1990. *Societies of brains: A study in the neuroscience of love and hate.* Hillsdale, NJ: Erlbaum.

Freire, P. 1970. *Pedagogy of the oppressed.* Trans. Myra Bergman Ramos. New York: Herder and Herder.

Grossberg, L. 1997. *Bringing it all back home: Essays on cultural studies.* Durham: Duke University Press.

—. 1998. The cultural studies' crossroads blues. *European Journal of Cultural Studies* 1 (1): 65-82.

Hall, B. 2006. Social movement learning: Theorizing a Canadian tradition. In *Contexts of adult education: Canadian perspectives,* ed. T. Fenwick, T. Nesbit and B. Spencer (118-127). Toronto: Thompson Educational Publishing.

Horton, M., and P. Freire. 1990. *We make the road by walking: Conversations on education and social change, e*ds. B Bell, J Gaventa, and J Peters. Philadelphia: Temple University Press.

Lashua, B. 2006. "Just another native?" Soundscapes, chorasters, and borderlands in Edmonton, Alberta, Canada. *Cultural Studies ⇔ Critical Methodologies* 6: 391-410.

Loeb, Paul, ed. 2004. *The Impossible will take a little while—a Citizens guide to hope in a time of fear.* New York: Basic Books.

Levitin, D. 2008. *The World in six songs: How the musical brain created human nature.* New York: Dutton.

Lewis, G. E. 2008. Foreword to *Writing through music: Essays on music, culture, and politics* by J. Pasler, vii-xi. Oxford: Oxford University Press.

Mezirow, J. 2000. *Learning as transformation: Critical perspectives on a theory in progress.* San Francisco: Jossey-Bass.

Monisha, B. 2008. 'Critical' peace education. *Encyclopedia of Peace Education.* http://www.tc.edu/centers/epe/PDF%20articles/Bajaj_ch16_22feb08.pdf (accessed Nov. 11, 2008).

Murray, E. 1986. Imaginative thinking and human existence. Pittsburgh, Pa.: Duquesne University Press.

Pasler, J. 2008. *Writing through music: Essays on music, culture, and politics.* Oxford: Oxford University Press.

O' Sullivan, E. 1999. Dimensions of power: Education for peace, social justice and diversity. In *Transformative learning: Educational vision for the 21st century* (134-176). Toronto: University of Toronto Press.

Reardon, B. 1988. *Comprehensive peace education: Educating for global responsibility.* New York: Teachers College Press.

Tomaselli, K. and A. Shepperson. 2004. Cultural studies is the Ccrisis: Culturalism and dynamic justice. *Cultural Studies ⇔ Critical Methodologies* 4 (2): 257-268.

Tomaselli, K.G. 2000. Recovering praxis: Cultural studies in Africa. *European Journal of Cultural Studies* 1 (3): 387-402.

United Nations Educational, Scientific and Cultural Organization. *Declaration and Programme of Action on a Culture of Peace.* http://www.unesco.org/cpp/uk/declarations/2000.htm.

—. *Peace, Human Rights and Democracy Education.*

http://www.unesco.org/education/ecp/publicat/brochure/english/intro.h
tml.

Williams, R. 1981. *Culture*. Glasgow: Fontana Paperbacks. .

Willis, P. 1978. *Profane culture*. London; Routledge.

Willis, P., S. Jones, J. Canaan, and G. Hurd. 1990. *Common culture: Symbolic work at play in the everyday cultures of the young*. Philadelphia: Open University Press.

Wright, H. K. and K. Maton. 2004. Cultural studies and education: From Birmingham origin to global presence. *Review of Education, Pedagogy, and Cultural Studies* 26 (2-3):73-89.

CHAPTER ELEVEN

DIVERSITY, OPPRESSION, AND THE CHALLENGING QUEST FOR SUSTAINABLE PEACE

ELAVIE NDURA-OUÉDRAOGO

A quick glance at school demographics across the United States, a trip to the local grocery store, and the faces and voices portrayed in the local, national, and international media provide compelling testimonies of increasing human diversity. Whether characterized as a trend or a state of being, such diversity problematizes traditional concepts of *mainstream*, *majority*, and *minority*. It calls for renewed and enhanced attention to voice, agency, relationships, and the shared quest for self-sustaining communities. Indeed, it challenges our understanding of democracy and citizenship in education and broader society. Banks (1997,88) posits that "citizens in a democratic pluralistic society must interact and engage in public discourse with people from diverse racial, ethnic, gender, and social-class groups." Just as different forms of violence impact all members of society in some way or another, the quest for peace must engage all people from all societal strata. Referring to our respective neighborhoods as global communities is an understatement. If we are to learn anything from the 2008 presidential campaign and the subsequent historic election of Barack Obama as President of the United States of America, and from the recent economic crisis as well, it should be a shared understanding of our interconnectedness as members of the human race. It is this understanding that frames the issues discussed and recommendations outlined in this chapter within the context of the enduring quest for peace.

The compelling testimonies of increasing human diversity are often punctuated with cries of intolerance, injustice, and violence. These are cries of a nation that welcomes diversity, and yet, is challenged by it. They are cries of a nation stratified by race, ethnicity, religion, class gender and sexual orientation. They are cries of a nation that hopes to turn the page, move beyond its history of inequity and oppression, and step into a new transformative era of equity and social justice. The election of Barack Obama potentially opens a door to this new era. Thus, there is hope. But there is also much work to be done to build self-sustaining communities that validate human diversity, communities that are grounded in the promises of equity, social justice, and peace.

This chapter contributes to the critical and courageous conversations that are needed to build and sustain these emerging communities. After the theoretical framework is developed, troubling images of U.S. society will be discussed. A discussion of ways that these troubling images challenge the quest for sustainable peace will follow. The paper concludes with a discussion of signs of hope and ways to face the challenge to sustain that hope.

Theoretical Framework

The overall goal of this chapter is to further our understanding of the central role that cultural diversity, social justice, and relevant continued courageous conversations play in our shared quest for cultures of peace. From the cultural and physical genocide suffered by Native Americans to slavery, to modern-day racism and many other forms of oppression, the United States continues to be challenged by the same human diversity that characterizes its beauty and richness. The historic election of Barack Obama as the fist African-American and biracial president of the U.S. is seen by many as an indication that the nation has crossed the bridge of divisiveness and discrimination into a new era of inter-group unity, justice, and equity. It is safe to argue that in reality, this memorable event helps create spaces for truly courageous conversations, as it is through these that a future of equity, social justice, and peace can be engineered. It is an opportunity for the U.S. to affirm and heed Shipler's (1997) challenge that "a key test for any society is whether or not it is self-correcting. And to be self-correcting, it must be open and truthful about itself." Such openness and truthfulness begins with understanding that peace means more than the absence of war, because it implies individuals and communities working together to resolve conflicts, respect standards of justice, satisfy everyone's basic needs, and affirm human rights. In addition, peace implies a respect for life and for the dignity of each human being, without discrimination or prejudice (Harris and Morrison 2003).

Navanethem Pillay, United Nations High Commissioner for Human Rights, extrapolates the meaning of human nights:

The comprehensive vision of human rights set forth in the Universal Declaration...contemplates a world with the full realization of civil, political, economic, social and cultural rights without distinction...a world in which every man, woman and child lives in dignity, free from hunger and protected from violence and discrimination, with the benefits of housing, health care, education and opportunity...Development, security, peace and justice cannot be fully realized without human rights...Each of these pillars are undermined when discrimination and inequality— both blatant and in subtle ways-- are allowed to fester and poison harmonious coexistence. (Navanethem Pillay, UN High Commissioner for Human Rights, September 2008)

Bajaj (2008, 1) similarity argues that "comprehensive peace includes the oft-discussed domains of both 'negative' and 'positive' peace that, respectively, comprise the abolition of direct or physical violence, and structural violence constituted by systematic inequalities that deprive individuals of their basic human rights." She further indicates that critical optimism "aimed at promoting solidarity and diminishing the distance between social groups—whether they are stratified by race, ethnicity, religion, class, or any other ascriptive characteristic" can contribute relevant and important insights about peace. Nevertheless, as Bajaj (2008, 3) argues, "[t]he cultivation of hope alone without a critical understanding of the social conditions that constrain action and diminish optimism among the marginalized can be counter-productive."

What does social justice have to do with diversity and peace? Broadly defined, social justice "embodies essential principles of equity and access to all opportunities in society, in accordance with democratic principles for all persons and points of view." (College of Education and Human Development 2008) Within the context of education, it has been defined by Nieto (2000, 183) as follows:

A concern for social justice means looking critically at why and how our schools are unjust for some students. It means analyzing school policies and practices-the curriculum, textbooks and materials, instructional strategies, tracking, recruitment and hiring of staff, and parent involvement strategies-that devalue the identities of some students while overvaluing others.

The quest for social justice is a quest for transformative action. As McDonald and Zeichner (2009) explain, social justice programs explicitly attend to societal structures that perpetuate injustice, and they foster both individual and collective action toward mitigating oppression. As we celebrate and draw hope and inspiration from Obama's ascension to the presidency, we ought to recognize that we still live in a society challenged by enduring divisions and inequalities, as our nation continues to struggle with the structural integration of people of color, immigrant populations, and other marginalized groups.

Troubling Images of U.S. Society

Shipler's (1997) call for openness and truthfulness is not a quest for blame or condemnation. Rather, it is an invitation to constructively and collaboratively examine the difficult and quite humbling social realities that shape and underlie the human existence, relationships, dreams, and achievements in the U.S. and society in general. It is an invitation to engage in courageous and even painful conversations about these realities and to transform them for the common good. What are these realities in the United States of America? In *The State of American Children*, the Children's Defense Fund (2005) depicts some of the troubling images of the U.S., a nation otherwise known for its wealth and possibilities, even as it battles the current rather challenging economic recession. It is commonly said that the quality and success of any family or society can be easily inferred from its treatment of its youth. Thus, the following examples of troubled images focus on the children and youth of the United States. According to the children's Defense Fund's (2005), Black and Latino children are exponentially more likely to be born into poverty and to live in extreme poverty. They are more likely to be uninsured even when their parents work full-time throughout the year. They are significantly more likely than their White peers to be incarcerated. In fact, one in three Black men between the ages of 20 to 29 is under correctional supervision or control. Although they represent 16 percent of all children, Black children comprise 32 percent of the foster care population and are thus at a higher risk for dropping out of high school, for experiencing homelessness, and for being involved in the criminal justice system. Overall, Black and Latino children lag behind their White peers in all standard measures of academic achievement.

The challenge to affirm and manage rich human diversity in the U.S. is further demonstrated by widespread and persistent intolerance and violence. The U.S. Department of Justice Federal Bureau of Investigation (2007) reported almost eight thousand hate crimes in 2006. Over half (52%) of the hate crimes were motivated by racial bias. Nineteen percent of the hate crimes were motivated by religious bias. Sixteen percent of the hate crimes were motivated by sexual orientation bias. Thirteen percent of the hate crimes were motivated by ethnic and national origin bias. One

percent of the hate crimes involved bias against a disability. The minor
fluctuations from the previous 2005 report provide little cause for
celebration. The 2005 FBI report indicates that more than nine thousand
hate crimes were reported in the U.S. in 2004. Fifty four percent of the
2004 hate crimes were motivated by racial bias, 16% by religious bias,
16% by sexual orientation bias, 13% by ethnic and national origin bias,
and one percent by disability bias. Although the total number of reported
hated crimes went down in 2006, the statistics do show that the U.S.
society is still gravely challenged by racial, religious, sexual orientation,
and ethnic diversity.

Oppression: Roadblock to the Quest for Sustainable Peace

In his widely acclaimed book, *Race Matters*, Cornell West (1994, 23)
warns that "life without meaning, hope, and love breeds a coldhearted,
mean- spirited outlook that destroys both the individual and others." We
must therefore ponder ways in which our social, political, and economic
institutions create oppressive structures that annihilate marginalized
individuals and groups, thus laying an insurmountable roadblock in our
path to peace. This is where open and truthful conversations must begin, in
order to understand the violence that continues to besiege our schools and
communities. We must be willing to deconstruct and eliminate all forms of
violence in order to maximize human potential and build a peaceful
society. Francis (2006) describes three forms of violence: "direct violence"
is physical, emotional, and psychological; "structural violence" denotes
deliberate policies and structures that cause human suffering, death, and
harm; and "cultural violence" refers to cultural norms and practices that
create discrimination, injustice, and human suffering.

A prerequisite to effectively confronting and lifting the challenge that
oppression poses to the quest for peace is the willingness to examine ways
that our social system may be oppressive to many people and
communities. Recently, a professional colleague from another institution
stated publicly that he doesn't like the term "oppression" and that he'd
rather conceptualize it as "misunderstanding." Such a tendency to reach
for a softer construct may stem from attempts to avoid critical and
potentially painful conversations about the nature, scope, and implications
of oppression in our society.

In the event that the statistics cited above from the Children's Defense
Fund do not sound a siren loud enough to call us all to the urgent task of
societal transformation, the following questions should be considered. In
what ways does the stratification of U.S. society into "dominant

privileged" and "dominated disadvantaged" groups (Howard 2006; Spring 2004) impact people's lived experiences? In what ways may systemic inequity and injustice impede individuals' potential to develop self-efficacy dispositions? To what extent have educational policies and practices contributed to the problems of intolerance and oppression? In what ways could structural and cultural violence lead to direct violence? In what ways do endemic poverty, discrimination, and prejudice create silencing and oppressive educational and social systems that impede the progress of both the disadvantaged and the privileged? These queries begin to suggest paths to peace that include the patterns of justice that serve to define any society.

Conclusion: Facing the Challenge to Sustain Hope

Clearly, then, the quest for peace and the struggle for social justice go hand in hand. Equity and social justice are the cornerstones of the peace discourse. If we are indeed genuinely concerned about the violence that threatens the survival of our families, schools, and communities, we must build social systems that empower all citizens to raise critical questions and support social justice in our pluralistic society. Such citizens will reject politically correct discourses that promote individual and structural hypocrisy. They will courageously dedicate their talents, time, and resources to the development and implementation of programs that seek to eradicate racism, classism, sexism, and all other forms of oppressive injustice. Broadly speaking, such citizens will be active agents of peace who labor to build culturally diverse communities devoid of fear, tension, and suspicion (Ndura 2007). Within the context of education, educators who are committed to equity, social justice, and peace ought to exhibit similar dispositions and skills. They should face and accept their own cultural identity (Nieto 2000), and seek to understand ways in which their identity influences their classroom relationships and practices (Ndura 2004a, 2006). They should engage in reflective self-analysis to identify, examine, and reflect upon their attitudes toward different ethnic, racial, gender, and social-class groups (Banks1997), becoming social activists who challenge racism and other biases (Ndura 2004b, 2006; Nieto 2000). They should teach students to work together rather than against each other (Miller 2005), providing opportunities for students to learn about the cultural similarities and differences that underlie the human experience. They should engage students in learning experiences that foster positive identity exploration and clarification, implementing teaching practices that foster kindness, fairness, and responsibility (Duhaney 2000). This call for reflective self-analysis and active engagement with diversity reaches beyond educators to all citizens concerned with human rights, social justice, the common good, and peace.

This paper does not intend to minimize or undermine the notable progress that U.S. society has achieved since the onset of the Civil Rights movement in the 1960s, and many other transformative events and actions that have moved us a step closer to an equitable society. Spring (2008) highlights some of the critical events in his 13th edition of *American Education*. For example, racial restrictions were rescinded from the 1790 Naturalization Law in 1952. In 1974, the U.S. Supreme Court required schools to provide special help to students whose first language is not English. Indian students were granted freedom of religion and culture in 1974. In 1954, *Brown v. Board of Education* overturned the separate but equal doctrine. The 1964 Civil Rights Act ended school segregation. In 1975, the Education for All Handicapped Children Act (now Individuals with Disabilities Act or IDEA) was passed. Gender discrimination in educational programs was outlawed in 1972 through Title IX or the Higher Education Act. And of course, the world witnessed the historic election of Barack Obama, the first African American (and biracial) person, as President, a sign of the positive shifting of race relations in this country.

Thus, there is hope on the horizon. As a nation, the challenge before us is to stand together to transform our painful history and magnify our hopeful present to forge a nation with liberty and justice for all. This will require us to work together, politics aside, to break the oppressive chains that hold the majority of the nation's Black men trapped in an annihilating justice system. We must forge inter-group coalitions to create schools where "No Child Left Behind" actually means that all children have equitable access to quality teachers, curricula, and materials that affirm their humanity and empower them to perform to their highest potential. We must work together to create a society where poverty is not an inheritable generational curse, because as such it disempowers and oppresses the mind, soul, intellect, and body.

In the epilogue to *Race Matters*, Cornel West (1994, 155-156) strongly argues that "[t]he persistence of poverty generates levels of despair that deepen social conflict; the escalation of paranoia produces levels of distrust that reinforce cultural division." He adds that "[r]ace is the most explosive issue in American life precisely because it forces us to confront the tragic facts of poverty and paranoia, despair and distrust." Such endemic poverty, paranoia, despair, and distrust is documented in many works whose authors have penetrated forgotten schools and neighborhoods throughout the U.S. The images of the forgotten and dilapidated schools and lives in Jonathan Kozol's *Savage Inequalities* (1991) and *Amazing Grace* (1995) vividly reflect this nation's challenge to affirm diversity and to empower individuals and families to achieve the "American Dream." *Amazing Grace* (1995, 3) opens with the haunting image of Mott Haven, "whose 48,000 people are the poorest in the South Bronx. Two thirds are Hispanic, one third black. Thirty-five percent are children." In *Growing Up Empty*, Loretta Schwartz-Nobel (2002) exposes the reality of the hunger epidemic in the U.S. through the lives of the working poor who have jobs but do not make enough money to support their families; immigrants who labor under dehumanizing conditions and with almost no benefits; a formerly middle-class dentist's wife abandoned by her husband, reduced to stealing to feed her starving children; and soldiers who fight for the country while their hungry young wives and children have to beg for food. Similar and equally wrenching stories of dehumanizing poverty are depicted in Lisa Dodson's (1998) *Don't Call Us Out of Name*, Barbara Ehrenreich's (2001) *Nickel and Dimed*, and David Shipler's (2004) *The Working Poor*.

In all these works the harsh realities are accentuated by individuals' membership in non-dominant groups as stratified according to race, ethnicity, gender, age, and social class. It is clear that transforming such realities to help improve people's lives will take concerted and unified efforts across groups, driven by a firm conviction that the strength of our communities and of our nation will be determined by our commitment to seek the common good. Thus, Cornell West (1994, 159) concludes that we are at a crucial crossroad in the history of this nation, whereby we either hang together by combating these forces that divide and degrade us or we hang separately. He wonders whether we have "the intelligence, humor, imagination, courage, tolerance, love, respect, and will to meet the challenge."

The election of Barack Obama to the presidency inspires hope because it strongly suggests that we have chosen to "hang together" and reclaim a unified nation for the common good. As Obama and his administration toil dutifully to shift and heal a nation that has been wounded by centuries of oppressive discrimination, hope fills the air and dreams of nonviolence and peace fill the imagination. Obama's presidency may not fully relieve the enduring suffering of the nation's disadvantaged, but it nonetheless provides a potential space for all of us to openly and truthfully recognize the long and ragged road to peace. Each time a baby is born into poverty, each time another hate group is formed, each time another young Black man is incarcerated, each time a person of color is denied employment due to a past offense for which time has been fully served, each time a child drops out of school, each time a child suffers from neglect and violence, we as a nation move farther and farther back from the promises of liberty, justice, and peace. Luckily the opposite is also true, and every action we take to address and overcome these challenges yields positive potential for creating a more just and peaceful world.

References

Bajaj, M., ed. 2008. *Encyclopedia of peace education*. Charlotte, NC: Information Age Publishing.

Banks, A. J. 1997. Educating citizens in a multicultural society. New York: Teachers College Press.

Children Defense Fund. 2007. *America's cradle to prison pipeline*. Washington, D.C. www.childrensdefense.org (accessed November 10, 2007)

College of Education and Human Development. 2008. *Core values*. http://cehd.gmu.edu/about/values (accessed April 24, 2008).

Dodson, L. 1998. *Don't call us out of name: The untold lives of women and girls in poor America*. Boston: Beacon Press.

Duhaney, M. Garrick. 2000. Culturally sensitive strategies for violence prevention. *Multicultural Education* 7(4): 10-17.

Ehrenreich, B. 2001. *Nickel and dimed*. New York: Henry Holt and Company.

Francis, J. D. 2006. Linking peace, security and developmental regionalism: regional economic and security integration in Africa. *Journal of Peacebuilding & Development* 2(3): 7-20.

Howard, R. G. 2006. *We can't teach what we don't know: White teachers, multiracial schools*. New York: Teachers College Press.

Kozol, J. 1991. *Savage inequalities: Children in America's schools*. New York: Harper Perennial.

—. 1995. *Amazing grace: The lives of children and the conscience of a nation*. New York: Crown Publishers.

McDonald, M., and K. M. Zeichner. 2009. Social justice teacher education. In *Handbook of social justice in education*, ed. W. Ayers, T. Quinn, and D. Stoval (595-610). New York: Routledge.

Miller, S. 2005. Building a peaceful and just world—Beginning with children. *Childhood Education* 82(1): 14-18.

Ndura, E. 2004. Teachers' discoveries of their cultural realms: Untangling the web of cultural identity. *Multicultural Perspective* 6(3): 10-16.

—. 2006. Transcending the majority rights and minority protection dichotomy through multicultural reflective citizenship in the African Great Lakes region. *Intercultural Education* 17(2): 195-205.

—. 2007. Calling institutions of higher education to join the quest for social justice and peace. *Harvard Educational Review* 77(3): 345-350.

Nieto, S. 2000. Placing equity front and center: Some thoughts on transforming teacher education for a new century. *Journal of Teacher Education* 51(3):180-187.

Pillay, N., 2008, September. Address on the occasion of the opening of the 9th Session of the Human Rights Council. http://www.unhchr.ch/huricane/huricane.nsf/view01/8F6C6D5B6EE3 E7F6C12574BE004A5FB8?opendocument. (accessed September 11, 2008).

Shipler, K. D. 1997. *A country of strangers: Blacks and Whites in America*. New York: Knopf.

Shipler, D. 2004. *The working poor: Invisible in America*. New York: Vintage Books.

Spring, J. 2008. *American education*. 13th ed. Boston: McGraw Hill.

Schwartz-Nobel, L. 2002. *Growing up empty: The hunger epidemic in America*. New York: Harper Collins.

U.S. Department of Justice Federal Bureau of Investigation. 2005. Hate crime statistics 2004. http://www.fbi.gov/ucr/hc2004/tables/HateCrimes2004.pdf.(accessed September 5, 2006)

U.S. Department of Justice Federal Bureau of Investigation. 2007. Hate crime statistics 2006. http://www.fbi.gov/ucr/hc2006/index.html.(accessed April 23,2009).

West, Cornel. 1994. *Race matters*. New York: Vintage Books.

PART III:

POLITICS, ECONOMICS, AND THE ENVIRONMENT

As an educational and societal aim, peacebuilding faces many obstacles and, as we have seen, many opportunities. When we consider this from the perspective of politics and current events, the prospects for peace can sometimes look even more dismal. Still, as the chapters in this section point out, even the most problematic and intractable conflicts (for example, Iraq and Darfur) offer great potential for peacemaking efforts to take hold and perhaps even flourish. These analyses are grounded in the tangible aspects of politics, and also ask us to consider the ways in which economics can serve as a tool for creating peace rather than simply as a method for institutionalizing conflict. In order to achieve this result, a consideration of the environment as a touchstone for peacemaking and conflict resolution becomes essential. Indeed, the path to peace is here for the walking.

CHAPTER TWELVE

IRAQ'S WAR ECONOMY:
BARRIERS AND OPPORTUNITIES

CHERYL DUCKWORTH

Much has been said, and no doubt will continue to be said, about the decision by the Bush Administration to invade Iraq in 2003. One particular focus of analysts has been the mangled efforts at stabilization and reconstruction. Leadership (or the lack thereof), national intelligence, and decision-making processes have come in for particular scrutiny. So too has the terrible violence, often defined as ethnic or sectarian, that has not yet abated. I will not rehearse this debate here (in the interest of transparency, I opposed the war from the beginning). This chapter will instead contribute to the post-war discussion by asserting that a genuine war economy has indeed taken hold in Iraq. A war economy is an economy that has become significantly mobilized around a particular violent conflict. As a consequence, resources, means of production and employment are all significantly dependant on the conflict, making the conflict far more intractable than it might otherwise be. I will examine how Iraq's war economy impacts the various peace processes currently unfolding in Iraq and offer possibilities for a way forward. Given that the mainstream media so often refers to the conflict in Iraq as "ethnic violence", which I view as a misnomer that obscures other systemic drivers of this conflict, now seems a particularly important historical moment to further examine the economic particulars of Iraq and how they are impacting current peace processes there. I will also briefly consider what the implications may be for peace building in general.

There is growing consensus that the economic dynamics fueling and financing various intractable, violent conflicts must be a central consideration in shaping peace building policy. Several main debates appear to have emerged in the literature on war economies; I will briefly place myself in these debates before proceeding to examine the war economy in Iraq. Paul Collier's dichotomy regarding "greed and grievance" has come in for some considerable criticism. A number of scholars have noted, quite fairly, that one cannot reductively identify "the cause" of a conflict as the greed of the combatants. Agbonifo, for example, argues that "The reductionist categories of greed and grievance not only obfuscate the place of religion, and an amoral political economy in the decision-making calculus of anti-state elements but, also, downplay the destructive effects of conventional development" (Agbonifo 2004). Given the centrality of Islam to many Iraqis, and its prominent place in the new Constitution, which asserts that "Islam is the official religion of the State and is a foundational source of legislation" (Iraqi Constitution), clearly religion, ethnicity and culture cannot be ignored even in the "economic" analysis that I am undertaking here. Analyses which wholly ignore either, in my view, are incomplete. This is an especially salient observation for understanding the violence unfolding in Iraq, given how marked it has been by factional divisions between the Shiites, Sunnis and Kurds.

Agbonifo also highlights the role of international organizations (licit and otherwise) in war economies, an aspect of analysis that he feels the "greed or grievance" dichotomy obscures.

Scholars such as Arowobusoye (2005) and Goodhand (2004) have been similarly clear in calling for a regional and global understanding of war economy dynamics. After all, international financial institutions, neighboring countries and diasporas have all played a role in financing violent conflict. Without "excusing" so-called war lords of, for example, the Democratic Republic of Congo or Sierra Leone, I believe that a primary emphasis on the more powerful global and regional economic actors is reasonable. My own analysis of Iraq will reflect this, giving attention to global and regional economic forces, such as UN sanctions and CPA policies in the service of global neoliberalism, as well as the domestic economy.

Evidence of a War Economy

The Bush administration and the Coalition Provisional Authority (CPA) did not so much create as inherit and facilitate Iraq's war economy. Ballentine and Nitzschke note that two important characteristics of a war economy include, "the destruction or circumvention of the formal economy and the growth of informal and black markets, effectively blurring the lines between the formal, informal, and criminal sectors and activities" (Ballentine and Nitzschke 2005). They further identify war economies as "highly decentralized and privatized, both in the means of coercion and in the means of production and exchange" (Ballentine and

Nitzschke 2005). A third common feature, disturbingly relevant to Iraq, is the use of civilians, "by combatants to acquire control over lucrative assets, capture trade networks and Diaspora remittances, and exploit labour" (Ballentine and Nitzschke 2005). I will emphasize these three features of Iraq's war economy, attempting to integrate as well recent regional and Iraqi history and the ethnic and tribal rivalries which currently interact with the war economy.

One of the sharpest analyses I have yet seen is by Christopher Parker and Peter W. Moore, examining the emergence of a war economy in Iraq with particular attention to the role of the CPA's policies, as well as global neoliberalism in general, in encouraging such. I find much to admire in their analysis, yet they turn far more attention, it is fair to say, to analysis of the problem than development of solutions (they state they do not feel there are any). Outrageously, they may well be correct but I will, towards the end of this chapter, draw on conflict resolution theories to offer thoughts for a way forward nonetheless. They begin by noting the very need for examination of Iraq's war economy. One feature of neoliberalism is the tendency to view itself as natural and inevitable; perhaps this explains why so many other aspects of this conflict have received more attention than the war economy. As they write, a "war economy is firmly rooted, yet it has gone largely unexamined in the stacks of books and articles dissecting Washington's grandiose venture gone bad" (Parker and Moore 2007). With specific regard to Bremer's CPA, they argue, "Armed with ideological assumptions and economic quick fixes, U.S. occupation officials pursued policies that, at a minimum, aggravated the severe social dislocation wrought by war, privatization and sanctions before 2003" (Parker and Moore 2007). Chandrasekaran, while a bit less explicitly than Parker and Moore, also repeatedly emphasizes the hasty privatization of numerous sectors demanded by the CPA. Parker and Moore also highlight Hussein's "state retreat" from the economy throughout the 1980s and 1990s which resulted in "plummeting living standards" (Parker and Moore 2007). I am, of course, not positing a direct correlation between privatization of public sectors and war economies; if such were true, we should see war economies far more extensively than we do. I am, however, emphasizing that such rapid privatization by the CPA, in the context of a growing civil war, watered already fertile soil in which a war economy could take root.

This proved particularly true given the inequalities violently institutionalized by Saddam Hussein's Sunni Ba'ath Party. As Parker and Moore write, "Mainstream accounts of the 1980s and 1990s preserve the centrality of the state by charting the rise of what Charles Tripp has referred to as the 'shadow state'—a web of informally regulated networks that leveraged statist agency (e.g., the ability to make and enforce internationally binding contracts or employ nominally legitimate coercion) to create domestic enclaves for the private accumulation of capital and power" (Parker and Moore 2007). Such private accumulation of capital fits well with Ballentine and Nitzschke's definition of a war economy above, especially the use of civilians to consolidate political and economic control. Trade routes were one mechanism of this control: "All of this trade was organized through bilateral protocols ensuring the political control to reward allies and punish rivals" (Parker and Moore 2007). Specifically, the military and security forces of the state, as Parker and Moore describe, served monetary purposes for Hussein and his forces. This appears to have been a state-institutionalized war economy. To paint a picture of how severe the social dislocations and threats to life and livelihood were, some numbers: "In 1980, Iraq was a net creditor and considered home to one of the region's most advanced economies. By early March 2003, as U.S. and British forces amassed on its southern border, it had become one of the world's poorest and most underdeveloped countries. Average annual income had fallen from between $3,600 and $4,000 in 1980 to between $500 and $600 by the end of 2003" (Parker and Moore 2007).

Many analyses of the current state of Iraq, I think quite rightly, also emphasize the economic devastation of eight years of war with Iran as well as the sanctions put in place after the first Gulf War. Clearly the devastation of the economy resulting from the Iran-Iraq war and years of international sanctions are critical factors in understanding what the CPA inherited (Graham-Brown 1999). This is especially true given the accounts that argue that such historical and cultural specifics were not given heed by the war's planners (Ricks 2006, 1-111). These sanctions, along with the economic devastation of war and crashing standards of living as the statist economic regime retreated, all interacted to form the context of the current war economy.

One fundamental feature of a war economy is the dependence of a major portion of society on the war itself for their daily bread. Parker and Moore confirm that, indeed, some 20% of Iraq's labor force was "employed in the armed forces" during the Iran-Iraq war. As noted above, this was accompanied by what Leslie Gill might call an "armed retreat" of the Iraqi state in rapid privatization which especially impacted the agricultural sector, of obvious importance to food security. Nor were the beneficiaries of this privatization arbitrary, or those who might have benefitted in more normal market processes. Parker and Moore specify,

"The main beneficiaries of Saddam's *infitah* were by and large the same people who, by virtue of their connections to government power brokers, had profited from the massive amounts of government spending on construction during the oil boom of the 1970s" (2007). Even popular policies such as nationalizing Iraq's oil, as Hussein did in 1972, enriched Hussein without resulting in investment or economic growth for the Iraqi people, a predictable result from a kleptocracy (Slugglet 2008, 607). Hence the CPA and the current Iraqi government both inherited an already highly militarized socio-economy and an impoverished people. Biddle, Pollack and O'Hanlon cite current unemployment numbers as high as 40% (Biddle et al, 2008)! Many analyses, such as F. J. West's, who served as Asst. Secretary of Defense under Reagan, note the poverty of those arrested for attempting (or succeeding at) an IED or other attack against Coalition forces (West 2008). This highlights both how necessary it is to distinguish between those ideologically committed to violence in the name of Islam, and those feeding their families. This is difficult work, no doubt. The line between a "committed extremist" and someone trying to feed her family may well be dotted, not solid. As I will argue throughout the remainder of this chapter, processes such as community dialogue and economic recovery, in the right policy context, can be mutually reinforcing. Ultimately, both markets and communities are built on trust. Hence, transforming Iraq's war economy and healing the trauma of the ethnic strife which continues to unfold can be synergetic processes. This is a crucial observation for peace builders in Iraq and similarly divided societies (Pakistan and Afghanistan rush to mind). I will emphasize, however, that this possibility is not at all automatic. Reconciliation will need to be built through problem-solving, dialogue and a policy bias for the involvement of every stakeholder possible.

Criminality, Security and the War Economy: Economics by Other Means?

The interaction of sectarian violence and criminality in post-invasion Iraq provides a brutally stark picture of what the "economics of ethnicity" can look like in fragile or failing states. As noted above, a goal of this chapter is to move beyond the "greed or grievance" dichotomy and detail how ethnicity and class are interacting in a particular context. While a wealth of daily local and provincial interactions can illuminate, for reasons of space and clarity I will focus on three in particular: Iraqi Kurdistan, al Sadr's Madhi Army and the Sons of Iraq (SOI). One reason privatization has proved such a common feature of war economies is that it weakens control of the State who might otherwise be able to control, for example, drugs, arms or even human trafficking. This is particularly salient given that often states emerging from a civil war or an occupation are fragile to begin with. A critical need is for such states to be able to provide security and services which might begin to address human needs and thereby establish some sort of genuine legitimacy. Indeed, countries undergoing such a transition as Iraq's depend precisely on such legitimacy. Hence it is worth remembering that what the state, viewed as legitimate by some but not by others, deems criminal is highly contested. Trust in the State and its ability to deliver for the common people, if not outright mistrust of Baghdad's intentions and integrity, remains problematic.

Historically, tensions between the central government and regional systems have been dominant in so-called Iraqi Kurdistan. Some of the particulars of this region's economy further illuminate the specifics of this war economy, and implications for today's peace processes. So individualized was the control of oil smuggling (into Turkey) that Leezenburg identifies two specific people who consolidated control: Uday Hussein (of course, Saddam Hussein's now dead son) and Nechirwan Barzani (Leezenburg 2005, 638). After the 1991 invasion, harmful sanctions were applied. Food security, in particular, was impacted. Writes Leezenburg, "Misguided policies, protracted conflicts and the international market, not to mention the enticements of an oil economy, have not wholly destroyed the local agriculture; but they have seriously jeopardised the prospect of self-sufficient agriculture, in Iraqi Kurdistan as elsewhere in Iraq" (Leezenburg 2005, 637). Given the violence in much of the rest of Iraq, and the violence with which Iraqi Kurds have been historically treated, it is difficult to see incentive for Iraqi Kurds, presently quite autonomous, to cede much of this control to the Central Government. This is especially so given that the state of the agricultural sector and the industrial sector in the Kurdish region remain weak at best, making control of the oil resources even more difficult to compromise. In another example of how thorny such a genuine sharing of wealth is likely to be, the most recent successful oil deal was not between the government of Iraq and Turkey but rather between the Kurdish Regional Government and Turkey. Predictably, the Central Government deemed it illegal ("Back to Business" 2008). Such disagreements need not *ipso facto* doom Iraq's nascent democracy; the relationship between the federal government and states to this day remains a point of contention for the U.S. Still, the U.S. is not currently threatened by continuing domestic violence and private militias which are still not thoroughly integrated into either the police or national military. Nor is there yet, according to Ali Allawi, former Iraqi Defense and Finance Minister, an official settlement on how power and wealth will be shared among the provinces, which very much reflect the country's ethnic divisions, and the central government, as Allawi explained in a recent interview with the BBC's Steven Sakur. That these tensions have not abated was emphasized by the recent January elections, which took place in fourteen of Iraq's eighteen provinces; notably, three of four Kurdish provinces did not hold elections. Massoud Barzani, who heads the semiautonomous Kurdish region, had announced that anyone supporting the councils being encouraged and courted by Maliki "would be deemed traitors" ("Iraq's Top Cleric" 2009).

Media coverage of the "ethnic violence" and looting throughout Iraq has been extensive. Most recently, the media is reporting that violence has been declining. Because this violence, I argue, is rooted in a war economy, understanding its nature and origins is necessary here. This requires disentangling what I argue are misunderstandings regarding the absolute success of "the surge". While welcome news, of course, I must emphasize that, in addition to the surge, several other factors which could soon change seem to have been responsible for this improved security. In the same BBC interview referenced above, Allawi observed that violence is down because *the ethnic cleansing worked*. A second reason is that the Sons of Iraq, it has been widely reported, have allied with U.S. forces. Any study of the U.S. experience in Afghanistan, however, should remind us that the "enemy of our enemy" is not automatically our friend. A drop in the rates of violence is an opportunity to be seized, but not evidence that can be trusted of actual conflict resolution.

This disentangling brings me now to Moqtada al Sadr, of course the Shiite militia leader who battled coalition forces previously, having led several uprisings against the occupation; he has held to a cease fire since Aug. 2007 but his Madhi Army (JAM) still patrols some Shiite neighborhoods in Baghdad. The Council on Foreign Relations reports that his support is anywhere from three to five million strong, but estimates of his militia range widely, anywhere from three thousand to, according to Sadr himself, sixty thousand ("al Sadr"). The lesson here for policy makers surely is how little reliable information we have about al Sadr or the JAM. Given his more recent emphasis on social involvement and seeing supporters in political office, my read of al Sadr is something very like an Iraqi Hezbollah. His movement won 32 of 275 Parliamentary seats in 2005 ("al Sadr").

Of the Madhi Army, West writes, "But in Khadamiya, in northwest Baghdad, and in Sadr City to the east, JAM operates as a shadow government, extorting money while sneering at the Maliki clique that accommodates them" (West 2008). Sadr is especially relevant to my discussion of the interaction between sectarianism and a war economy because of the criminal enterprises al-Sadr's supporters have been involved in and the fact that so much of his support comes from impoverished and disenfranchised Shiites. His legitimacy is in the eye of the beholder. Prime Minister Maliki and his Dawa Party are often perceived as privileged and removed from the concerns of Iraq's poor, a perception surely not helped by the post-war difficulties in restoring security and basic services such as sanitation and reliable electricity. What concerns me here, of course, is that it appears all al Sadr would have to do is simply no longer adhere to the ceasefire. It is possible that he will not break the ceasefire; it is also possible that he will decide that it is no longer wise or in his interests to hold to it. Though he did not campaign in the January elections, likely his future choices will depend on the outcome of the national elections to be held at the end of this year. Given that the (Sunni) Sons of Iraq are private militias that may or may not be successfully integrated into the formal police and military forces, I see little reason to assume that the cease fire will hold indefinitely. Al Sadr and other Shiite leaders have viewed Sunni militias as a threat and vice-versa. This was reflected in the violence surrounding the elections. A Shiite candidate allied with al Maliki, Haitham Kadhim al-Husaini, was gunned down Jan 16, 2009. News sources such as the *Washington Post* and Al Jazeera English did not identify the shooter. Shortly thereafter, a Sunni candidate, Hassan Zaidan al-Luhaibi, and several of his relatives, were killed by a young suicide bomber. Forty-eight hours before the Jan 31 elections, three more Sunni candidates were killed: Hazem Salem Ahmed, Omar Faruq al-Ani and Abbas Farhan ("Poll Candidates Killed" 2009). There has been no suggestion that I have seen that al Sadr was behind either attack, but such recent electoral violence clearly suggests continued struggle for power, and the economic security it brings. This violence has only continued to escalate. The end of April has been especially bloody, with one hundred and sixty people killed in attacks over the 23rd and 24th ("Iraq Resists Pleas" 2009).

I argue that the lull in violence may well be connected to the war economy I have been detailing. For example, Iraqi Gen. Hohan al-Furayji argued that jobs were at the heart of the "peace", not a shift in social, political or economic systems towards conflict resolution. He observed, "If enough had been done to create jobs for the young men then we would not have the situation we have now with the militias. I don't think the British and the Americans have done enough. The militias have exploited the lack of money among the young. I have interviewed people who carried out murders for $500, serious criminal acts for $15" (Sengupta 2007). West also noted that Maliki has been loath to offer police jobs to Sunnis, "running the risk of engendering the very militia he wants to avoid" (West 2008). The (very relative) "successes" of the surge may be due to it providing jobs to the militia-men paid to fight al Qaeda. Given the dire economic state Iraq is in, the incentive, perhaps even the necessity, of joining the Awakening as a survival strategy seems clear. The Sons of Iraq were until recently on the U.S. payroll; the progress of Iraq's economy, especially non-military and security sectors, will matter greatly for sustainable peace.

What Is to Be Done?

Iraq is an important case study in and of itself, but it also has implications for peace building broadly. One such implication is that policy makers moving forward will be faced with what I view as a classic tension between moving forward from *peacekeeping* to *peace building*. I draw here on Galtung's distinction between peacekeeping (akin to negative peace, or an absence of violence) and peace building and peacemaking (building positive peace through reconciliation, building trust and undertaking the necessary social, political and economic reforms). There is not an automatic, linear progression between each of these "stages" of conflict resolution. In fact, in my analysis highly escalated conflicts which involve the culture, political structures and economy of a society, such as in Iraq, suggests a tension between the negative peace so prized now in Iraq and the positive peace which is what will offer a lasting resolution. Peacekeeping, of course, is nearly always undertaken by an armed force. As detailed above, the formal security sector in Iraq remains plagued by private militias. Naturally, the Iraqi government must address this but I would go a step further. The size of the security sector, formal and informal, in Iraq's economy itself must ultimately be reduced. Navigating this Catch-22 will be extremely tricky because of the incidences of violence throughout the country, which remain far too high. Human security and peace are inextricably linked and Maliki will need to ensure security to the best of his ability if any peace building is to be possible. Yet again, these are not wholly sequential, linear processes. If other economic opportunities are not available, or if each of Iraq's sectarian groups do not see a profit for themselves in a whole and unified Iraq, the central government may well fail; a diverse economy with a variety of industries is needed.

The approach to peace building that is, in my view, the most likely to succeed (though there are never guarantees) will incorporate trust-building dialogues and community development at the most local, neighborhood level. School curriculum must immediately and explicitly confront challenges and stereotypes which various groups in Iraq may hold of one another (something I have consistently recommended for schools worldwide). Development projects can be designed around super-ordinate goals, goals around which all groups in Iraqi society can come together and from which all will benefit. Rebuilding infrastructure and other projects will, after all, legitimately benefit Sunnis, Shiites, and Kurds alike. These proposals confront the reality that there is precious little trust after decades of brutal minority rule followed by armed occupation. The temptation will be to "deliver results" on security, and once again, I do not at all dispute the importance of this. Yet allowing security to remain privatized at the expense of beginning to build trust will only sow the seeds of the next conflict. For example, the U.S. and Iraqi government funding for the Awakening's Sons of Iraq, that has privileged some tribes over others, can only further exacerbate tribal and sectarian divisions, and further entrench the current war economy, if the SOI is not perceived as serving the national interest ("Tribal Rivalries" 2009). As such, this policy does not serve U.S. or Iraqi peace and security objectives.

While clearly effective and professional law enforcement that allows people to feel safe is a critical aspect of building a culture of peace in Iraq, lost in this discussion too often is the reality that law enforcement is one aspect of a whole social system. It will be important for policy makers to resist the temptation to believe that the criminal violence is solely a law enforcement dilemma. As Totsi notes, "...the process of law enforcement itself...can, by its nature, only ameliorate or relocate a problematic situation, not solve it comprehensively" (Totsi 2004, 4). It is no substitute for the difficult, slow work of reconciling a society brutalized for at least several generations now, consciously divided along ethnic lines. Such divisions, indeed, extend to the British occupation of Iraq in the early 20th Century and remained a dominant feature of Hussein's regime, as well as the post-war period.

In her analysis of the war economies of Somalia and Bosnia, Mary Kaldor noted the ineffectiveness of "top down" or Track One processes of peace making (Kaldor 2001, 90-92). This is because legitimacy had not been sufficiently established. This remains true for Iraq, and is precisely why I am arguing that multi-track, civil society peace processes are likely to be the most successful for allowing Iraq to emerge from its war economy and toward a culture of peace. Track One (governmental)

conflict resolution too often assumes that a signed peace treaty genuinely
suggests a transformation of the systems which are at the root of the
conflict. These processes have been elite, and have not mobilized the
grassroots of their societies. Given that Iraq has only been officially
sovereign since 2004, and considering the terrible levels of violence
particularly between 2004 and 2007, there has hardly been ample time for
indigenous, local processes of conflict resolution. Guided by Abu-Nimer, I
argue that it is vital that such processes be supported and that they center
on processes and systems indigenous to Iraqi culture. Given the leadership
role that the U.S. will likely have in the coming years, and the wealth of
Western NGOs undertaking community development work, the temptation
will be to impose Western assumptions and processes regarding conflict
resolution. This will fail. In the context of a society emerging from
dictatorship, civil war and a war economy, no doubt the social contract is
battered, but indigenous processes of resolving or at least managing
conflict are in place. No society can reproduce itself without them. This
concept is what connects the importance of local, community-led peace
building to emerging from a war economy. Ultimately a war economy
must be replaced with a functioning market economy. Like any other
social institution, markets depend on a minimum of trust. In the particular
context of civil war and a war economy, processes of reconciliation and
forgiveness, though it may not be obvious, hence become vital to
economic growth.

One might reasonably wonder whether or not transitioning to a market
economy will in fact contribute to building a culture of peace in Iraq.
Given the inequities and volatilities of the market, especially markets
which function outside of a democratic, wisely regulated context, I can
only answer no. In fact, without the right policy context, which would
include social safety nets and strong financial and regulatory institutions,
continued deregulation and state retreat could well deepen the inequalities
which are such a driver of this conflict. This is especially true in the
context of the current global recession. Growing inequalities are not,
however, unavoidable. If the public, and indeed the private, sectors are
willing to invest in social safety nets, infrastructure and industries,
expanding freedoms and capabilities for Iraqi citizens should, over time,
form a vital part of building a culture of peace in Iraq. As Galtung
suggests in his *Peace by Peaceful Means,* human freedom and security
tend to be improved when a multiplicity of options and systems are
available to citizens. He refers to this as "eclectic" development theory, in
which societies can blend blue (capitalist), red (socialist), green (local
agricultural economies), pink (a blending of red, blue and green often

found in social democratic systems) and yellow (a blending of blue and red currently seen in China and other Asian countries). While space does not permit a full exploration of Galtung's thinking here as it applies to Iraq, a general point about development and peace building should emerge clearly: the major traditional schools of development are perhaps not as incompatible as often assumed, and a dynamic multiplicity of systems offers people options in an unpredictable and still violent environment. Behind Galtung's thinking here is the truism of peacemaking that applies to Iraq and beyond: human needs are diverse and so systems designed to meet those needs should reflect that diversity. As he writes, "One general formula emerges: *eclecticism.* If human beings possess infinite potential for diversity…then we are doomed to fail if we cannot mirror at least some of that variety" (Galtung 1996, 183).

With Iraq newly sovereign, an opportunity to begin building legitimacy has emerged, but given the tenacity of most war economies, and the deep mistrust that the continuing violence in Iraq implies, the government's task is Herculean. As the *Economist* reported, no one has yet moved into the official Palace because of the disagreements as to who has that right. Further, this new sovereignty means that the Iraqi government will have to decide the fate of 18,000 detainees. Most of these detainees are Sunni ("Iraq is Sovereign" 2009). Many are currently being released but what they will decide to do with this freedom remains an open question ("Vow to Fight" 2009). These are just a few of the most recent and relevant minefields the Iraqis, and all involved in peace building processes in Iraq, will have to navigate. I emphasize this here because such decisions speak directly to what I view as the only true way to transform a war economy, which is the genuine sharing of wealth and power. This calls for precisely the kind of slow, patient community development and trust-building that so-called "Track One" (governmental) peace processes have in the past been blind to or even contemptuous of (Kaldor 1999, 112-137; McDonald and Diamond 1996).

Elections are a vital aspect of building this "virtuous cycle", and much will depend on how they proceed. Sistani's call for participation in the Jan. 2009 provincial elections was surely helpful. Yet candidates were killed, and if the upcoming national elections are viewed as corrupt, they will not be able to foster the public trust essential to emerging from a war economy which has seen successful ethnic cleansing. There are reports of Hussein's Ba'ath party secretly being reconstituted ("Tribal Rivalries" 2009). The perception of Maliki as less than neutral with regard to sectarian divides bodes ill; he continues to resist any suggestion of reintegrating Ba'athists ("Iraq Resists Pleas" 2009). He must explicitly embrace a multicultural view of Iraq if a culture of peace can emerge. Tribal leaders retain a considerable amount of power, apparently even vetting a list of the Islamic Party's candidates ("Iraq Election Highlights" 2008). A recent Global Policy opinion poll documented worsening perceptions of the provision of basics such as schooling, medical care, electricity, water and crucially, security. U.S. forces and militias shared nearly equal blame for the lack of security (20% to 18% respectively), yet more optimistically, the number of Iraqis who viewed the security situation as better rose from 11% in Aug. 2007 to 36% in March 2008. Also favorably, reported confidence in the Iraqi Army and police forces has grown. As noted before, the elections are exacerbating tensions as various groups angle for power. I dwell on these poll numbers because of the importance of building and repairing interethnic, intertribal (and intra-tribal) trust to creating a culture of peace in Iraq which will allow it to emerge from a war economy which, as this chapter has demonstrated, has existed long before the invasion of March 2003 ("Iraq Poll 2008").

Another vital step for allowing Iraq to emerge from its war economy is completing the withdrawal of all U.S. and other Coalition troops. 61% of Iraqis believe that the presence of U.S. troops worsens security in their country ("Iraq Poll 2008"). The completion of this withdraw should have two positive effects. One, it robs the most militant leaders, and any Al Qaeda in Iraq who remain, of their strongest message. Secondly, and obviously dependent on the ability of the Iraqi government nationally and locally to deliver security and services, the withdrawal should also strengthen the legitimacy of the Iraqi government in the eyes of its citizens because of its effective exercise of sovereignty. Former President Bush, in compromising on the Status of Forces Agreement of early Jan. 2009, bequeathed President Obama solid groundwork for such a withdraw.

I argued above that "national" war economies are best understood in their regional and global context. Hence, I would be remiss if I did not address again Iraq's position in the global economy in general. Had the U.N. Security Council yet developed an effective means for regulating global arms flows, war economies, to include Iraq's, would be far less common. The U.S., Russia, France and China all were major arms dealers to Iraq (as well as to numerous other war economies to include Sudan and Sierra Leone) (Barton 2003, Graham-Brown 1999). It is essential that the Security Council develop a policy for such regulation—yet I must note here the irony that the very countries most at fault themselves comprise 4/5ths of the Security Council. It does not pay for current practices to change. Therefore, the citizens of each of these countries, through education and mobilization, must hold their own governments to account, thereby gaining some sort of leverage over such a large and elite organization as the Council. In our interdependent, interconnected age, the work of building a culture of peace in Iraq is hardly Iraq's alone.

References

Abu Nimer, M. 1996. Conflict resolution in an Islamic context: Some conceptual questions. *Peace and Change.* 21: 22-40.

Agbonifo, J. 2004. Beyond greed and grievance: Negotiating political settlement and peace in Africa. *Peace, Conflict and Development* 4 (4). http://www.peacestudiesjournal.org.uk/docs/greedandgrievance.PDF (accessed November 2008).

Arowobusoye. O. Why they fight: An alternative view on the political economy of civil war and conflict transformation. *The Bergdorf Handbook for Conflict Transformation.* http://www.berghof-handbook.net/uploads/download/dialogue3_arowobusoye.pdf.

Back to Business. 2008. *The Economist.* 9 Dec.

Ballentine, K. and H. Nitzschke. The political economy of civil war and conflict transformation. *The Bergdorf Handbook for Conflict Transformation.* http://www.berghofhandbook.net/std_page.php?LANG=e&id=22&parent=5.

Barton, F. and B. Crocker. 2003. A wiser peace: An action strategy for a post-conflict Iraq. Center for Strategic and International Studies. http://www.csis.org/media/csis/pubs/wiserpeace_i.pdf

Biddle, S., K. Pollack and M. O'Hanlon. 2008. How to leave a Stable Iraq. *Foreign Affairs.* 87 (5). http://www.foreignaffairs.org/20080901faessay87503/stephen-biddle-michael-e-o-hanlon-kenneth-m-pollack/how-to-leave-a-stable-iraq.html (accessed November. 2008).

Chandrasekaran, R. 2006. *Imperial life in the emerald city: Inside Iraq's Green Zone.* New York, NY: Vintage Books.

Dagher, S. 2009. Another politician is killed as Iraqi voting draws near. *The New York Times.* 19 January. http://www.nytimes.com/2009/01/19/world/middleeast/19iraq.html?_r=1&ref=world.

Dagher, S. 2009. Iraq resists pleas by US to placate Baath party. *The New York Times.* 25 April. http://www.nytimes.com/2009/04/26/world/middleeast/26baathists.html.

Fadel, L., 2009. Vow to fight raises questions: How long will Iraq's calm last? *McClatchy.* 30 March.

http://www.mcclatchydc.com/world/story/65083.html.

Galtung, J. 1996. *Peace by peaceful means.* London: Sage Publications.

Goodhand, J. 2004. From war economy to peace economy? *Journal of International Affairs* 58: 155-174.

Graham-Brown, S. 1999. *Sanctioning Saddam: The politics of intervention in Iraq.* I.B. Tauris Publishers: London.

Irani, G. 1999. Islamic mediation techniques for Middle Eastern conflicts. *Middle East Review of International Affairs* 3 (2) http://meria.idc.ac.il/journal/1999/issue2/jv3n2a1.html (accessed January 2009).

Iraq's Top Shiite Cleric Urges Participation in Upcoming Vote. *The Washington Post.* Jan 20, A20. http://www.washingtonpost.com/wp-dyn/content/article/2009/01/19/AR2009011902839.html

Iraq Election Highlighting Ascendancy of Tribes. *The Washington Post.* Jan 25, World, Middle East. http://www.washingtonpost.com/wp-dyn/content/article/2009/01/24/AR2009012402051_3.html.

Iraqi National Constitution. http://www.uniraq.org/documents/iraqi_constitution.pdf

Iraq is Sovereign. Sort of. 2009. *The Economist.* 5 Jan.

Iraq Poll 2008. Online at http://www.globalpolicy.org/security/issues/iraq/poll/2008/0308opinion.pdf.

Jabar, F. Post-conflict Iraq: A race for stability, reconstruction and legitimacy. *United States Institute of Peace.* Online at http://www.usip.org/pubs/specialreports/sr120.pdf.

Leezenberg, M. 2005. Iraqi Kurdistan: contours of a post-civil war society. *Third World Quarterly.* 26 (4): 631-47.

McDonald, J. and Dr. L. Diamond. 1996. *Multi-track diplomacy: A systems approach to peace.* Sterling, VA: Kumarian Press.

"Muqtada al-Sadr". Council on Foreign Relations. http://www.cfr.org/publication/7637/.

The New York Times. 20 January 2009. Tribal rivalries persist as Iraqis seek local posts. http://www.nytimes.com/2009/01/20/world/middleeast/20anbar.html?emc=eta1

Parker, C. and P. W. Moore. 2007. The war Economy of Iraq. *Middle East Report 243.* http://www.merip.org/mer/mer243/parker_moore.html (accessed November 2008).

Perezalonso, A. 2006. Not just about the oil: Capillary power relations in the U.S. as motives behind the 2003 war on Iraq. *Peace, Conflict and Development* 9 (9) (accessed December 2008).

Poll Candidates Killed in Iraq. 2009. *Al Jazeera English.* 29 January. http://english.aljazeera.net/news/middleeast/2009/01/20091291753387 01596.html.

Ricks, T. 2007. *Fiasco: The American military adventure in Iraq.* New York, NY: Penguin Books.

Sakur, S. Interview with Ali Allawi. BBC Hardtalk. 18 Dec. 2008. http://news.bbc.co.uk/2/hi/programmes/hardtalk/7786441.stm.

Sengupta, K. 2007. The man left to pick up the pieces in Basra. *The Independent.* Sept 7, World, Middle East. Online http://www.independent.co.uk/news/world/middle-east/the-man-left-to-pick-up-the-pieces-in-basra-401617.html

Shadid, A. 2009. The political dance of Iraq's South. *The Washington Post.* Jan 19, A1. http://www.washingtonpost.com/wp-dyn/content/article/2009/01/18/AR2009011802545.html?hpid=topnews.

Slugglet, P. 2008. Imperial Myopia: Some lessons from two invasions of Iraq. *Middle East Journal* 64 (4). http://www.mideasti.org/middle-east-journal/article/imperial-myopia-some-lessons-two-invasions-iraq (accessed January 2009).

Tosti, P. 2004. Forecasting crime and narcobusiness: Iraq after the war. *Conflict, Security &Development* 4: 91-95.

West, F.J. 2008. A report from Iraq. *The Atlantic.* 30 Jan.

CHAPTER THIRTEEN

THE RESPONSIBILITY FOR SECURITY: HOW A REFORMED SECURITY COUNCIL OUGHT TO COUNTER THREATS TO THE PEACE

JOHN W. LANGO

A truly global culture of peace ought to be built partly by means of the United Nations (Weiss and Daws 2007). Of course, grassroots activism by nongovernmental organizations (NGOs) and civil society organizations is essential for building cultures of peace. But the United Nations is also essential, so long as the world remains dominated by the international system of states. Ideally, bottom-up peace activism should be harmonized with top-down UN peace actions. Towards this goal, representatives of NGOs (e.g., Amnesty International and Human Rights Watch) in the NGO Working Group on the Security Council have been meeting regularly with Security Council ambassadors (Global Policy Forum 2008).

In this chapter, I shall focus on peace actions by the Security Council. It might be objected that the Security Council is presently unable to collaborate sufficiently with other actors in building a global culture of peace, especially because of the policies and politics of the five permanent members. To answer this objection, a proposal about Security Council reform is eventually sketched. More explicitly, then, my focus is on the question of how a properly reformed Security Council ought to counter threats to the peace. The word "ought" is used here as a moral term. I am a specialist in moral philosophy, and my purpose is to examine moral issues.

In the words of the UN Charter, the 192 Members of the United Nations "confer on the Security Council primary responsibility for the maintenance of international peace and security" (Article 24). In particular, according to Chapter VII of the UN Charter, the Security Council "may take such action by air, sea, or land forces as may be necessary to maintain or restore international peace and security" (Article 42). Notably, the Korean War and the Gulf War were authorized beforehand by Security Council resolutions. Indeed, the Security Council is widely stereotyped as the legitimate source of war actions. Arguably, for example, when the conflict in the Darfur region of the Sudan became genocidal, the Security Council ought to have authorized armed humanitarian intervention there.

Consequently, it might be thought that the term "Security Council peace actions" is an oxymoron. To dispel this thought, it is crucial to recognize that the UN Charter mandates that the use of armed force must be a last resort. For, according to Chapter VI, the parties to a peace-endangering dispute should "first of all" attempt to settle their dispute "by negotiation, enquiry, mediation, conciliation, arbitration, judicial settlement, resort to regional agencies or arrangements, or other peaceful means" (Article 33). Significantly, Chapter VI empowers the Security Council to "call upon the parties to settle their dispute by such means" (Article 33). Thus the term "Security Council peace actions" encompasses Security Council resolutions calling upon the parties to settle their peace-endangering dispute by means of negotiations, Security Council resolutions calling upon the parties to submit their peace-endangering dispute to binding judicial settlement, and so forth.

For instance, Security Council Resolution 1828 (31 July 2008) about the conflict in Darfur includes such a peace action:

> [The Security Council] Welcomes the appointment of Mr. Djibrill Yipènè Bassolè as Joint AU-UN Chief Mediator, who has its full support; calls on the Government of Sudan and rebel groups to engage fully and constructively in the peace process, including by entering into talks under the mediation of Mr. Bassolè; demands all the parties, in particular rebel groups, to finalize their preparations for and to join the talks; and underlines also the need for the engagement of civil society, including women and women-led organizations, community groups and tribal leaders.
> (Security Council resolutions are available at http://www.un.org/documents/scres.htm). Although widely stereotyped as the legitimate source of war actions, the Security Council is also a legitimate source of peace actions.

In addition to Security Council peace actions under Chapter VI of the UN Charter, there can be Security Council peace actions under Chapter VII. For Chapter VII empowers the Security Council to "decide what measures not involving the use of armed force are to be employed to give effect to its decisions" (Article 41). Historically, the most valuable type of such nonmilitary measures has proven to be peacekeeping operations (O'Neill and Rees 2005). For instance, in Resolution 1769 (31 July 2007), the

Security Council authorized the establishment in Darfur of a joint peacekeeping operation (UNAMID) by the African Union (AU) and the United Nations. The term "Security Council peace actions" encompasses Security Council resolutions authorizing peacekeeping operations.

Historically, another type of nonmilitary measures that the Security Council is empowered by Chapter VII to employ has been economic sanctions (Article 41). For example, in Resolution 1591 (29 March 2005), the Security Council authorized the imposition of targeted economic sanctions (i.e., travel bans and the freezing of assets) on individuals in the Sudan "who impede the peace process" in Darfur.

Prohibiting the Use of Armed Force

Clearly, the Security Council is empowered by Chapter VII of the UN Charter to permit the use of armed force. However, the empowerment to permit is also the empowerment to prohibit. By implication, then, the Security Council is also empowered by Chapter VII to prohibit the use of armed force. There can be Security Council war actions permitting the use of armed force, but also there can be Security Council peace actions prohibiting the use of armed force.

Furthermore, there is a critical difference between the action of prohibiting and the omission of merely not permitting. For example, the Iraq War was not permitted by a Security Council resolution. (A U.S. sponsored draft resolution that would have authorized the Iraq War was withdrawn, because it would have been vetoed by France and Russia.) By contrast, imagine a Security Council resolution prohibiting the Iraq War. (Obviously, such a resolution would have been vetoed by the United States; indeed, there is need for Security Council reform.)

Despite political obstacles, Security Council resolutions prohibiting the use of armed force comprise a vital type of Security Council peace actions. For instance, in the aforementioned Resolution 1769 about Darfur, there is the following such peace action: "[the Security Council] Demands an immediate cessation of hostilities and attacks."

Importantly, this Chapter VII empowerment to prohibit the use of armed force can serve to bolster the peaceful means of Chapter VI (and the nonmilitary measures of Chapter VII). For the Security Council is both empowered by Chapter VI to call upon the parties to a peace-endangering dispute to use peaceful means and empowered by Chapter VII to prohibit their use of armed force. For example, in Resolution 1828 (31 July 2008), there is the clause: "[the Security Council] Reiterates there can be no military solution to the conflict in Darfur, and that an inclusive political settlement and the successful deployment of UNAMID are essential to re-establishing peace in Darfur."

Equally importantly, the Chapter VII empowerment to permit the use of armed force can also serve to bolster the peaceful means of Chapter VI. For the Security Council ought to authorize the use of armed force only as a last resort. And so, when the Security Council calls upon the parties to a peace-endangering dispute to settle their dispute by peaceful means, there can be the following (explicit or implicit) threat: if the parties fail to settle it by peaceful means, the Security Council will authorize the use of armed force to settle it. The Security Council is empowered by Chapter VII to pressure states to settle their disputes peacefully by the threat of military measures. In short, the peaceful means of Chapter VI may be bolstered by Chapter VII pressures.

Similarly, the Chapter VII empowerment to permit the use of armed force can serve to bolster the nonmilitary measures of Chapter VII. For instance, in the aforementioned Resolution 1769 authorizing the hybrid AU/UN peacekeeping operation in Darfur (UNAMID), it is stated that: "[the Security Council] decides that UNAMID is authorized to take the necessary action [. . .] in order to [. . .] support early and effective implementation of the Darfur Peace Agreement, prevent the disruption of its implementation and armed attacks, and protect civilians." Note that the phrase "necessary action" includes necessary uses of armed force (Lango 2009b).

Also, the Chapter VII empowerment to permit the use of armed force can serve to bolster Security Council peace actions prohibiting the use of armed force. For example, in Resolution 1591 (29 March 2005), there is an action of prohibiting: "[the Security Council] Demands that the Government of Sudan [. . .] immediately cease conducting offensive military flights in and over the Darfur region." Although the Security Council has not yet (as of March 2009) bolstered this peace action sufficiently by Chapter VII pressures, imagine a resolution with the following threat: if the Government of the Sudan continues to conduct these flights, the use of armed force will be authorized against Sudanese military aircraft. (Usually, such a threat needs to be made, whether explicitly or implicitly, in order to enforce a "no-fly zone.")

However, it is crucial again to recognize that the UN Charter mandates that such uses of armed force must be a last resort. For, according to Chapter VII, the Security Council may resort to the use of armed force only when the nonmilitary measures (of Article 41)—and, by implication, the peaceful means (of Chapter VI)—"would be inadequate or have proved to be inadequate" (Article 42).

In summary, rather than Security Council war actions, the focus in this chapter is on Security Council peace actions. The Security Council war powers of Chapter VII of the UN Charter are crucial, but so are the Security Council peace powers of Chapter VI and the Security Council nonmilitary measures of Chapter VII. Before resorting to war actions, the Security Council must determine that peace actions are inadequate. For instance, before resorting to armed humanitarian intervention (e.g., in the Darfur conflict), the Security Council must determine that such peace actions as peace agreements and peacekeeping operations are inadequate.

The Acceptance of Principles

Having discussed the UN Charter, I shall now discuss just war theory. Complementing legal issues about Security Council peace actions, I shall also consider moral issues. The legal empowerments of the Security Council in the UN Charter ought to be grounded on moral principles. Just war theory is a moral theory, and just war principles—among which are the principles of just cause, legitimate authority, right intention, proportionality, reasonable chance of success, and last resort—are moral principles. Ideally, these principles ought to morally constrain agents from using armed force unjustly. Presumably, then, they ought to morally constrain the Security Council from authorizing the use of armed force unjustly. The UN Charter empowers the Security Council to authorize the use of armed force only as a last resort. Comparably, the just war principle of last resort ought to morally constrain the Security Council from using armed force if every reasonable peaceful means or nonmilitary measure has not been attempted first.

Frequently, however, discussions of just war theory are oriented from the standpoint of individual states, and just war principles are formulated as state-centric principles. Consider, in particular, how the last resort principle has been formulated as a state-centric principle: "when conflicts of interest occur between two states, the use of force may be justified only as the last resort, that is, only when all nonmilitary means of conflict resolution have been tried" (Coppieters et. al. 2002, 101).

Traditional state-centric just war principles should be generalized, so as to be applicable to agents of all sorts—for example, regional organizations (e.g., NATO), insurgent groups (e.g., the Taliban), and the Security Council; additionally, they should be generalized, so as to be applicable to all sorts of military actions—for instance, counterinsurgencies (e.g., by NATO in Afghanistan), insurgencies (e.g., by the Taliban), and Security Council war actions (Lango 2007). Because the Security Council has the primary responsibility for the maintenance of international peace and security, the discussion of just war theory in this chapter is primarily oriented from the standpoint of the Security Council. Instead of being primarily state-centric, the generalized just war principles should be primarily UN-centric (Lango 2005). Furthermore, only the last resort and just cause principles can be considered. There is no space to consider other just war principles.

In particular, the following generalized last resort principle is presupposed: before resorting to the use of armed force, every reasonable peaceful means or nonmilitary measure must be attempted (Lango 2006). Note that this principle is qualified by the term "reasonable." Rather than every possible peaceful means or nonmilitary measure, what the last resort principle morally requires is that every reasonable peaceful means or nonmilitary measure must be attempted, before resorting to the use of armed force (Childress 1982, 75). This generalized last resort principle should be primarily UN-centric.

But why should the Security Council accept just war principles? Moral ideas are expressed in the UN Charter. Crucially, a moral idea of principles governing the use of armed force is expressed in the Preamble: "to ensure, by the acceptance of principles and the institution of methods, that armed force shall not be used, save in the common interest." By signing the UN Charter, the 192 UN Member States have committed themselves to abide by this moral idea. Therefore, the UN Member States on the Security Council ought to abide by it. But which principles about the use of armed force should the Security Council accept?

An authoritative answer to this question is contained in the Report of the Secretary-General's High-level Panel on Threats, Challenges and Change—namely, that, when deliberating about authorizing or endorsing the use of armed force, the Security Council should utilize "five basic criteria of legitimacy" (High-level Panel 2004, par. 207). Subsequently, then Secretary-General Kofi Annan summarized these legitimacy criteria and recommended "that the Security Council adopt a resolution setting out these principles and expressing its intention to be guided by them when deciding whether to authorize or mandate the use of force" (Annan 2005, par. 126).

Apparently, members of the High-level Panel were influenced by the just war tradition (Evans 2008, 140). For the five legitimacy criteria are tantamount to generalized just war principles of just cause, right intention, proportionality, reasonable chance of success, and last resort. For example, closely resembling the generalized last resort principle stated above, there is a legitimacy criterion entitled "last resort": "Has every non-military option for meeting the threat in question been explored, with reasonable grounds for believing that other measures will not succeed?" (High-level Panel 2004, par. 207).

However, the Security Council has not yet (as of March 2009) adopted a resolution of the sort envisaged by Kofi Annan. The Security Council ought to adopt such a resolution. The Security Council ought to accept suitably generalized just war principles.

Just Cause and Seriousness of Threat

The just cause principle is the most fundamental of the just war principles. To begin with, consider how it has been formulated state-centrically: "The [interstate] war must be fought in a just cause" (Graham 1997, 57). To generalize it, so that it is applicable to all sorts of agents and military actions, it could be reformulated thus: armed force must be used in a just cause. Specifically, consider how it could be reformulated UN-centrically: the Security Council must authorize the use of armed force in a just cause.

What causes are just? Traditionally, the primary type of just cause has been self-defense by a state against aggression by another state. Supplementing the traditional concept of state security, there is an emerging concept of human security. After the end of the Cold War, cases of genocide, ethnic cleansing, and other crimes against humanity have occasioned an emerging norm called "the responsibility to protect" (R2P) (Evans 2008). Controversially, another type of just cause is the defense of human beings against extreme violations of their basic human rights (e.g., "enslavement or massacre") (Walzer 2006, 90). Are there other causes that are just? A general answer to this question has been proposed roughly as follows. When there is a sufficiently "serious and weighty" responsibility to counter a threatened harm, there is a just cause for the use of armed force (Childress 1982, 75).

In the High-level Panel Report, one of the five basic criteria of legitimacy is comparably general—namely, the criterion entitled "seriousness of threat": "Is the threatened harm to State or human security of a kind, and sufficiently clear and serious, to justify prima facie the use of military force?" (High-level Panel 2004, par. 207). This threat-seriousness criterion is tantamount to a generalized just cause principle.

A wide range of kinds of threatened harms to the security of states and human beings is acknowledged in the High-level Panel Report: poverty, infectious disease, environmental degradation, conflict between states, conflict within states, weapons of mass destruction (WMD), terrorism, and transnational organized crime. The United States has been preoccupied with the threat of terrorism. However, many states are threatened much more by poverty, infectious disease, environmental degradation, and internal conflict. All of these kinds of security threats are potentially threats to the peace.

Which threatened harms of these kinds are sufficiently clear and serious? The UN Charter empowers the Security Council to "determine the existence of any threat to the peace" (Article 39). Consequently, in accordance with the threat-seriousness criterion, the Security Council could determine the existence of a threat to the peace of any of the stated kinds, decide that it is sufficiently clear and serious, and authorize the use of armed force to counter it. Indeed, the (legal) power of the Security Council is "extraordinary" (Matheson 2006, 33).

Such power, if unbridled, is troubling. For example, the Security Council could determine that the possession of WMD by Iran is a threat to the peace, decide that this threatened harm is sufficiently clear and serious, and authorize a coalition of states led by the United States to use armed force to counter it.

Similarly, some U.S. military actions have been troubling. Notably, concerning the possession of WMD by enemy states, and shortly before the Iraq War, the United States apparently invoked a state-centric just cause principle. For, in The National Security Strategy of the United States of America of September 2002, it is declared that: "The purpose of our actions will always be to eliminate a specific threat [of WMD] to the United States or our allies and friends. The reasons for our actions will be clear, the force measured, and the cause just" (U.S. White House 2002, 16).

Just Cause Hawks versus Last Resort Doves

When just war principles are applied to cases, there is a signal danger: "A one-sided and exaggerated emphasis on just cause" (Coates 1997, 146). More broadly, a person who tends to lopsidedly and unduly emphasize the just cause principle can be termed a just cause hawk. Just cause hawks tend to underrate or neglect other just war principles (e.g., Patterson, 2007). For instance, a just cause hawk could reason as follows. The just cause principle is a very stringent moral principle (i.e., it is a "deontological" principle), but the last resort principle is only one of several "prudential tests" (Johnson 1999, 34). Emphatically, when there is a just cause, the use of armed force is virtually justified. As a prudential test, the last resort criterion only "urges a sober caution" (Orend 2006,

241): armed force must not be used too hastily (Orend 2006, 58).
Therefore, when there is a just cause—and assuming that additional just
war principles are satisfied (e.g., the legitimate authority principle)—the
cautious and deliberate use of armed force is fully justified. For example,
when an enemy state of the United States is found by U.S. intelligence
work to possess nuclear weapons, the use of armed force by the United
States is virtually justified. The last resort principle only urges a sober
caution.

By contrast, a person who tends to emphasize equally the just cause
principle and the last resort principle (with due regard to other just war
principles) can be termed a last resort dove. In what follows, the topic of
how a last resort dove should reason is explored.

Ideally, even when the just cause principle is satisfied, the last resort
principle ought to morally constrain agents from using armed force
unjustly. Instead of being a merely prudential test, the last resort principle
is also a very stringent moral principle (i.e., it is a deontological principle).
It is not enough merely to counsel a sober caution. Instead, the last resort
principle should be meaningful operationally.

In general, a cardinal purpose of just war principles is to morally
constrain agents from using armed force unjustly. The words "morally
constrain" can be elucidated in terms of a notion of burden of proof. When
agents deliberate about whether to use armed force, they should make the
moral presumption that they must not. To override this presumption, they
have the burden of proving that just war principles are satisfied (Childress
1982, 64-73). Even when they have proven that the just cause principle is
satisfied, they still have the burden of proving that other just war
principles are satisfied.

In particular, even when agents have proven that the just cause principle
is satisfied, they have the burden of proving that the last resort principle is
satisfied. Therefore, when deliberating about whether to use armed force,
they should presume that it is reasonable to attempt some peaceful means
or nonmilitary measure first. To override this presumption, they have the
burden of proving that it is not reasonable to attempt any peaceful means
or nonmilitary measure first. To make the last resort principle meaningful
operationally, there is need for objective and impartial standards of
reasonableness, standards for determining whether it is no longer
reasonable to attempt any peaceful means or nonmilitary measure first
(Lango 2006).

For each type of pacific means or nonmilitary measure, there should be
specific reasonableness standards. For example, in order for negotiations
to be just, representatives of the parties to the negotiations ought to be

chosen correctly and the terms of the peace agreement ought to be fair. Accordingly, among the reasonableness standards for negotiations, there should be procedural standards and standards of fairness. To make the last resort principle meaningful operationally, there is need for such standards for determining whether it is no longer reasonable to attempt to use the pacific means of negotiation (cf. Ross 2008, 187-215).

Comparable remarks hold of the High-level Panel's legitimacy criteria. When the threat-seriousness criterion is satisfied, the use of armed force is prima facie justified. For the use of armed force to be actually justified, the last resort criterion and the other legitimacy criteria also have to be satisfied. The words "prima facie justified" can be interpreted in terms of the notion of burden of proof. When the Security Council deliberates about whether to authorize the use of armed force, it should presume that it must not. To override this presumption, it has the burden of proving that the five legitimacy criteria are satisfied. And, having proven that the first legitimacy criterion is satisfied—thereby proving that the use of armed force is prima facie justified—it still has the burden of proving that the other four legitimacy criteria are satisfied. In particular, concerning the last resort criterion, it has the burden of proving that it is not reasonable to attempt any peaceful means or nonmilitary measure first. Instead of merely a sober caution, there must be operationally meaningful proofs.

Peace Advocacy to the Security Council

In review, the UN Charter mandates that the use of armed force must be a last resort. For, according to Chapter VII, the Security Council may resort to the use of armed force only when nonmilitary measures and, by implication, peaceful means "would be inadequate or have proved to be inadequate" (Article 42).

This legal requirement—and the last resort criterion proposed in the High-level Panel Report—can be grounded on a suitably generalized just war principle of last resort. In terms of the notion of burden of proof, the words "would be inadequate" should be interpreted (or supplemented) as follows. When deliberating about whether to authorize the use of armed force, the Security Council must presume that peaceful means or nonmilitary measures would not be inadequate. To override this presumption, it has the burden of proving that every reasonable peaceful means or nonmilitary measure would be inadequate.

For example, before authorizing armed humanitarian intervention in the conflict in Darfur, the Security Council has the burden of proving that such peace actions as the current peace negotiations under a Joint AU-UN

Chief Mediator and the hybrid AU/UN peacekeeping operation (UNAMID) are inadequate (cf. International Crisis Group 2006).

To build a global culture of peace, grassroots peace activists should advocate and promote Security Council peace actions that would be adequate. In particular, concerning any threat to the peace that is proven to be sufficiently clear and serious, representatives of NGOs in the NGO Working Group on the Security Council should strive to communicate to Security Council ambassadors cogent and convincing reasons for resorting to peace actions before authorizing the use of armed force.

Nonviolent actions comprise a type of peace actions. Various specific methods of nonviolent action can be divided into three broad categories: nonviolent protest and persuasion, noncooperation, and nonviolent intervention (Sharp 2005). Should the Security Council counter threats to the peace by means of such nonviolent actions? To build a global culture of peace, grassroots peace activists should strive to persuade the Security Council that this question ought to be answered affirmatively (Lango 2009a).

Nevertheless, sometimes, when a threat to the peace is proven to be sufficiently clear and serious, the use of armed force ought to be authorized by the Security Council. Sometimes the presumption that peaceful means or nonmilitary measures would not be inadequate can be overridden by sound proofs. Under such extreme circumstances, and in support of such proofs, grassroots peace activists should provide reasons why Security Council peace actions would be inadequate and the use of armed force ought to be authorized. For instance, when the genocide began in Rwanda (in April 1994), "Human Rights Watch and FIDH [the International Federation of Human Rights Leagues] fought together with other human rights and humanitarian organizations to oblige policymakers, the press and the public to recognize the genocidal nature of the killings and to honor moral and legal obligations to intervene to halt the genocide" (Des Forges 1999, 28).

Reforming the Security Council Morally

In review, the question of how a properly reformed Security Council ought to counter threats to the peace has been addressed. What remains for consideration is the topic of Security Council reform. To be minimally reformed, the Security Council ought to genuinely and sincerely accept the High-level Panel's legitimacy criteria, and, as Kofi Annan recommended, "be guided by them when deciding whether to authorize or mandate the use of force" (Annan 2005, par. 126).

Frequently, the UN Secretary-General is perceived as having "moral authority" (Evans 2008, 176). By contrast, members of the Security Council are often perceived as being motivated primarily by national interests. Whereas the General Assembly with its 192 members is representative of almost all of the world's states, the Security Council with its 15 members is far less representative, and is dominated by the five permanent members with their veto power (i.e., Britain, China, France, Russia, and the United States). Among developing states especially, there is suspicion, concerning the idea of armed humanitarian intervention, "that noble principles are convenient cloaks for hegemonic interests" (Thakur 2006, 269). Hence a Security Council resolution endorsing the legitimacy criteria might be widely perceived as insincere and hypocritical.

Ideally, the Security Council should be transformed, so that it is invested with considerable moral authority. Without amending the UN Charter, the peoples of the United Nations have the legal authority to initiate this moral transformation. For the members of the General Assembly are empowered by the UN Charter to elect the Council's nonpermanent members. Indeed, among the provisions in the UN Charter for this election is a provision about: "due regard being specially paid [. . .] to equitable geographical distribution" (Article 23). However, there also is a provision about: "due regard being specially paid [. . .] to the contribution of Members of the United Nations to the maintenance of international peace and security and to the other purposes of the Organization" (Article 23). To begin to transform the Security Council morally, the General Assembly ought to comply with the latter provision strictly.

In light of this provision, a proposal for initiating the moral reform of the Security Council is sketched incompletely as follows. To counterbalance the five permanent members, the General Assembly ought to elect five nonpermanent members that are stable democracies, obey international laws, pursue alternatives to war, reject nuclear weapons, support environmentalism, and respect human rights—for example, Botswana, Canada, Costa Rica, Japan, and the Netherlands. Instead of serving their own national interests, the five nonpermanent members elected by the General Assembly ought to pledge to serve the best interests of everyone everywhere. Concerning threats to the peace, these five nonpermanent members ought to pledge to make objective and impartial moral judgments. To epitomize the traditional military function of the Security Council, the five permanent members might be called "the Circle of Warriors"; and, to epitomize the moral purpose of objectivity and impartiality, these five nonpermanent members might be called "the Circle of Judges." Just as the words and actions of the Secretary-General can have significant moral authority, so the words and actions of this Circle of Judges could have significant moral authority.

In conclusion, instead of Security Council war actions, the focus in this chapter is on Security Council peace actions. Even when the just war principle of just cause is satisfied, the Security Council ought to be morally constrained by the other just war principles from authorizing the use of armed force unjustly. In particular, in accordance with the UN Charter, the last resort principle ought to morally constrain the Security Council from authorizing the use of armed force if every reasonable peaceful means or nonmilitary measure has not been attempted first. To build a global culture of peace, grassroots peace activists should advocate and promote reasonable peace actions to the Security Council—for instance, effective peace agreements, robust peacekeeping operations, and principled nonviolent actions.

References

Annan, K. 2005. *In larger freedom: Towards development, security and human rights for all*. Report of the Secretary-General. United Nations General Assembly A/59/2005 (21 March 2005). http://www.un.org/largerfreedom/.

Childress, J. F. 1982. *Moral responsibility in conflicts: Essays on nonviolence, war, and conscience*. Baton Rouge: Louisiana State University Press.

Coates, A. J. 1997. *The ethics of war*. Manchester: Manchester University Press.

Coppieters, Bruno, R. Apressyan, and C. Ceulemans. 2002. Last resort. In *Moral constraints on war: Principles and cases*, ed. B. Coppieters and N. Fotion. Lanham, MD.: Lexington Books.

Des Forges, A. 1999. *Leave none to tell the story: Genocide in Rwanda*. New York and Paris: Human Rights Watch and International Federation of Human Rights.

Evans, G. 2008. *The responsibility to protect: Ending mass atrocity crimes once and for all*. Washington, D.C.: The Brookings Institution Press.

Global Policy Forum. 2008. NGO Working Group on the Security Council: Information statement, http://www.globalpolicy.org/security/ngowkgrp/statements/current.htm

Graham, G. 1997. *Ethics and international relations*. Cambridge, MA: Blackwell.

High-level Panel. 2004. *A more secure world: Our shared responsibility*. Report of the Secretary-General's high-level panel on threats, challenges and change. New York: United Nations, http://www.un.org/secureworld/. Also available in print form.

International Crisis Group. 2006. Getting the UN into Darfur. Africa Briefing No. 43. Nairobi/Brussels (12 October 2006), www.crisisgroup.org.

Johnson, J. T. 1999. *Morality and contemporary warfare*. New Haven: Yale University Press.

Lango, J. W. 2005. Preventive wars, just war principles, and the United Nations. In *Current debates in global justice*, ed. G. Brock and D. Moellendorf (247-68). Dordrecht: Springer.

——. 2006. The just war principle of last resort: The question of reasonableness standards. Asteriskos: *Journal of International and Peace Studies* 1: 7-23. Also available at http://www.igesip.org/asteriskos/1_2/galego/art1.pdf.

——. 2007. Generalizing and temporalizing just war principles: Illustrated by the principle of just cause. In *Rethinking the just war tradition*, ed. M. Brough, J. W. Lango, and H. van der Linden. Albany: State University of New York Press.

——. 2009a. Before military force, nonviolent action: An application of a generalized just war principle of last resort. *Public Affairs Quarterly* 23: 115-133.

——. 2009b. Military operations by armed UN peacekeeping missions: An application of generalized just war principles. In *The moral dimension of asymmetrical warfare: Counter-terrorism, western values, military ethics*, ed. T. van Baarda and D. Verweij (115-133). Leiden: Martinus Nijhoff.

Matheson, M. J. 2006. *Council unbound: The growth of UN decision making on conflict and postconflict issues after the cold war*. Washington, D.C.: United States Institute of Peace Press.

O'Neill, J. T., and N. Rees. 2005. *United Nations peacekeeping in the post-cold war era*. London: Routledge.

Orend, B. 2006. *The morality of war*. Peterborough, Ontario: Broadview Press.

Patterson, E. 2007. *Just war thinking: Morality and pragmatism in the struggle against contemporary threats*. Lanham, MD: Lexington Books.

Ross, D. 2008. *Statecraft: And how to restore America's standing in the world*. First paperback edition. New York: Farrar, Straus and Giroux.

Sharp, G. 2005. *Waging nonviolent struggle: 20th century practice and 21st century potential*. Boston: Porter Sargent.

Thakur, R. 2006. *The United Nations, peace and security: From collective security to the responsibility to protect*. Cambridge: Cambridge University Press.

U.S. White House. 2002. *The national security strategy of the United States of America* (September 2002), www.whitehouse.gov/nsc/nss.pdf.

Walzer, M. 2006. *Just and unjust wars*. 4th ed. New York: Basic Books.

Weiss, T. G., and S. Daws, eds. 2007. *The Oxford handbook on the United Nations*. Oxford: Oxford University Press.

CHAPTER FOURTEEN

CAN YOU EAT PEACE?
ADDRESSING DEVELOPMENT NEEDS
AND PEACE EDUCATION IN GUJARAT, INDIA

SUPRIYA BAILY

A popular bumper sticker emerged about a decade ago urging people to "envision whirled peas." Not only were the words a pun on the need for world peace, but also the visual attached to the pun was a tornado of swirling green peas, engaging people to laugh and to then think about the upheaval and chaos that ensues when there is no world peace. As witty as it seemed then, it also appears that to think about a more peaceful world, it may be in our best interests to think about peas, or carrots, or grains, or other basic needs that many parts of the planet are still lacking.

The connection between peace education and human developmental needs is the lack of resources available to always do both. In a world where basic needs are still barely accessible to large swathes of people, it becomes almost impossible for peace education programs to claim a share of already inadequate resources. Though international organizations like the United Nations Children's Fund (UNICEF) and the United Nations Educational, Scientific and Cultural Organization (UNESCO) have spearheaded efforts to create strong peace education programs and curricula, the reality is that in many communities the threat of violence, intolerance, and conflict with neighbors takes a backseat to addressing the basic needs that communities increasingly focus upon first to allow their citizens greater opportunities for development. Unfortunately, in areas where development needs are still barely provided for, there are often greater tensions between the "us" and the "them." The divisions that are created between people "linked with distinct racial or ethnic or other non-economic identities are made more tangible and serious through their association with poverty and inequality.... It is mainly through those associations that economic deprivation and social humiliation can become a lethal cause of violence" (Sen 2008, 15).

In exploring these ideas, this chapter seeks to use the case of a state in India, namely Gujarat, as an example of how social, economic, and political differences have allowed the region to explode in violence and how the lack of resources affects not only the relationships between the groups that are fighting but also hinders any role peace education might have in the region. Often we hear about the needs of peace education programs in post-conflict situations, in refugee camps, or in post-war situations, but there is also a need for peace education programs in regions of the world that are part of largely peaceful societies and where the conflict is neither national in scope nor international in reach. Peace education and development programs compete for the same limited resources, and this chapter seeks to present the reality of a case caught up in such a vortex of human suffering and chaos. How can poor and developing communities incorporate peace education programs alongside development programs? Is there a continuum, which if followed, would allow optimal success? What roles do poverty, unemployment, and limited resources play in understanding the need to live peaceably with others who have historically been strict adversaries? The case of Gujarat represents not only what is happening in India, but opens a window to other countries where development programs and localized intolerance create a vacuum requiring the need for effective peace education programs. By setting the stage on the current situation in Gujarat, and in systematically exploring the challenges, this chapter seeks to build an argument in a critical framework that addresses the process of meeting two needs in a rapidly modernizing, democratic, and developing country.

Peace Education in India

It may be ironic that Gujarat, the case explored in this chapter, is also the home state of India's most famous man of peace. Mohandas K. Gandhi, or Mahatma Gandhi, was born in Gujarat and might have established one of the first foundations of peace education as we know it today. Any efforts towards peace education in India are fundamentally inspired by his teachings and writings, and he has helped transform the definition of peace from purely the absence of war to the more broad and holistic idea where peace is "nonviolence restored with justice and equity" (Prasad 1998, 4).

As his ideas on non-violence or *ahimsa* reverberated around the world, his critique on the Indian educational system is less well known and addresses a point on what we now call peace education. Gandhi felt the educational system was devised to increase the inequity both socially and economically for citizens and he believed that education should incorporate not only a local medium of instruction, vocational training, and understanding of technology and industrialization but also religious tolerance (Tamatea 2005). Gandhi's recognition that social justice lay at the heart not only of global peace but also local development and equity, shows the congruence of his thinking. This aligns not only the theoretical bases of peace education but also human development theories, which he was already beginning to synthesize.

Today, peace education programs have evolved from the early ideas of educating people about the threat of nuclear weapons and the role of disarmament to building a culture of positive peace (Harris 2004). Theorists in peace education like Galtung and Freire who emerged after Gandhi's death in 1948 further shaped his ideas linking peace education to social justice and through a bottom-up approach to development and peace. Galtung addressed how "structural violence, the inequitable denial of resources, causes violence…and (Galtung) expanded the field of peace studies beyond the study of the interstate system that leads to war to the study of cultural violence, human rights and development" (Harris 2004). Later Freire incorporated the roles of the oppressed and the oppressor in the search for human freedom and addressed the influence of education in allowing people to seek out their own freedom and agency (Harris, 2004).

Evolving from these theories, peace education has come to be defined as "the process of promoting the knowledge, skills, attitudes and values needed to bring about behavior changes that will enable children, youth and adults to prevent conflict and violence, both overt and structural; to resolve conflict peacefully; and to create the conditions conducive to peace" (Fountain 1999, 1). The overall expectation of incorporating a peace education program is to provide people with the skills and knowledge that will help them to make decisions that will guide them towards peaceful solutions, rather than ones that will allow for more violence to occur at the individual, community, and national level.

Returning to India, the role of peace education, or as it was called earlier, Gandhian education, did not have much of a place in the Indian context before 1959. There were no centers established to study peace, and almost no research conducted to explore the ideas and concepts of peace (Prasad 1998). After 1961 however, there has been the progressive development of research, the creation of centers and the transfer of ideas that have promoted peace education, evolving from a defense and military background to a more political one looking at India's status as a nonaligned country in the cold war era, to currently studying the role of social change and non-violence (Prasad 1998).

Peace education in India then has been a field of study cobbled together, with a sense of history and reverence in its relationship with the "father of India," M.K. Gandhi. Yet there has been little grassroots work in the arena, which has limited its access and increases the need to allocate additional resources for peace education since it has not become an integral part of how the country looks at education. The fact remains, that peace education can sometimes be seen as a luxury, developing countries can still ill afford when their priorities remain focused on basic developmental needs.

Setting the Stage—The Current Situation in Gujarat

To understand what is happening in Gujarat today and to explore the how human development needs take precedence over peace education programs, one must understand three things about Gujarat. Firstly, one must understand the economic and social indicators that highlight Gujarat's developing status. Secondly, there needs to be an understanding of the recent history of natural disasters that are unpredictable and devastating in the toll they take on lives and limited resources, and finally the third level of understanding should be through the conflicts that are emerging as a result of increasing divisions between two of the largest religious groups in the state, namely the Hindus and the Muslims.

Gujarat is located on the west coast of India beside the Arabian Sea. It has a narrow international border with Pakistan in the northwest and has the longest coastline in the country. Even with a large part of the state covered by two deserts, agriculture plays a prime role in the economy of the state, and the state shows healthy economic growth at over ten percent per year which is two percent more than the national rate of growth (Socio-Economic Review SEC 2008).

Gujarat faces high levels of poverty, illiteracy, and gender discrimination (Krishna et al. 2005). On the state government website, only 69 percent of the population over the age of six is considered literate. Males have a literacy rate of 76 percent, while female literacy rates hovers near the 58 percent mark (SEC 2008). The state population makes up approximately 6.1 percent of the national population, or approximately 50 million people (SEC 2008). Gujarat also maintains the population figures of the major religious groups with Hindus making up the majority of the population at just over 45 million people. Muslims are next with about 4.5 million people living in Gujarat. Jains number around 525,000; Christians around 284,000; Sikhs, 45,000; Buddhists, 17,000; and other religions or unstated in the census number around 62,000 (SEC 2008). These numbers are important to note, as they relate to the inter-group violence that will be explored further in this chapter.

Gujarat has suffered from two devastating earthquakes over the last nine years. In 2001, an earthquake measuring 7.9 on the Richter scale was the worst natural disaster in India in over 300 years. Over 20,000 people were killed, 167,000 were injured and four districts in the state were decimated, while 21 other districts were severely affected by the earthquake (Global Education 2009). In 2006 a smaller earthquake measuring 5.5 on the Richter scale also caused high levels of loss both to people and property in the state. These earthquakes are part of the story of the state highlighting the tenuous nature of development and poverty reduction programs.

In addition to the toll of these natural disasters, Gujarat has also suffered from communal violence and terrorism as well. Primarily the people involved determine the differences between the two forms of violence - in situations of communal violence perpetrators tend to people who reside and interact in close proximity. Terrorism tends to be seen more as the violence inflicted on people by outside enemies and not people who you see at the teashop or in the local markets. It is primarily the Hindu and Muslim populations who lie at the heart of the communal violence Gujarat has seen in recent years. In 2002, Gujarat became the state that was home to two of eight cities in the entire country responsible for nearly 50% of all deaths in Hindu-Muslim confrontations up until that time (Varshney 2002). The fact remains that Gujarat is a complicated state, with issues related to development, natural disasters that have played havoc as well as the specter of rising animosity between two of the largest religious groups in the country. To understand the need for peace education, one must also understand how these three factors affect the productive development of relationships across a cultural and religious divide.

Understanding Communal Violence in a Development Framework

Intolerance, bigotry, and religious violence are not the hallmarks a country like India wishes to present to the world and overwhelmingly the country has maintained its strong secular traditions evidenced by the fact that in the elections of 2004 Indian voters elected a Muslim as President, a Sikh as Prime Minister, and a Christian as the leader of the opposition party (Sen 2008). India has been methodical about presenting an image of a country that is on the cusp of tremendous growth and modernity. Still uneven development has meant that not all of its citizens are experiencing the same levels of opportunity, which has led to large pockets of inequity and frustration.

Communal violence is different from terrorism, which is unfortunately also not new to India. The recent attacks in Mumbai come on the heels of other attacks around the country, but there is another side to the religious violence in India, which is not as well-documented in western media, and falls under the less threatening term of "communal violence." Inter-religious, inter-caste, and inter-faith violence between one community group in India and another can be broadly defined as communal violence and there has been a rising level of attacks on people of different faiths whether they are Christians, Hindus, or Muslims or one of the other religions of India. There has been a long history of communal violence in India where the term "communalism" itself is a term specific to the Indian context where people have a "strong identification with a community of believers…(which) not only has religious affiliation but also social, political, and especially economic interests in common which conflict with the corresponding interests of another community of believers—the enemy, who shares the same geographic space…(where) the "real" cause of violence generally embraces some version of a class struggle between the poor and the rich" (Kakar 2000, 878).

Gujarat has been at the heart of much of the violence over the last seven years. In 2002, 58 people, who were primarily Hindus, were killed on a train in Eastern Gujarat, while traveling on a religious pilgrimage. Over the next three months, violence against Muslims took the form of brutal murders, rapes, arson, and looting as retaliation for the attacks on the pilgrims (South China Morning Post 2007). Petrol bombs, acid throwing, and violent beatings characterized the attacks, and the lingering fear, suspicion and anger remains a vivid part of how people live in Gujarat today.

Added to this a political element, where the ruling party in Gujarat is the Bharatiya Janata Party (BJP) who have touted themselves to be the "champions the rights of India's Hindus" (The Economist 2008), have not leaned hard on the courts to bring the guilty to justice. The situation remains tense and the opportunities that India seeks to build as it takes a bigger role on the world stage will remain shadowed by the nature of the communal violence in Gujarat and some of the other states in India. The economic situation fans the flames of the continued tension where the foundations of the formal and informal economies remain shuttered and/or destroyed. Over 17,000 businesses were affected by the violence, and only a small percentage of those businesses were insured (Sharma 2002). Fallout from the violence has continued to plague those hoping to find work, where business owners have been unwilling to take a chance in the fragile peace, and have therefore decamped to other states where the likelihood of communal violence destroying their businesses is far less (Sharma 2002).

The Impact of Development on Communal Disharmony

On the development front, India has established wide-ranging programs and is actively seeking to build a strong foundation to be considered an active player on the world's stage. The tangible goals of education, health, employment, and opportunity are results that citizens are eager to support and encourage greater investment in. As one of the oldest members of the World Bank, India has centered its focus on reducing poverty, engaging in greater trade, equalizing gender and social disparities, and implementing a broad universal primary education program (World Bank 2008).

Gujarat, as a middle income state, has a new focus with the 2009-2012 World Bank plan for India, namely fighting poverty in parts of the state that are falling behind, and managing to maintain economic growth despite the faltering global economy (World Bank 2008). Poverty reduction remains a vital part of Gujarat's plan for the future. In the study by Krishna et al. (2005) they found that though there was economic growth in the state, there were many rural villages where "poverty has remained virtually unchanged over this (25 year) period; 65 per cent of people in these villages were poor 25 years ago by their own reckoning, and 62 per cent are poor now in terms of the same criteria. Lack of food and clothing, inadequate and leaky shelters, assets insufficient to send their children even to primary school, and dependence on high-interest private debt characterize the conditions of poverty among villagers of this region" (Krishna et al. 2005, 2). They also have found that "Muslims constitute another population group that is poorer on average than other households in this region" (Krishna et al. 2005, 26). In their case study, they found that Muslim families were faced with significantly higher levels of stagnation at poverty levels than other groups, and far fewer have "escaped" from poverty. Additionally, Muslim families have faced violence that has also prevented them from moving forward and for many of them who descended back into poverty the researchers found that "arson and looting in the recent past constituted the primary reason for descent" (Krishna et al. 2005, 26).

These situations lead to greater levels of frustration and anger among group members and can enhance "the already existing discrepancy between more and less privileged groups. It activates or intensifies the experience of injustice" (Staub 2003, 2). In earlier communal violence in another Indian city the "poverty-stricken neighborhoods of Hyderabad have a long history of riots between the religious groups, and the presence of all the conditions for violence - economic, political, historical, demographic, social-psychological" (Kakar 2000, 898).

In a qualitative case study conducted in Gujarat in 2007, the Hindus and Muslims interviewed in the study talked about how the economic adversity faced by the members of both communities hindered their ability to regain trust in each other after the communal violence of 2002. The continued lack of business opportunities and continued economic hardship remains a hindrance for the two groups to seek out effective measures for peace (Shankar and Gerstein 2007).

Besides the general lack of economic opportunities, the people of Gujarat also face other economic challenges, which are not unusual for India in general. High expenses for social obligations like marriage and death ceremonies, health care, and low levels of access to reputable credit hinder the poor from moving ahead (Krishna et al. 2005). These economic factors affect peoples' frustration, limit their hopes for opportunities for the future, and increase the likelihood of being willing to blame "others" for ones misfortunes.

It has not helped that political entities are using religious differences as a wedge between Hindus and Muslims for political leverage. From 1992 when politicians called for the demolition of the mosque, Babri Masjid, in the name of the Hindu god Rama, tensions between the two groups simmered and boiled over (Kakar 2000). Politicians in Gujarat continue to promote the divisiveness among the religions to not only further their own aims, but have used their influence and power to hinder the appropriate extension of justice for the people of Gujarat and news reports claim intimidation of witnesses from politicians as well as the use of the issue to raise money for political purposes (South China Morning Post 2007).

Applying Strategies and Best Practices
from an International Context to Gujarat

There is a lot to learn from the case of Gujarat. If India, in spite of its long history of peace and nonviolent movements still struggles in balancing an agenda for peace alongside an agenda for developmental needs, it can only be more difficult for other countries that do not share the same history. For practitioners in the field of peace education, an additional challenge makes the situation more complex. To transform peace education from theory to practice and from rhetoric to action remains difficult if not downright impossible given the limited resources of the country. To counter criticisms of peace education programs being more about talk than action, some suggestions of best practices include:

1.   Conduct a situation analysis before the program is designed to assist in the correct monitoring and evaluating of the program after implementation (World Health Organization 1998). This answers the questions of who are the populations to be served by implementing a peace education program? Will the entire community be involved or will it be restricted to school-age students?

2.   Provide adequate opportunities for teachers and staff to be trained in the concepts and skills required to educate for peace. Teachers who do not adequately understand the concepts will not be able to translate those concepts to others; therefore training is vital (Metis Associates 1990).

3.   Use real-life situations to teach students. Teachers should focus their attention on putting context to the curriculum and make situations more relevant to the students they teach (Tolan and Guerra 1994).

4.   Allow young people the opportunity to use the skills they are learning to engage in the broader community (Tolan and Guerra 1994). This would increase the value for students participating in the program as well as to counter any initial hostility or hesitation on their part.

5.   Enlist the support of the community including politicians, educators, local and business leaders as well as religious leaders in the implementations of programs (WHO 1998). If the program is to succeed there must be a strong sense of ownership by the community.

The issue with these best practices is that they do not take into account the costs of developing curricula, hiring trainers, establishing offices, implementation, oversight and evaluation. The competition for limited resources is fierce when you pit developmental needs next to peace education programs. Yet if anything is illustrated by the case of Gujarat, a middle-income state in a rapidly modernizing and developing country is that the flames of unequal development fan conflicts bubbling over due to communal disharmony.

There is substantially less research being done in Gujarat in the post-communal violence period as it relates to how people are moving on with their lives (Shankar and Gerstein 2007). As researchers and development professionals return to Gujarat and as international aid organizations like the World Bank infuse greater resources into Gujarat, it would take far fewer resources for these entities and individuals to incorporate a needs assessment for peace education in their programs for Gujarat. The situation in Gujarat shows that there is a link between poverty, lack of access and communal violence, but without the implementation of some of these best practices, it challenges the ability for the state to build a culture of peace and economic stability.

In terms of teachers and teacher training, the National Council of Education Research and Training (NCERT) in India recognized the need for peace education. The idea that teachers should understand the basis of peace education and apply that to their teaching by recognizing that "conflicts are pervasive in society and are held in place due to uneven distribution of socio-economic as well as political power, religious and regional differences" (NCERT 2009) cuts to the heart of what is happening in Gujarat and it is a step towards incorporating a long-term plan to build a cadre of teachers who can not only teach peace education but also nurture the establishment of a culture of peace as they transition from teacher training institutes to schools. Unfortunately, there is still no evidence to determine if the institutes are effectively incorporating the peace education curriculum in programs around the country. News reports cite a six-week program held in the national capital of New Delhi over the summers of 2006 and 2007, but that again is not as extensive as what might currently be needed (MSN 2009).

Another suggested best practice is to engage leaders both in and outside of the community to address the need for peace education. There is some evidence that political leaders are starting to understand the divisive nature of inequity and violence. In 2006, the Prime Minister, Manmohan Singh, stated "High growth has not made as much of an impact on poverty reduction as we would have liked...Too many of our people lack access to basic services especially education, health, housing and clean drinking water...(what) I am drawing your attention to can be termed as our equity concerns. Equity is the foundation on which our democratic polity has to rest and thrive...the basis on which our citizens develop a sense of ownership of the state and its organs. Inequity can lead to large-scale migration, disaffection and discord" (Staff writer 2006, 5). The ability to engage political rhetoric has to be followed by effective actions to promote both development and confidence. Measures that allow for improved living conditions, as well as addressing broad societal issues like corruption and ineffective law enforcement will also allow citizens to regain trust in the government if they are to be able to feel safe in their homes and as a result feel more welcoming of peace initiatives geared towards reducing hostilities with neighbors.

Peace education can be helpful to providing a positive view of the other group –rather than differentiating the "us" from the "them", but in working with people to develop a sense of common purpose. Communities can help in creating peaceful societies where the alternate basic needs of respect and caring (Staub 2003) are structured into the goal of other basic needs—namely, food, shelter, education and job opportunities. Unfortunately financial resources at a disadvantage when talking about poor regions of the world, and it appears that there are few short-term solutions that could blend incorporating peace education with development planning. Part of the rationale in highlighting the case of Gujarat is to advocate for longer term solutions that cost less and can have longer term impact on the other regions of the world that find themselves in similar situations.

One long-term solution emerges from the fact that development practitioners and peace educators do not necessarily overlap in their expertise. Professionals involved in the role of development initiatives come from a multitude of backgrounds and disciplines, from economics to education, and from health to history. The work of poverty reduction relies on the involvement of engineers, city planners, and even those involved in law enforcement, but unfortunately, peace educators are not necessarily invited or involved in many of these actions. Due to this minimal investment, the responsibility might need to be placed in colleges, universities and training institutions that incorporate the curricula of peace education in training these professionals. Peace studies need to be folded into many more disciplines, including ones that historically have not seen a need for an option like peace education.

Peace education also suffers from a negative reputation among people that it is unrealistic to expect decades, if not centuries of hostilities to be made up in the matter of a short time, and in the manner of a few exercises, superficial reflection, and a kumbaya moment. Obviously, peace education when done correctly is much more than that, but when resources are limited, a piece of curricula might be used as a "symbolic" effort, made to appease a donor or a particular stakeholder. Peace educators should resist such efforts and exert greater pressure on development entities to work in tandem for the benefit of the community.

Additionally, there is little known about the impact of this type of violence in the long-term on young people. Scholars and researchers might find it a relevant and timely challenge to explore how young people see their futures in Gujarat and how the experiences of the communal violence has affected them to get a better grasp on how the progression of animosity and bitterness might or might not be affecting the next generation. It is clear that building a culture of peace takes time and patience and it is important to start to look at the intersection between development, opportunity and hope for peace with the younger generations so that they are allowed a chance to grow and develop with losing their lives or their livelihoods to communal violence. Understanding the impact on the younger people also allows a chance for peace educators to teach to those specific reactions and build a sense of understanding the rivalries and lengthy hostilities and allow for greater depth and knowledge to create a more peaceful community.

Conclusion

In this chapter, I have tried to answer three questions through this exploration of one case in India. In reverse order, the third question tried to explore the role that poverty, unemployment and limited resources play in understanding the need to live peaceably with others who have historically been strict adversaries. In the case of Gujarat, we have seen people suffering from high levels of stagnation and limited opportunity and this among other reasons, has resulted in greater levels of enmity and violence between Hindus and Muslims. Communal violence is something India continues to fight, and is not a hallmark of this secular, diverse, and increasingly influential country. There is a sense on the part of progressive activists, that to continue to improve the lives of the people in Gujarat, there must also be a clear expectation of creating a culture of peace since recent events have shown that no matter how much development works, the peace is still tenuous.

The second question looks whether a clear progression that might allow for optimal success moving from introducing, implementing and completing development programs to introducing, implementing and completing peace programs. Here the answer is less murky and it appears that best practices signify the need for concurrent peace building programs alongside development programs. The presence of multiple local, state, national and international actors involved in basic education means that there might be a way to allocate additional resources to compliment development programs in order to engage people to think about moving forward in a manner that promotes a culture of peace. It seems that for any real change to occur in Gujarat, resources need to be allocated by some entity to allow for peace educators to do their job, but realistically, the case of Gujarat may not be one we can fix immediately. Taking some of the other long-term solutions might prevent other Gujarats from occurring.

Finally, the primary question addressed how poor and developing communities need peace education programs working alongside development programs. The answer in the case of Gujarat is that there really is no clear evidence to show that development programs are involved in addressing peace education programs, but that does not mean that the two must continue to remain independent. The situation in Gujarat still shows high levels of mistrust and suspicion but it might be more important for development professions to adopt some of the curriculum and programming of peace education alongside their plans for growth.

Sen (2008, 7) says that it is not "hard to see that the injustice of inequality can generate intolerance and that the suffering of poverty can provoke anger and fury," but he goes on to say that poverty by no means signifies the propensity towards violence. He uses the example of the city of Kolkata, which is one of the poorest cities in India but also has the lowest rate of violent crime in the country with only 0.3 homicides per 100,000 people. This is much lower than the other Indian and world cities: 2.9 in New Delhi, 2.3 in Paris, 5.0 in New York, 17.0 in Mexico City, and as high as 21.5 in Johannesburg and 34.9 in Rio de Janeiro. The point he makes is that Kolkata is one of the most mixed cities in India, where the "understanding of multiplicity of our identities can be a huge force in combating the instigation of violence based on a singular identity, particularly religious identity, which is the dominant form of cultivated singularity in our disturbed world today" (Sen 2008, 11).

Sen, one of the most influential writers, scholars and activists on poverty and identity recognizes that the ideas for peace don't emerge from the hopelessness of our situations, the deprivation of our needs or the anger at the "other," but come from our recognition that we all have multiple identities and we align ourselves with the "other" based on our understanding of ourselves. For development to be successful in Gujarat, and for the creation of a culture of peace, it appears that we might need to continue to look at ways we can envision not only whirled peas, but also world peace, and put the onus of that responsibility on both development professionals and peace educators alike to help promote the change we seek.

References

Bush, K., D. and Saltarelli, D. 2000. *The Two Faces of Education in Ethnic Conflict: towards a Peacebuilding Education for Children.* Florence, Italy: UNICEF.

Fountain, S. 1999. *Educational initiatives working paper - Peace education in UNICEF.* New York: UNICEF.

Global education. The Indian Gujarat Earthquake 26 January 2001 - Case Study.

http://www.globaleducation.edna.edu.au/archives/secondary/casestud/i
ndia/2/earthquake.html

Harris, I. 2004. Peace education theory. *Journal of Peace Education* 1: 5-
20

Kakar, S. 2000. The time of Kali: Violence between religious groups in
India. *Social Research* 67: 877-899.

Krishna, A., M. Kapila, M. Porwal, and V. Singh. 2005. Why growth is
not enough? Household poverty dynamics in Northeast Gujarat, India.
Journal of Development Studies 41:163-1192.

Metis Associates. 1990. *The Resolving Conflict Creatively Program,
1988-1989: Summary of Significant Findings.* New York: New York
City Board of Education.

MSN, 2008. India teachers get training in peace education.
http://education.in.msn.com/schoolcolleges/article.aspx?cp-
documentid=1215662

National Council for Education Research and Training (NCERT). 2006.
Position Paper. National Focus Group on Education for Peace. New
Delhi: NCERT.

Prasad, S. N. 1998. *Development of Peace Education in India (since
Independence).*Sweden: Lund University.

Sen, A. 2008. Violence, identity and poverty. *Journal of Peace Research*
45:5-15.

Shankar, J., and L. H. Gerstein. 2007. The Hindu-Muslim conflict: A pilot
study of peacebuilding in Gujarat, India. *Peace and Conflict:Journal of
Peace Psychology* 13:365-379.

Sharma, K. 2002. Victims look for work. *India Together.*
http://www.indiatogether.org/opinions/kalpana/thinthread.htm

Socio-Economic Review (SEC). 2008. *Gujarat State.* Gandhinagar, India:
Government of Gujarat.

South China Morning Post. 2007. Where wounds refuse to heal. *South
China Morning Post.* February 25.

Staff writer. 2006. PM's speech at National Development Council Meet.
India e-News.

State Government of Gujarat. 2009. State Profile.
http://www.gujaratindia.com/stateprofile/profile1.htm

Staub, E. 2003. Notes on cultures of violence, cultures of caring and
peace, and the fulfillment of basic human needs. *Political Psychology*
24: 1-21.

Tamatea, L. 2005. The uses of Gandhi in education in Bali: Different
responses to globalization—implications for social justice. *Journal of
Peace Education* 2: 139-159.

Tolan, P.H., and N.G. Guerra. 1994. What Works in Reducing Adolescent Violence: An Empirical Review of the Field. Monograph prepared for the Center for the Study and Prevention of Youth Violence. Boulder, CO: University of Colorado.The Economist. 2008. Terror in India. *The Economist.* November 29, US Edition.

Varshney, A. 2002. *Ethnic conflict and civic life: Hindus and Muslims in India.* New Haven, CT: Yale University Press.

World Bank. World Bank strategy for India set to boost support for Infrastructure and poorer states. http://web.worldbank.org/WBSITE/EXTERNAL/NEWS/0,,contentM DK:22009243~pagePK:64257043~piPK:437376~theSitePK:4607,00.h tml

World Health Organization (WHO). 1998. *Violence Prevention: An Important Element of a Health-promoting School.* Geneva: WHO.

CHAPTER FIFTEEN

PAX GAIA:
THE ECOLOGY OF WAR, PEACE,
AND HOW TO GET FROM HERE TO THERE

RANDALL AMSTER

As human cultures grow and evolve, so too does our understanding of the ways in which the various facets of our lives are interconnected. From the impetus of globalization and the networks of technology and communication, to the challenges of resource depletion and planetary climate change, there is a nascent yet pervasive understanding that we are all part of a whole system. The potential for this emerging sensibility to promote greater unity and empathy is palpable, even as conceptual and pragmatic difficulties with a "one world" model are likewise prevalent. Still, the notion of a holistic framework is appealing to many, and in some instances it has begun to take on an air of inevitability. Navigating this state of affairs is a cutting-edge crucible for all disciplines of human thought, particularly as we seek to imagine and create those elusive "cultures of peace," and the field of Peace Studies itself is certainly no exception in this regard.

Indeed, Peace Studies as both a body of knowledge and a set of action-oriented principles stands in good stead to directly embrace these issues and challenges. Thoroughly interdisciplinary by nature—including in its rubric strands of history, political science, psychology, sociology, criminology, religion, and philosophy, among others—Peace Studies already is prone to holistic thinking about social problems and potential solutions. Moreover, as an academic field with a value-based perspective woven into its very moniker—to wit: Peace!—there is a deeper sense in the discipline of being comfortable engaging ethical issues in a manner that is neither premised on achieving an unattainable objectivity nor consumed by academic tendencies to bifurcate theory and action. Simply put, Peace Studies is a natural arena for ecological thinking, in the sense of *ecology* as an understanding of interrelationships and mutual dependencies.

Still, and perhaps somewhat ironically, the field has been a bit slower than some to directly embrace environmentalism among its many cross-disciplinary forays. This is not entirely the case, of course, and there are many fine examples in the literature and history of the field expressing connectivity with environmental matters, including Johan Galtung's consideration of primitive war and the implications of "rank-disequilibrium," Elise Boulding's writings on utopian communities and their relationship to the land, and Gandhi's explicit focus on the material conditions of life as a precondition for a more peaceful world. But by and large the discipline has confined itself to considerations of more anthropocentric (and equally compelling) matters, such as the prevention of warfare and the establishment of human rights. While some have begun the dialogue to bridge human and "more than human" issues, a fuller articulation of the ecological implications of Peace Studies has commenced but has yet to be exhaustively undertaken. This work seeks to address some of the fundamental aspects of this potential evolution of the field, hoping to spur greater interest and suggest avenues of critical inquiry and engagement.

Roots and Renderings

In a landmark article published in 1967 on "Ecology and Peace Research," Gutorm Gjessing looked at the intersections of historical resource innovations such as agriculture and the domestication of horses with conflict and warfare. Positing that "[m]odern war is turned more upon the command of raw materials and markets than upon ideologies" (1967, 131), Gjessing concluded that "strengthening a mere representative political democracy" would alone be insufficient to alleviate conflict, but rather we would need to develop "values which make for cooperation rather than competition" (1967, 136). Gjessing's insights began to move the Peace Studies field explicitly in a direction of linking human concerns with environmental issues.

In 1974, Edward Goldsmith wrote on "The Ecology of War," exploring the connection between resource shortages and conflict, and pointing out the centrality of commodities such as oil and water in potential future conflicts. Goldsmith further opined on the economic impetuses for war, noting that internal national struggles are often due to "our efforts to bring the other countries of the world into the orbit of our industrial society, that we may more easily persuade them to part with their resources and buy our finished products" (1974, 12). Goldsmith concluded his influential essay with a call for action that still resonates today (1974, 17):

> Self-righteous exhortations in favour of peace or pious declarations of the universal brotherhood of man can serve no purpose save to mask the real issues. The problem can, in fact, only be solved by methodically and systematically de-industrialising and decentralising society, thereby recreating those conditions in which new cultural patterns can re-emerge, once more to regulate aggression both between individuals and between the societies into which they are organized.

Journalist Philip Shabecoff likewise noted the centrality of our economies and how they might better exist in balance with the natural world, concluding that the path to social and ecological sustainability—what he termed "A New Name for Peace"—would lay in large measure upon how well we could "minimize competition and aggression among individuals and nation-states and replace it with cooperation" (1996, 216).

In his 2000 book, *The Ecology of War & Peace*, Tom Hastings enunciated in an explicit manner what a "peace ecology" ought to represent. Hastings looked specifically at the environmental impacts of warfare and at the ecological issues that promote the rise of conflict, subjects that have taken a prominent place in the discipline, and concluded that "[o]nly when we in the field of Peace Studies can replace that sense of futility with a new cause for confidence in an array of better methods will our culture then care more deeply" about such matters (2000, xxi). Beyond this, Hastings (2000, 99) began to map out the full import of this nascent disciplinary innovation toward peace at all levels:

> What would an ecology of peace look like? It would have to be diverse enough to value all life and each human culture within the life of our species. It would have to be stable enough to withstand the strains of periodic shortage and suffering. An ecology of peace would need many and varied elements of immunological response to occasional outbreaks of jingoism, xenophobia, manipulative genius and even to emergent virulent violence.

Extending these points further, Richard Matthew and Ted Gaulin elaborated on "The Ecology of Peace" in 2002, shortly after the terrorist attacks of 9/11. They began by pointing out that early environmentalists often opposed war because of its potential for grave ecological destruction, and that some of the key early figures in American peace movements were likewise motivated by environmental concerns in their work. Connecting the dots to the then-present, the authors observed that "the environment even appears to be relevant to the recent terrorist attacks on the U.S., as research ... has shown that in Pakistan environmental degradation is a significant source of political instability and that it fuels frustration that contributes to Islamic extremism" (2002, 39). More to the point of the peace side of the ecology question, they (2002, 36) cogently note that

> it is widely accepted in the environmental community that conservation measures and programs geared towards sustainable development may reduce the likelihood of violence and help preserve conditions of peace. For example, protecting the environment can eliminate a growing cause (scarcity) of social tension and dissatisfaction. It can relieve pressure on other conflict-inducing social variables such as poverty and population flows. It can serve as a topic that can bring diverse parties into the same room for discussion and confidence-building. And protecting the environment may also prove to be an essential part of the groundwork for rebuilding peace in environmentally stressed areas....

Similar themes have been articulated in the area of "environmental peacemaking," as in Ken Conca and Geoffrey Dabelko's influential 2002 book by that name, where a serious attempt is made to systematically adduce precisely how environmental cooperation can help forestall conflict and preserve peace. Rather than relying upon anecdotal evidence or lofty desires, this argument proceeds in a manner more akin to Goldsmith's call for concrete interventions, seeking to avoid well-meaning generalizations by articulating two necessary elements for environmental peacemaking to have traction: (1) "it must create minimum levels of trust, transparency, and cooperative gain among governments that are strongly influenced by a zero-sum logic of national security," and (2) "it must lay the foundation for transforming the national-security state itself, which is too often marked by dysfunctional institutions and practices that become further obstacles to peaceful coexistence and cooperation" (2002, 10-11). Similarly, Steven Daniels and Gregg Walker (2001) have proposed a method of "collaborative learning" to facilitate public participation in the process of resolving resource conflicts, noting that individuals and management agencies alike hold great potential in this regard.

In his work on "peace parks," Saleem Ali (2007, 3) also emphasizes the positive sense of peace ecology by exploring "how environmental issues can play a role in cooperation—regardless of whether they are part of the original conflict." Examining specific international conservation efforts, Ali reminds us that "[p]ositive exchanges and trust-building gestures are a consequence of realizing common environmental threats," and that "a focus on common environmental harms (or aversions) is psychologically more successful in leading to cooperative outcomes than focusing on common interests (which may lead to competitive behavior)" (2007, 6). This work seeks to bring together strands of environmentalism, conflict resolution, psychology, and resource management in a manner that encapsulates and reiterates the aims of the Peace Studies discipline.

Finally, in terms of mapping out these disciplinary antecedents, Christos Kyrou presented a paper in 2006 on "Peace Ecology: An Emerging Paradigm in Peace Studies," where he argued that Peace Studies and Environmental Studies shared many common assumptions and affinities including a belief in diversity, interdependence, non-violence, and the importance of "place." Kyrou concluded that Peace Ecology is reliant upon two key and mutually-inclusive principles, namely the "capacity to maintain ecological integrity with humans residing responsibly in and as part of nature" and an "effectiveness in managing conflicts constructively while eliminating the various forms of violence" (2006, 10). As Alan Weisman (2008, xv) concurs in the Introduction to Thich Nhat Hanh's book *The World We Have: A Buddhist Approach to Peace and Ecology*, and as a fitting synthesis of the emerging paradigm, things are indeed this simple—and urgent: "The environment unites every human, of every nation and creed. If we fail to save it, we all perish. If we rise to meet the need, we and all to which ecology binds us—other humans, other species, other everything—survive together. And that will be peace."

What We Do, and Why

Drawing upon these teachings and insights, it becomes evident that peace scholars and practitioners have long been concerned with what has more recently come to be known as "sustainability." Implicit in the field's efforts to transcend warfare and establish human societies based on egalitarian and empathetic principles, there has also been a critical engagement with concepts such as "structural violence" that include a focus on the distribution of resources and opportunities alike (see Barash, ed., 2000). This fits quite closely with the emerging sustainability literature that often seeks to create a world in which everyone has access to basic goods including food, shelter, education, healthcare, meaningful work, creative diversions, and the capacity to take part in decisions that affect them. Digging a bit deeper, the impetus toward sustainability suggests that social systems are only viable in a longer-term sense when they promote just and peaceful relations with ourselves, each other, and the biosphere itself. As such, sustainability may be taken to equate with personal wellbeing plus social justice plus a healthy environment. Taken together, and acknowledging the work of progenitors in the field, these interlocking aims can be seen as comprising the basis for an emerging Peace Ecology.

Strands of this holistic perspective have appeared most directly around the issue of warfare and its implications, and the investigation of these issues has been a source of much scholarship in recent years. "Resource conflict" has often been viewed as both a leading cause and consequence of warfare (Westing, Fox, and Renner 2001; Wagner 2003), and the environmental impacts of militarism have been included among the casualties of conflict in cases such as the Vietnam War (Tully 1993), the first Gulf War (Loretz 1991; Adley and Grant 2003), Azerbaijan (Turyalay and Hajiyev 1994), Kosovo (Weller and Rickwood 1999), and Bosnia (Clancy 2004), among others (see generally Austin and Bruch, eds., 2007). In her book *The Ecology of War*, Susan Lanier-Graham notes that "[t]he environment has always been a victim in warfare" (1993, 3), dating back at least to Old Testament descriptions of Samson burning the Philistines' crops and Abimelech sowing the ground with salt after a military victory in order to render it infertile—with the former tactic repeated in the Peloponnesian War in 429 B.C. and the latter by the Romans in Carthage circa 150 B.C. Despite often being thought of as "good wars," Lanier-Graham points out that the American Revolution and World War II both possessed elements of "environmental warfare" (the destruction of the enemy's resources as a conscious tactic of war) and "scorched-earth tactics" similar to those described in the biblical narratives. Westing, Fox, and Renner (2001, 4) also note practices of "deliberate degradation . . . of the natural or built environment for hostile military purposes."

Specifically, investigations of this sort have looked at issues such as the enormous cost of warfare and its resource-draining tendencies; the resultant despoliation of resources including infrastructure, water systems, forests, transportation, and agricultural sites; impacts upon animal populations and habitats; and the long-term toxifying and disease-causing effects of warfare on environments and peoples. In fact, in 2008 the United Nations Environment Programme launched a "Post-Conflict and Disaster Management Branch" focusing on such matters in an attempt to forestall future conflicts, noting on its website that "[b]ecause conflicts and disasters are so closely intertwined with the environment, proper environmental management and governance are essential for long-term peace, stability, and security in any conflict- or disaster-prone country." Likewise in the Peace Studies literature, warfare consistently has been condemned as a wasteful and unnecessary endeavor that, in the end, almost inevitably will lead to more war (cf. Beer 1981, 68). In short, warfare emphatically is not a sustainable practice and in fact works directly against the interests of individuals, societies, and nature alike.

From Political Economy to Peace Ecology

Investigation of the workings of "political economy" has also been an essential component of Peace Studies. Looking at matters ranging from voting rights and democratic policies to living wages and workers' rights, the field has in its history been directly engaged with the ways in which people sustain themselves economically and participate in the political underpinnings of their lives. Many of the leading figures in the field— from Jesus Christ and Mohandas Gandhi to Martin Luther King, Jr. and Dorothy Day—have specifically focused their efforts on crucial issues of race, class, gender, and the like. The history of movements for women's rights, social welfare, workplace safety, ending segregation, stopping war, promoting diversity, and saving the environment are all part of the Peace Studies literature and lexicon on nonviolent change. And the manner in which peace is seen as something much more than simply preventing warfare directly implicates (as noted above) basic sustenance issues such as food, clothing, and shelter.

An important evolution of this work is sometimes expressed under the rubric of "the political ecology of war" (Le Billon 2001). In this arena, "resource wars" are seen partly as a manifestation of competition over scarce materials, but also as a symptom of valuable commodities being maldistributed around the world oftentimes to the disadvantage of peoples in resource-rich Third World locales. As the groundbreaking work of Thomas Homer-Dixon points out, "environmental scarcity has often spurred violence [and] in coming decades the incidence of such violence will probably increase as scarcities of cropland, freshwater, and forests worsen in many parts of the developing world," a scenario that will "further exaggerate the world's already gaping differentials between rich and poor societies and between the powerful and weak people within those societies" (2001, 177-81). At the end of the day, not only will scarcity and degradation often lead to internecine conflicts, but moreover "as global environmental damage increases the gap between the industrialized and developing worlds, poor nations might militarily confront the rich for a fairer share of the planet's wealth" (Homer-Dixon 2001, 3; see also Bannon and Collier 2003, Le Billon 2006). Indeed, undoubtedly aware of such eventualities, the U.S. military has described in its 2008 Army Modernization Strategy document a global future of "perpetual warfare," "persistent conflict," and "resource competition" over items including "food, water, and energy" (Clonan 2008).

Thus we arrive on the threshold of an era where fostering and implementing the tenets of Peace Ecology will be more critical than ever. As Michael Klare presciently observed at the dawn of this historical turn, "the wars of the future will largely be fought over the possession and control of vital economic goods—especially resources needed for the functioning of modern industrial societies.... [R]esource wars will become, in the years ahead, the most distinctive feature of the global security environment" (2001, 213). In quintessential Peace Studies fashion, Klare fleshes out the full implications of this moment, including a reinvigoration of terrorism as the "presence of foreign troops in resource-producing regions will often stir up resentments" and as "recurring conflict over resources will also squander vast quantities of critical materials—especially oil—and cause significant damage to key sources of supply" (2001, 222-23), further exacerbating the problem and contributing to even more conflict—a point echoed by Lanier-Graham (1993, 132) in noting that "wars fought to retain precious environmental resources would probably destroy them in the process." Klare further opines that with the 9/11 attacks, "the United States, too, became the victim of resource-related conflict" (2001, ix), and concludes his assessment with a call for "alternatives to war" including "the equitable distribution of the world's existing resource stockpiles ... as well as an accelerated, global program of research on alternative energy sources and industrial processes" (2001, 223). In more recent work, Klare (2009) elaborates on the need for a collaborative diplomatic initiative to promote radical energy alternatives that are both environmentally sensitive and necessary to manage inherent geopolitical resource conflicts. Here again we see the essence of a robust Peace Ecology emerging, a point echoed in the literature describing how justice can emerge even in cases of resource scarcity (e.g., Sachs and Santarius 2007), despite the obvious temptation to resort to violence.

In even more explicit terms, Vandana Shiva points out the terroristic aspects of Western military and economic policies, noting that in 2001 when she joined myriad others in remembering the victims of 9/11 she "also thought of the millions who are victims of other terrorist actions and other forms of violence" including "World Bank-imposed policies [that] weakened the food economy" and the "carpet-bombing [of] Afghanistan" (2002, xiii). Concluding her section on "The Ecology of Peace" with a hopeful note, Shiva (2002, xv) seeks to turn the ways of war into a chance for peace:

The ecology of terror shows us the path to peace. Peace lies in nourishing ecological and economic democracy and nurturing diversity. Democracy is not merely an electoral ritual but the power of people to shape their destiny, determine how their natural resources are owned and utilized, how their thirst is quenched, how their food is produced and distributed, and what health and education systems they have. As we remember the victims of [9/11], let us also strengthen our solidarity with the millions of invisible victims of other forms of terrorism and violence that threaten the very possibility of our future on this planet. We can turn this tragic and brutal historical moment into building cultures of peace. Creating peace requires us to resolve water wars, wars over food, wars over biodiversity, and wars over the atmosphere. As Gandhi once said, 'The earth has enough for the needs of all, but not the greed of a few.'

Putting It All (Back) Together

In the final analysis, it becomes clear that Peace Studies scholars and practitioners have already come a long way in terms of cultivating a perspective that is holistic and cognizant of the deep-seated interconnectedness of people and place, of culture and nature, and of societies and their environments. Indeed, in this sense Peace Studies has always been inherently ecological in its purview and aims. This has become eminently apparent in recent years with Al Gore winning the Nobel Peace Prize for his work on global warming, and before that in 2004 with Wangari Maathai for her groundbreaking Green Belt Project in Kenya which linked women's rights, economic self-sufficiency, resource conflict resolution, and environmental restoration. Maathai's insights into the impetus for and goals of her work are instructive, as related on *Democracy Now!* in 2007:

We were able to show the linkage between the way we manage our resources, whether we manage them sustainably or in an unsustainable way, [and] also the way we govern ourselves, whether we respect [the] human rights of each other, whether we respect the rule of law, and whether we promote justice, fairness and equity. These issues are very interrelated, because if we do not manage our resources responsibly and accountably, it means we allow corruption, we allow a few individuals to benefit from these resources, to enrich themselves at the expense of the majority of the people. And eventually, the majority of the people, who are left behind, who are not included, who are excluded, become very poor, and they will eventually react. And their reaction will threaten our peace and security.... [T]here is a link between the environment, which is symbolized here by the tree, and the way we govern ourselves and the way we manage the resources and the way we share these resources. This is a very new message that the world needs to embrace, because when we have a critical mass of people and governments who understand this, then we shall deliberately and consciously work for these three to be consciously cultivated, so as to promote the peace by preempting the causes of conflict....

When we talk about lofty ideals such as "building cultures of peace," we are thus by necessity also thinking about the pragmatics of creating and sustaining human societies in their material as well as their ideological needs. A peaceful culture is one in which people learn new ways of resolving conflicts and restoring relationships, distributing resources and opportunities in just ways, and promoting the health and well-being of all of its members. It is also a culture that relates to the balance of the biosphere in positive and healthy ways, that limits its ecological footprint and sees itself as part of nature rather than as its superior. As global conditions worsen and resource wars become pervasive, such notions move from the realm of hopeful idealism to practical necessity. Simply put, if we do not embrace a perspective that integrates ecological thinking into our daily practice, peace will remain but a distant hope rather than a tangible end. Luckily, peace advocates have long understood this, at least implicitly, and are now perhaps developing a language (and logic) that renders this insight explicit.

A Few Concrete Examples

By way of illustration, let me sharpen the point with some examples. In my own work in the fields of peace and justice studies, I have focused for more than a decade on issues of homelessness and public space (Amster 2008). In this analysis, the connection between the socio-political issue of homelessness was necessarily intertwined with a geographical understanding of the places where people at the margins of society were constrained to live. It also became apparent in this work that once-public spaces were fast becoming private ones either in principle or practice, and that in any event homeless people were not welcome to inhabit them any longer. This meant that parks, sidewalks, and downtown areas were becoming off-limits to people who had nowhere else to go. The implications of this began to appear as a form of warfare, namely a war on homeless people rather than a war on homelessness. It further became clear that the policy of spatial dislocation being enacted was potentially genocidal in its full dimensions by leaving millions of people at the lowest economic plateau quite literally with no place to be, offering them non-existence as the only real alternative to their present condition.

Against this, I discovered that homeless people and the tenuous communities they sometimes would form often utilized tactics of *placemaking* to resist these annihilative and quasi-militaristic trends. They also often deployed an ingenious "subsistence perspective" that included a strong ethic of reusing and recycling materials, sharing meager resources with one another, and living much of their life at the level of need. This suggested to me that an issue usually coded as a "social problem" was also one with an obvious ecological component, and that the two were in fact inseparable. Bringing peace and justice to the homeless was likewise an effort to promote a more peaceful and just environment, exemplified in the powerful example of "Dignity Village" in Oregon (in Tafari 2005):

> The transformation of Dignity Village, the longstanding homeless community, from the shantytown that it became after its fifth sweep, continues unto this day. What was birthed by an act of civil disobedience and protest by homeless people who began a campaign has changed into what we are today. And the zoning of the land on which Dignity stands has changed in its designation from industrial to campground. Dignity Village is now Oregon's first transitional homeless campground. What guides the transformation of this piece of ground is … the vision of a green, sustainable urban village where we may live simply and in harmony with our mother Earth and where we may do for ourselves and help ourselves and others. As our proposal so eloquently states, 'Dignity Village is the only place-based community in this town that practices grassroots democracy with an ecological vision. It is the only walkable community not invaded by cars, and it is the most cost-efficient, self-help model for transcending homelessness in the nation.'

Touting its "green" dwellings (including strawbale and cob houses), Dignity Village brings together social and environmental justice as "a model for the future, while helping develop the tools with which to build the model and others like it" (Tafari 2005). Due to the relative material scarcity of their lives and their general condition of dispossession, homeless people can sometimes appear as 'urban nomads' in a rapidly globalizing world, pursuing "the realization of human freedom" by rejecting "the constraints of bourgeois society" and instead becoming "a source of alternative values" (Kohn 2004, 178). As such, homeless communities can invent new forms of social and ecological relationships, simultaneously challenging the socio-spatial structures inherent in mainstream society and modeling new people-place visions. What appeared to be primarily a cultural phenomenon had thus taken on critical ecological concerns as well, finding resonance with other exemplars of peaceful, collective self management such as those taking hold around what are sometimes called "common pool resources" (Ostrom 1990) and in particular concerning the cooperative sharing of water (Rodriguez 2006).

Similarly, after Hurricane Katrina devastated the Gulf Coast, grassroots relief entities sprung up to fill the void left by governmental neglect and mismanagement. Among these was the Common Ground collective in New Orleans, whose network of volunteers were "involved in all aspects of relief work and community building including skilled labor, health care, soil remediation, housing rights advocacy, technical assistance and . . . community organizing" (Haletky 2006, 91). This dual emphasis on "social and environmental justice" in the relief effort mirrors the simultaneous natural and manmade aspects of the storm and its aftermath (Jones 2008, 22). Indeed, there has been increased theorizing about the relationships among global climate change, calamities such as hurricanes, social justice, and human conflict (e.g., Zhang et al. 2007; Hoerner and Robinson 2008). In a big-picture sense it is apparent, as Peter Vintila (2007, 1) points out, that "war is very, very dirty," it "cost[s] a great deal of money," and it "also acts to extinguish the cultural space [needed for] successful climate change treaty making."

As a possible antidote to this deplorable situation, consider the Demilitarized Zone (DMZ) between North and South Korea, which has become a massive wildlife and bird sanctuary that is in the process of moving toward formal protection. Having remained relatively untouched for more than 50 years, the DMZ is a rich habitat made up of marshes and grasslands, inhabited by many rare and endangered species including Asiatic black bears, leopards, lynx, and "nearly the entire world population of red-crowned cranes" (Lanier-Graham 1993, 73). The implications of this are self-evident, namely that de-militarization leads to species diversification and a thriving ecosystem, whereas militarism yields precisely the opposite: desertification and resource depletion.

Conclusions

Building a culture of peace, of course, requires more than simply pointing out what has gone wrong in the world. Equally (if not more) important is the articulation of positive examples that integrate peaceful human societies with just ecological outcomes. The Peace Studies rubric has reflected an awareness of the need for such illustrations, including among its adopted brethren figures such as Henry David Thoreau and Aldo Leopold. The field has often examined the workings of intentional communities and other "back to the land" efforts as important experiments in peacemaking. Beyond this lay significant evolutions in our understanding and articulation of exemplars of Peace Ecology in practice, including those described here. Above all, Peace Ecology emphasizes the inherent interconnectedness of all things; as Martin Luther King, Jr. once famously said, "Injustice anywhere is a threat to justice everywhere." While he was referring to social and political concerns at the time, there is little doubt that the principle reflected in his teachings holds true today as we expand our framework and analysis. Equally clear is that the road from a war mentality (and economy) to a peace mindset (and ecology) is likely to be arduous initially but will certainly pay great dividends both for ourselves and the future. In the end, a Peace Ecology asks that we embrace this challenge, counseling that a more just and sustainable world is quite literally in our hands—and in what we choose to create with them (cf. Erickson 1990).

And that brings me to a final element that is crucial to a vibrant and fully-formed Peace Ecology: actions oftentimes speak louder than words. Theoretical and academic expositions of the field are certainly essential to illuminate the central issues involved and help to develop guideposts for concrete actions. But sometimes these notions can also serve to reify the current state of affairs by implying that the world's problems can primarily be resolved through more pacific intercourse among nation-states and international entities. While such bodies surely ought to play a role in moving the world toward peace and sustainability, it is equally important to remember that individuals and communities also possess the power to promote these changes, as Thich Nhat Hanh (2008, 4-5) cogently and pressingly reminds us:

> We all have a great desire to be able to live in peace and to have environmental sustainability. What most of us don't yet have are concrete ways of making our commitment to sustainable living a reality in our daily lives. We haven't organized ourselves. We can't only blame our governments and corporations for the chemicals that pollute our drinking water, for the violence in our neighborhoods, for the wars that destroy so many lives. It's time for each of us to wake up and take action in our own lives.

Peace Ecology has been pointing in this direction for many years now. The time is ripe to turn theory into practice, crisis into opportunity, and, ultimately, war into peace.

References

Adley, J., and A. Grant. 2003. The environmental consequences of war. *Sierra Club of Canada*, http://www.sierraclub.ca/national/postings/war-and-environment.html (accessed December 11, 2008).

Ali, S. H. 2007. Introduction: A natural connection between ecology and peace? In *Peace parks: conservation and conflict resolution*, ed. Saleem H. Ali, 1-17. Cambridge, MA: MIT Press.

Amster, R.. 2008. *Lost in space: The criminalization, globalization, and urban ecology of homelessness*. New York: LFB Scholarly.

Austin, J. E., and C. E. Bruch, eds. 2007. *The environmental consequences of war: Legal, economic, and scientific perspectives*. Cambridge, England: Cambridge University Press.

Bannon, I., and P. Collier, eds. 2003. *Natural resources and violent conflict*. Washington, D.C.: World Bank.

Barash, D. P., ed. 2000. *Approaches to peace*. New York: Oxford University Press.

Beer, F. A. 1981. *Peace against war: The ecology of international violence*. San Francisco: W.H. Freeman & Co.

Clancy, T. 2004. The war on Bosnia. *World Watch* 17 (2): 12-23.

Clonan, T. 2008. U.S. generals planning for resource wars. *Irish Times*, September 22.

Conca, K, and G. D. Dabelko, eds. 2002. *Environmental peacemaking*. Baltimore, MD: Johns Hopkins University Press.

Daniels, S. E., and G. B. Walker. 2001. *Working through environmental conflict: The collaborative learning approach*. Westport, CT: Praeger Publishers.

Democracy Now! 2007. *Unbowed*: Nobel Peace Laureate Wangari Maathai on climate change, wars for resources, the Greenbelt Movement and more (October 1), http://www.democracynow.org/2007/10/1/unbowed_nobel_peace_laur eate_wangari_maathai (accessed January 25, 2009).

Erickson, B. 1990. *Call to action: Handbook for ecology, peace, and justice*. New York: Random House.

Gjessing, G. 1967. Ecology and peace research. *Journal of Peace Research* 4 (2): 125-138.

Goldsmith, E. 1974. The ecology of war. *The Ecologist*, May.

Haletky, N. 2006. Rebuilding on common ground: Social and environmental justice in New Orleans. *Urban Action*,

http://bss.sfsu.edu/urbanaction/ua2006/pdf/ua2006-Haletky.pdf
(accessed January 22, 2009).

Hanh, T. N.. 2008. *The world we have: A Buddhist approach to peace and ecology*. Berkeley, CA: Parallax Press.

Hastings, T. H. 2000. *Ecology of war and peace*. Lanham, MD: University Press of America.

Homer-Dixon, T. F. 2001. *Environment, scarcity, and violence*. Princeton, NJ: Princeton University Press.

Hoerner, J. A., and N. Robinson. 2008. A climate of change: African Americans, global warming, and a just climate policy in the U.S. *Environmental Justice and Climate Change Initiative*, http://www.rprogress.org/publications/2008/climateofchange.pdf (accessed January 29, 2009).

Jones, V.. 2008. *The green collar economy: How one solution can fix our two biggest problems*. New York: HarperOne.

Klare, M. T. 2002. *Resource wars: The new landscape of global conflict*. New York: Owl Books.

—. 2009. *Rising powers, shrinking planet: The new geopolitics of energy*. New York: Holt Paperbacks.

Kohn, M. 2004. *Brave new neighborhoods: The privatization of public space*. New York: Routledge.

Kyrou, C. N. 2006. Peace ecology: An emerging paradigm in Peace Studies. Paper presented at the annual meeting for the International Studies Association, March 22-25, in San Diego, CA.

Lanier-Graham, S. D. 1993. *The ecology of war: Environmental impacts of weaponry and warfare*. New York: Walker & Co.

Le Billon, P. 2001. The political ecology of war: Natural resources and armed conflicts. *Political Geography* 20: 561-84.

—. 2006. *Fuelling war: Natural resources and armed conflicts*. New York: Routledge.

Loretz, J. 1991. The animal victims of the Gulf War. *The PSR Quarterly*, http://fn2.freenet.edmonton.ab.ca/~puppydog/gulfwar.htm (accessed January 25, 2009).

Matthew, R. A., and T. Gaulin. 2002. The ecology of peace. *Peace Review* 14 (1): 33-39.

Ostrom, E. 1990. *Governing the commons: The evolution of institutions for collective action*. Cambridge, UK: Cambridge University Press.

Rodriguez, S. 2006. *Acequia: Water-sharing, sanctity, and place*. Sante Fe, NM: SAR Press.

Sachs, W. and T. Santarius. 2007. *Fair future: Limited resources and global justice*. London: Zed Books.

Shabecoff, P. 1996. *A new name for peace: International environmentalism, sustainable development, and democracy*. Hanover, NH: University Press of New England.

Shiva, V. 2002. *Water wars: Privatization, pollution, and profit*. Cambridge, MA: South End Press.

Tafari, J. 2005. The ongoing transformation of Dignity Village. *Street Spirit* (March), http://www.thestreetspirit.org/March2005/dignity.htm (accessed January 2, 2009).

Tully, J. 1993. Vietnam: War and the environment. *Green Left Weekly* 106, http://www.greenleft.org.au/1993/106/5903 (accessed December 2, 2008).

Turyalay, S., and E. Hajiyev. 1994. Impact of the war on the environment. *Azerbaijan International* 2 (3): 57, Autumn.

Vintila, P. 2007. Climate change war or climate change peace. *PostKyoto Journal* (Spring), http://www.postkyoto.org/journal.pdf (accessed December 22, 2008).

Wagner, C. G. 2003. War crimes against nature. *The Futurist* 37 (3), May-June.

Weisman, A. 2008. Introduction to *The world we have: A Buddhist approach to peace and ecology*, by Thich Nhat Hanh, viii-xv. Berkeley, CA: Parallax Press.

Weller, P. and P. Rickwood. 1999. Kosovo: War on the environment. *The Ploughshares Monitor* 20 (3).

Westing, A. H., W. Fox, and M. Renner. 2001. Environmental degradation as both consequence and cause of armed conflict. Working Paper prepared for Nobel Peace Laureate Forum (PREPCOM subcommittee on Environmental Degradation), June.

Zhang, D. D., P. Brecke, H. F. Lee, Y. Q. He, and J. Zhang. 2007. Global climate change, war, and population decline in recent human history," *PNAS* 104 (49): 19214-19.

CONCLUSION

RANDALL AMSTER
AND ELAVIE NDURA-OUÉDRAOGO

The quest to envision, manifest, and ultimately build enduring cultures of peace is certainly among humankind's greatest challenges. From time immemorial, communities and cultures have struggled to define the terms of what a lasting peace would look like, and to take nascent steps toward cultivating and implementing the same. Perhaps at no other point in recorded history has this task been more urgent. The crises we presently face appear across the globe and at multiple levels of human experience—tangibly through economic recessions and the gravity of our ever-expanding arsenals of warfare, for instance, and intangibly through processes such as media hegemony and educational standardization. In this volume we have sought to address these many challenges from an array of perspectives and through interdisciplinary analyses at a multitude of levels including education, culture, and politics. In so doing, our aim has been to illuminate the nature and depth of the problems we presently face, and perhaps more importantly to suggest constructive pathways for promoting and sustaining cultures built upon the values of peace.

We have not taken up these issues lightly, and we are well aware that few would argue that the pursuit of peace is likely to be uncontroversial or easy to maintain. Despite its near universality as a fundamental aim of most human endeavors and as "something which we seemingly all aspire to" (Page 2008, xv), peace as a concept remains poorly understood. Often seen as well-intentioned but naïve at best and dangerously unrealistic at worst, those working and advocating for peace face many obstacles on a multitude of fronts. This eventuality has been accentuated in recent years, as the world has entered a new cycle of global conflict with deep roots in ideology and resource acquisition. At the same time, however, we have seen a reawakening of an international peace movement that does not merely strive to end warfare—in itself a monumental task, of course—but also seeks to build peaceful cultures on a much broader scale. This has led to innumerable innovations in basic spheres of life including education, art, politics, and economics. While perhaps not as well-reported as outbreaks of warfare and actions specifically contesting them, these proactive innovations are at least equally noteworthy.

It is in this spirit that we have presented the chapters contained in this volume. We do not contend that the topics and themes explored here are by any means exhaustive of the full dimensions of building cultures of peace, but rather we offer these as detailed examples of the types of innovative work being done across the academic disciplines to investigate pertinent issues and suggest pragmatic paths to peace. From the arts to sports, from education to politics, and from ethics to economics, scholars and practitioners everywhere are embracing the challenges and opportunities for creating a more just and peaceful world. The common thread among these explorations is, indeed, the strongly-held desire for peace and a willingness to take affirmative steps to help point the way there. This may well be the broadest notion of what "hope" represents in troubled times—namely the combination of sincere belief with well-informed action intended to achieve a positive end.

Again, we do not embrace these aims unaware of the magnitude of the challenges and crises we face as a civilization. As David Barash and Charles Webel (2009, 1) observe:

> Our planet is becoming increasingly polluted and threatened. The Earth is composed of finite resources whose limits may soon be reached and whose global warming may result in unprecedented catastrophes. Human societies contain gross maldistributions of wealth and power, which prevent the overwhelming majority of human beings from realizing their potential and ensure that vast numbers die prematurely. Our cultural systems perpetuate regrettable patterns of social and political injustice, in which racism, sexism, militarism, and other forms of unfairness abound, and in which representative government is relatively rare and torture and other forms of oppression are distressingly common.... Yet, despite all of these difficulties, the remarkable fact is that enormous sums of money and vast resources of material, time, and energy are expended, not in solving what we might call the 'problems of peace' but rather in threatening and actually making war on one another.

In this light, as Jonathan Schell (2003, 10) concurs, "it is difficult to make out, even in the distance, the outlines of a world at peace." Equally to the point, as Arundhati Roy (2003, 6) wonders, "how can there be a peace movement when, for most people ... peace means a daily battle for food, for water, for shelter, for dignity?"

Perhaps it is this basic recognition of the gravity and immediacy of the challenges before us that has sparked so much recent interest in the pursuit of peace. As Antony Adolf (2009, 1) observes, "we no longer have the luxury of seeing the actualization of peace as a noble if naïve vision of how things could have been or can be.... [T]he historically unimaginable destructive capacity of modern weapons, coupled with the inclinations of those who use them, have made risking war morally impermissible as well as rationally unthinkable." Once again, however, the crisis begets an opportunity, as Schell (2003, 10) contends: "Arms and man have both changed in ways that, even as they imperil the world as never before, have created a chance for peace that is greater than ever before." This is perhaps due to the obvious dangers posed by warfare but also the more subtle and insidious machinations of structural violence and oppression that are intimately connected to the workings of the pervasive martial culture that we see worldwide.

By connecting the two spheres of culture that often define the parameters of critical inquiry in the pursuit of peace—namely the militaristic and the socio-structural—recent scholarship and activism strives to not simply curtail the ways of war but also to create cultural frameworks that render war unappealing as a method of conflict resolution, if not outright unthinkable. This is where pedagogy in particular has great salience, and where the social and political realms likewise converge, in the understanding that what we ultimately seek is not merely an end to overt warfare and violence (although that would indeed be a very good start) but rather the proactive development of individuals, communities, and cultures that embody the values of peace and justice. This is quite likely to be an incremental enterprise, fueled in great measure by the impetus of pedagogy in all of its formal and informal manifestations, as Koichiro Matsuura (Director-General of UNESCO) recently observed (in Page 2008, xix): "Building a culture of peace throughout the world is a complex social process which involves long-term social and cultural changes. Education at all levels is integral to this." It will also necessitate a rethinking of our relationships to each other, and to the balance of life on the planet as well: "Cultures of Peace will require the best of our human capacities, including that we learn how to protect our global environment" (Brenes and Winter 2001, 157).

In this search for higher ideals may we find hope—not a remote, false hope, but one that is grounded in the best practices of humankind and the pragmatic implementation of positive values. Just as competitive, warlike, and destructive instincts can be fostered and inculcated through cultural apparatuses ranging from media and education to economics and law, so too can the virtues of cooperation, conflict transformation, creativity, and conservation be widely disseminated and pervasively embraced. As

Barash and Webel (2009, 1-2) note, "it does seem reasonable to hope …
that we will someday behave far more responsibly and establish a global
community based on the needs of the entire planet and the beings who
inhabit it, a planetary society that is just and sustainable…." To attain this
vision will require broad-based, multidisciplinary investigations into the
array of potential pathways to peace, informed by a spirit of hopefulness
that is grounded in experiential engagement with the pressing issues of our
time and that encourages positive action aimed at building cultures of
peace around the globe.

The authors presented in this volume take seriously the magnitude of
this lofty ideal, and ask that we all do the same. The vision of "world
peace" that is virtually universal among human desires awaits our overdue
engagement with both its challenges and opportunities. Our fervent hope is
that this work may serve as a starting point for the vibrant and much-
needed dialogue that we eagerly anticipate will ensue in the days ahead.

References

Adolf, A. 2009. *Peace: A world history*. Cambridge, UK: Polity Press.
Barash, D.P. and C. P. Webel. 2009. *Peace and conflict studies*.2nd ed.
    Thousand Oaks, CA: SAGE.
Brenes, A. and D. D. N. Winter. 2001. Earthly dimensions of peace: The
    Earth Charter. *Peace and Conflict: Journal of Peace Psychology* 7(2),
    157-171.
Page, J. 2008. *Peace education: Exploring ethical and philosophical
    foundations*. Charlotte, NC: Information Age Publishing.
Roy, A. 2003. *War talk*. Cambridge, MA: South End Press.
Schell, J. 2003. *The unconquerable world: Power, nonviolence, and the
    will of the people*. New York: Henry Holt.

CONTRIBUTORS

Cary D. Adkinson earned a B.A. in psychology from Southern Methodist University, and a Ph.D. from Sam Houston State University, and now serves as an assistant professor of criminal justice in the Department of Criminal Justice at Fayetteville State University. His research is in the area of insight criminology.

Randall Amster, co-editor of this volume and professor of Peace Studies at Prescott College, holds a J.D. from Brooklyn Law School and a Ph.D. in Justice Studies from Arizona State University. He publishes widely in areas including anarchism, ecology, homelessness, and social justice; serves on the Editorial Advisory Boards of the *Contemporary Justice Review* and the *Peace Studies Journal*; and is the Executive Director of the Peace & Justice Studies Association. His most recent books are *Lost in Space: The Criminalization, Globalization, and Urban Ecology of Homelessness* (LFB Scholarly, 2008), and the co-edited volume *Contemporary Anarchist Studies: An Introductory Anthology of Anarchy in the Academy* (Routledge 2009).

Antonette Aragon is an assistant professor from Colorado State University. Her research focuses on multicultural teacher education, anti-racist multicultural education, and the examination of marginalized students. She researches and develops curricula fostering cultural competencies for White teacher effectiveness to teach students who are racially, ethnically, linguistically, & socio-economically different from themselves.

Supriya Baily has spent over two decades working with peace and justice organizations in India and the United States. She received her doctorate in International Education and will be starting as Assistant Professor in Education at George Mason University in the summer of 2009. Her work has allowed her to engage with teachers, refugee populations, women, children and nongovernmental actors in different contexts by developing curricula, building and managing programs, using art and drama to highlight oppression and is currently building a research agenda to look at how the disenfranchised seek to become agents of their own change.

Robert E. Baker is associate professor in George Mason University's School of Recreation, Health and Tourism and director of the Center for Sport Management. He has extensive experience in interscholastic, intercollegiate, non-profit, and for-profit sport enterprises as an administrator and coach. His B.S. in Education and M.S. in Sport Administration are from Penn State University. His Ed.D. in Higher Education is from William & Mary.

Edward J. Brantmeier is an assistant professor at Colorado State University. His research focus includes multicultural peace education & cultural conflict and change. His co-edited book, Transforming Education for Peace, was published in 2008. Currently, he is completing two other book projects with colleagues: 147 Tips for Teaching Peace and Reconciliation and Spirituality, Religion, and Peace Education. He serves as a co-editor for a book series on peace education with Information Age Publishing.

Michael J. DeValve's publications and current research focus on the cultivation of compassion and diversity in justice organizations. Michael earned his M.A. (1998) and Ph.D. (2004) in Criminal Justice at Sam Houston State University, and is currently an assistant professor in the Department of Criminal Justice at Fayetteville State University.

Cheryl Duckworth is a global peace and security program leader and policy analyst who has served such organizations as the Institute for Multi-Track Diplomacy and the Center for International Education. She has lived in Zimbabwe and Paraguay, and her policy work has focused on civil society, international education and political economy. In addition to having led teacher trainings, she has published and presented globally. She recently completed her doctoral dissertation on development policy and the indigenous rights movement in Paraguay at the Institute for Conflict Analysis and Resolution, George Mason University. She currently teaches conflict resolution at George Mason University and teaches also at the NoVA Juvenile Detention Home School; she blogs at http://teachforpeace.blogspot.com. She can be reached at cheryl.duckworth@gmail.com.

Craig Esherick is assistant professor in George Mason University's School of Recreation, Health and Tourism. He is the former Head Men's Basketball Coach at Georgetown University and holds finance and law degrees from GU. Craig also served as an assistant coach of the Men's US

Olympic Basketball Team which won the bronze medal 1988 in Seoul, South Korea. He teaches Introduction to Sports Management, Sports Law and Sport Governance and Policy at GMU.

Tom H. Hastings is core faculty at Portland State University in the Conflict Resolution MA/MS program, director of PeaceVoice, and author of numerous books about nonviolence. He is a former co-chair of the Peace & Justice Studies Association, and is a founder of Whitefeather Peace Community in Portland, Oregon.

Pearl Hunt is a performing artist, educator and scholar. She is currently a PhD candidate in the Faculty of Education at the University of British Columbia. As an Instructor for the Humanities Department at Simon Fraser University, she developed a *music and social change* curriculum that integrates music with models of participatory learning to promote praxis-based, anti-oppressive education. Her latest music-based, multimedia project, "Postcards from Post Katrina," has been presented at Stanford University (Hunt 2008) and the International Conference on Multicultural Education, Vancouver, British Columbia (2009).

John W. Lango is Professor of Philosophy at Hunter College of the City University of New York. He received his Ph.D. in philosophy from Yale University. He specializes in metaphysics, ethics, and political philosophy. Concerning metaphysics, he has written articles on the philosophy of time and the metaphysics of Alfred North Whitehead. He is the author of *Whitehead's Ontology*. Concerning ethics and political philosophy, he has written articles on just war theory, the last resort principle, nonviolent action, UN peacekeeping missions, armed humanitarian intervention, and other subjects. He is a coeditor of *Rethinking the Just War Tradition*.

Cindy Maguire is Assistant Professor of Art and Art Education and Director of the Art Education Program at Adelphi University. Before joining Adelphi, she was a Senior Research Associate in urban arts education at the Annenberg Institute for School Reform, as well as an adjunct faculty member in Pratt Institute and New York University's Art Education Programs. Cindy taught visual arts education in the Los Angeles City Schools for over eight years. Her research interests include cultural studies, art education pedagogy and curriculum, peace and social justice education, and service-learning in the arts. She is a practicing visual artist.

Julie Morton studied American Cultural Studies at Bates College and received her master's from Prescott College in Peace and Conflict Studies. As part of her master's program, she designed an online middle school conflict transformation unit for Colorado University's Conflict Information Consortium. Julie currently teaches literacy in Thornton, Colorado, after working in middle schools in Vermont and Hungary.

Elavie Ndura-Ouédraogo, co-editor of this volume, is an Associate Professor of Educational Transformation at George Mason University. Her numerous interdisciplinary publications on critical multicultural and peace education and immigrants' acculturation have appeared in several books and various scholarly journals including *Harvard Educational Review*; *Multicultural Perspectives*; and *Journal of Peace Education*. She co-authored *147 Tips for Teaching Peace and Reconciliation* (Atwood Publishing, 2009) and co-edited *Seeds of New Hope: Pan-African Peace Studies for the 21st Century* (Africa World Press, 2009). She has delivered over 120 presentations, keynotes, and lectures at local, national, and international professional gatherings. She is a Board Member of the Peace and Justice Studies Association and the Peace Education Special Interest Group of the American Educational Research Association. She is the founder of the Burundi Schools Project.

Beverly Shaklee began her career in teaching some thirty years ago in a rural elementary classroom. She taught in four United State's school systems, served as full professor at Kent State University and began her work in international education in 1990. She has worked throughout the Caribbean, in post-apartheid South Africa and in post Soviet countries. She currently serves as professor of curriculum and instruction as well as Director of the Center for International Education at George Mason University. Dr. Shaklee is the author of over 100 publications in the field of education.

Stacia Stribling is an Instructor with the Initiatives in Educational Transformation Master's Program at George Mason University. Prior to joining the faculty at GMU, Stacia worked for eight years in the Virginia public school system teaching first and second grade. Her research interests include early childhood education, critical literacy, teacher professional development, and culturally responsive education. She has presented her research at numerous national and international conferences and has published in several professional journals. Stacia is currently a doctoral candidate at GMU; her major area of study is Early Childhood Education with a minor in Literacy.

Cris Toffolo, currently chair of the Justice Studies Department at Northeastern Illinois University, previously directed a justice and peace studies program at the University of St. Thomas. Recent publications include: *The Arab League; Emancipating Cultural Pluralism,* ed., and various articles. In addition to extensive curriculum development work, including for study abroad programs, Cris has worked with Amnesty International and with NGOs in both the USA and in South Africa. She earned a BA from Alma College, an MA in public policy from George Washington University, and an MA and PhD in political science from the University of Notre Dame.

Brian W. Yoder is a graduate research and teaching assistant at Colorado State University. He is also currently working as a school counselor at Polaris Expeditionary Learning School while finishing his Master's degree in counseling and career development. His passions include social justice, travelling, and outdoor pursuits.

INDEX

literacy, 3, 7, 45-55, 72-81, 83-4, 176-7, 230, 265

M

Maathai, Wangari, 250, 255
Manifest Destiny, 15
media, 31, 89, 101, 108, 112, 152, 154, 158, 184, 196, 202, 209, 232, 258, 260
Middle East, 28, 158, 210-1
mindfulness, 125-50
moral development theory, 3, 86, 97
morality, 7, 86-9, 93, 96, 100, 151, 225
multicultural education, 3, 8-10, 12-3, 65, 262
music, 3-4, 53, 101, 169-82, 264

N

Nhat Hanh, Thich, 30, 42, 49, 130, 132-3, 135, 139, 149, 246, 254, 257
No Child Left Behind, 45, 190
Nobel Peace Prize, 250
nonviolence, 3, 14, 152, 155, 163, 167, 177, 222-6, 234, 248, 264
nuclear, 54, 220, 223, 229

O

Obama, Barack, 45, 58, 118, 122, 125-6, 133, 149, 159, 184-6, 190-1, 208
oil, 200-1, 210, 243, 249
Olympics, 102, 108-11, 121-3, 264
oppression, 4, 10, 11, 15, 18-9, 23-4, 48, 53, 74, 85, 101, 157, 185-6, 188-91, 259-60, 262, 264

P

peace, 1-15, 22, 24-7, 29-42, 44-8, 52, 55-85, 90, 100-4, 107, 110-9, 121, 125-8, 141, 148-70, 173, 176-86, 188-9, 191-6, 200-19, 221-31, 233-40, 242, 244-66
Peace & Justice Studies Association (PJSA), 2, 262, 264
Peace Ecology, 246-9, 254
peace education, 3, 5, 8-9, 11-4, 25, 58-70, 73, 75-6, 153, 178, 227-30, 235-9, 263
peace movement, 258-9
peace professionals, 3-4, 151, 153, 162-3
peace studies, 2, 4, 59-60, 68, 70, 85, 151, 163, 167, 225, 229, 242-50, 253, 256, 262, 265
peacebuilding, 3-4, 14, 25, 74, 111, 116, 121, 195, 240
peacemaking, 5, 25, 48, 59, 74, 103, 170, 177, 195, 204, 207, 245, 254-5
pedagogy, 3, 7, 10-1, 26, 29-31, 36, 39, 40, 43, 58, 60-2, 68, 73, 75, 77, 83-9, 95, 97-8, 100, 170-3, 177-80, 260, 264
police, 4, 91, 125-8, 134-50, 162, 201, 203-4, 208
politics, 4, 15, 41, 43, 62, 74, 109, 148, 156, 163-8, 176, 178, 182, 190, 195, 210, 212, 258-9
political, 5, 12-3, 15, 22, 26, 34-7, 59, 61, 67-9, 75-6, 103-8, 118, 131, 152-6, 160-1, 167, 176, 179, 186, 188, 197, 199, 202-4, 209, 211, 214, 228-9, 232, 234, 236, 242-5, 248, 251, 254, 256, 259-60, 263-6
positive peace, 12, 126-7, 204, 229
poverty, 1, 94, 187, 189-91, 200, 218, 227-8, 230-1, 233-4, 236-40, 245
praxis, 2, 85, 153, 170-1, 178, 182, 264
prejudice, 2, 10, 19, 48, 51-2, 67, 76, 91, 116, 185, 189
privilege, 9-12, 14-5, 22-4, 26, 65